THE
SPEARHEADERS

THE
SPEARHEADERS
A Personal History of Darby's Rangers

JAMES ALTIERI

With a New Introduction by Mir Bahmanyar

NAVAL INSTITUTE PRESS
ANNAPOLIS, MARYLAND

This book has been brought to publication with the generous assistance of Marguerite and Gerry Lenfest.

Naval Institute Press
291 Wood Road
Annapolis, MD 21402

First Naval Institute Press paperback edition published in 2014.
ISBN: 978-1-59114-179-2 (paperback)
ISBN: 978-0-87021-089-1 (eBook)

Library of Congress Cataloging-in-Publication data for the hard cover edition is available.

♾ Print editions meet the requirements of ANSI/NISO z39.48-1992 (Permanence of Paper).
Printed in the United States of America.

22 21 20 19 18 17 16 15 14   9 8 7 6 5 4 3 2 1
First printing

This book is respectfully dedicated to:

The volunteers who fought with the First, Third and Fourth Rangers— Darby's Rangers; to their spirt of daring and initiative and to their strong belief in American ideals; and to every American and Allied soldier, sailor, airman, Commando and paratrooper who gave his fullest measure on the field of battle.

So Joshua arose, and all the people of war, to go up against Ai: and Joshua chose out thirty thousand mighty men of valour, and sent them away by night. And he commanded them, saying . . . ye shall rise up from the ambush and seize upon the city: for the Lord your God will deliver it into your hand.

Joshua 8:3-4, 7

ILLUSTRATIONS

These illustrations may be found following page 64:

The commanding officer of the U.S. Ranger unit, Lt. Col. William Orlando Darby.

Lieutenant Colonel Vaughan and Major Darby.

Rangers conducting bayonet drills under the watchful eye of their British instructors in Scotland.

Darby and Rangers inspecting an enemy vehicle after a successful ambush.

French prisoners of war, 1942.

The Rangers in a speed march across enemy terrain in Tunisia.

Ranger spatial scouts search out the enemy at El Guettar.

Prisoners of the German Afrika Korps.

Congratulations to the 1st Sgt. Donald (Butt) Torbett on the destruction of an enemy tank by Fox Company in Tunisia.

These illustrations may be found following page 128:

Rangers marching over the Tunisian hills.

Rangers in North Africa.

Sergeant Thompson before the Sened Raid.

D Company of the Rangers.

An Italian gun destroyed by Rangers in Tunisia.

Father Basil leads service for the Rangers in North Africa.

Night training at Arzew.

Prisoners of War.

Carlo Contrera at Arzew.

Capt. Charles M. "Chuck" Shunstrom.

These illustrations may be found following page 192:

Rangers overlook Arzew after the attack.

A "skull session" en route to Arzew. Rangers doing a final review of their operation orders.

Briefing aboard ship en route to Africa. Capt. Roy Murray, Jr., explains details of the impending invasion to Rangers of F Company.

Fox Company at Arzew.

Colonel Darby and Rangers on HMS *Princess Emma* at Arzew.

Rangers rehearse amphibious assaults after the attack on Arzew.

The battle at Arzew.

A Ranger guards a camp at El Guettar.

Relaxation after capturing the harbor of Arzew.

A mixed session of entertainment between Rangers and British Commandos.

FOREWORD

"I selected Rangers because few words have a more glamorous connotation in American military history. . . . On every frontier, the name has been one of hope for those who have required protection, of fear for those who have lived outside the law. It was therefore fit that the organization destined to be the first American ground forces to battle the Germans on the European continent in World War II should have been called Rangers, in compliment *to those in American history who have exemplified such high standards of individual courage, initiative, determination, ruggedness, fighting ability, and achievement.*" —Lucian K. Truscott, *Command Missions*, page 40.

It is an honor and privilege to introduce this time-worn tale of one of our Army's most distinguished combat formations. James J. Alteri's classic, *The Spearheaders*, recounts the formation and employment of the Ranger battalions from their inception early in World War II to their engagements in North Africa, Sicily, and Italy. Conceived to fight alongside the British Commandos and as the "spearhead" for American units involved in the liberation of Europe, the World War II Ranger battalions established a reputation for daring and boldness early in the war.

James Alteri was among those many soldiers selected from several U.S. units in England who were willing to take the challenge posed by this new and mysterious unit. He details the rigorous selection process and the realistic commando training. He recounts their participation in amphibious operations, weapons familiarization, and grueling foot-marches—all of which honed them into a fighting force that would spearhead the invasion of North Africa. Through these pages, the reader is introduced to the many men who brought this new style of fighting to life—the British commandos who administered the training and the Rangers—Walter Wojcik, Chuck Shunstrom, Randall Harris, and Roy Murray. Throughout the account looms the personality of William Orlando Darby. An artilleryman, Major Darby, or "El Darbo" as he was affectionately known, put his stamp on the Rangers through his personal involvement with all facets of their training. Always at the front of the most grueling movements, Darby pioneered the night raids that bought the Rangers their early and dramatic successes. Darby was fiercely loyal to his men. In these pages Alteri recounts with pride the number of offers for promotion that Darby spurned to stay with his Rangers. Their success in North Africa was rewarded with expansion, and soon many of the plank holders in the original Ranger battalion were holding key leadership positions in one of the three Ranger battalions composing the Ranger Force that would fight in both Sicily and Italy. Alteri himself eventually rose to command Fox Company of the 4th Battalion before the disaster at Cisterna led to the dissolution of the Ranger Force. In many ways, this book is a tribute to William O. Darby, who perhaps alone among the distinguished combat leaders of our Army will forever be associated with the American Ranger.

Ranger Mir Bahmanyar is to be commended for his perseverance in bringing this classic back into publication. I was fortunate to serve alongside Mir in Company B, 2nd Battalion, back in the late 1980s, and he, like James Alteri and the men recounted in this book, knows the cost of being a member of an elite unit. This reissue, I hope, will allow another generation of Rangers, returning from campaigns in the Hindu Kush and the Euphrates River Valley, to contemplate those who went before them and the challenges they may next face.

Colonel (Ret.) Mike Kershaw
Commander, 1st Ranger Battalion, 2002–2004
San Antonio, Texas

ACKNOWLEDGMENTS

I wish to express my deep gratitude to the many Rangers and other friends who encouraged me to write this book, and to those, also, who refreshed my memory by their invaluable contributions to the reconstruction of the numerous battle sequences not covered by my notes and diary or the official battle reports.

For the use of official photographs, my grateful appreciation goes to the Army Signal Corps, the Office of Chief of Information, and to Phil Stern, the Ranger Combat Photographer, who assisted me in collecting the photographs and allowed me to consult his diary of the North African campaign.

Every Ranger company in each of the three battalions—the First, Third and Fourth—could equal in spirit and action the story I tell here, which is mainly about the Rangers of Fox Company. To those Rangers, both living and dead, I offer my sincerest hopes that this book will measure up to their excellent spirit and superb achievements, which made the Rangers what they became.

James Altieri
Santa Barbara, California

INTRODUCTION
TO THE PAPERBACK EDITION

I met James J. Altieri many times, and the one thing that always stood out was his willingness to help anyone interested in the history of Darby's Rangers, America's first commando unit of World War II. Jim dedicated his civilian life to the preservation of the history of the fabled unit, and in *The Spearheaders* he preserves the colorful characters, hard training, and the attrition of sustained combat operations the men of the unit endured under their much-beloved commander, William O. Darby, who was killed in action in 1945.

Darby's Rangers came to an end during the invasion of Anzio, Italy, in February 1944. The 1st and 3rd Ranger Battalions, totaling 767 Rangers, were annihilated as a fighting force during the battle for Cisterna, with 700 men captured by the Germans. Jim fought alongside the 4th Ranger Battalion in their failed attempt to free their surrounded comrades. The reader will note that this defining battle does not receive the detailed attention that other events do. Clearly, it was painful for Jim to relive that battle.

James J. Altieri was born in Philadelphia, Pennsylvania, on March 4, 1920, and he passed away on April 18, 2008, in Newport Beach, California. A former steelworker at Lukens Steel Company near Philadelphia, Jim enlisted on October 8, 1941, and joined the 68th Field Artillery of the First Armored Division. While serving with the First AD in Northern Ireland, he volunteered for the 1st Ranger Battalion, which had been officially activated on June 19, 1942.

Jim was promoted from first sergeant to second lieutenant with the 4th Ranger Battalion on November 21, 1943, and to first lieutenant on February 25, 1944. He participated in six campaigns, seventeen battles, and four assault landings through North Africa, Sicily, and Italy, and he was wounded twice during the Volturno-Venafro Campaign. The 4th Ranger Battalion was deactivated in October 1944 at Camp Buckner, North Carolina. Jim was the recipient of the Bronze Star, the Purple Heart with Oak Leaf Cluster, and the Combat Infantryman's Badge.

He also served as a public relations officer for the Tennessee Military Authority. Jim was honorably discharged in 1946 as a captain. After World War II, he ran an unsuccessful campaign as the independent Democratic candidate for mayor in Philadelphia.

Jim stayed in touch with many Darby veterans, and he even managed to seal the records of the criminal trial in Los Angeles County of Ranger captain Charles M. "Chuck" Shunstrom, who had brazenly robbed a gas station at gunpoint in 1946.

Recalled to active duty in 1951, Jim served with the Army's Office of Information coordinating the production of Hollywood movies. In this position he supervised the feature-length color documentary, *This Is Your Army*. He was promoted to major.

After his service in World War II Jim continued his career as an author, writing *Darby's Rangers* (1945), which inspired the 1958 Warner Brothers film of the same name starring the iconic actor James Garner. He also wrote a subsequent memoir, *The Spearheaders* (1960), and several screenplays. He served as military technical adviser on films such as *Force of Arm* (1951) and *Darby's Rangers* (1958).

Jim continued his service to the Ranger community as a civilian, becoming president and chairman of numerous World War II Ranger associations. He also spearheaded the creation of the World War II Ranger Monument at Fort Benning, Georgia.

After Jim passed, his longtime friend Frank Lenaghan contacted me and I found in Jim's few belongings what looked like the original manuscript of *The Spearheaders*. I thought Jim would have liked to see it back in print, and his surviving relation, Robert Altieri, agreed. Susan Brook of the U.S. Naval Institute Press was kind enough to reprint the book, fifty-four years after its first release, as it is still a terrific account of men placed in terrible situations. I also thank Ranger Mike Kershaw for his fine Foreword for the classic tale found in *The Spearheaders*.

James J. Altieri was posthumously inducted into the U.S. Army's Ranger Hall of Fame in 2009. To this day, he and all of Darby's Rangers remain legends to Rangers, past, present, and future.

Rangers, lead the way!

Mir Bahmanyar
Toronto, Ontario

PART I

The Challenge

CHAPTER 1

THE shrill blasts of the first sergeant's whistle cut sharply through the North Ireland morning fog, and a hundred and thirty members of Battery A, Sixty-eighth Field Artillery, First Armored Division, stopped working at their varied details and double-timed to take their places at company formation. It was ten in the morning and I was cleaning my Springfield rifle. "I wonder what the hell is up now," I said, turning to my buddy, Carlo Contrera.·

"Another police-up detail," Carlo answered. "That's why they brought us over here—to police-up all the butts in the British Isles."

I had known Carlo since completing my basic training back at Fort Knox in January 1942. I liked him because he was always good-natured and ready with a wisecrack. He was of average height, stocky, with a strong, thick neck, and he wore his brown hair closely cropped. Brooklyn was his home and Brooklyn was his main topic of conversation. But unlike most Brooklynites he hated it! He was exceptionally popular among the fellows in the battery and could always be depended upon for a good laugh or a bitter gripe.

We took our places in the battery formation and stood at attention as our platoon sergeants made their report to Top Sergeant Burns, a big, hulking, lantern-jawed Regular Army man. Burns then assumed his familiar belligerent stance and said:

"Men, I got an important announcement to make." But this did not stir anyone because we all knew by now that anything the sergeant said was considered important. "I have a letter here from

15

higher H.Q. which states that all men of excellent physical condition among the troops stationed here in North Ireland *may apply* for service in a new type of combat unit to be formed along the lines of the British Commandos. It also says that this outfit requires a high type of soldier with excellent character who is not averse to seeing dangerous action. All volunteers must be athletically inclined, have good wind and stamina, be good swimmers and mentally adapted for making quick decisions in the face of unforeseen circumstances."

As he spoke I felt my heart pounding! *This was it.* I had always admired the Commandos. To me they seemed the perfect type of fighting men. I had read accounts of their daring raids at Tobruk, along the Norwegian coast and at St. Nazaire and Boulogne. I had read about their tough, realistic training, how they were handpicked and were resourceful fighters in any situation. The prospects of taking part in swift night sorties on enemy coast fortifications and then returning to rest up awhile and live in civilian billets as gentlemen also appealed to me. I needed no second thought to decide that I was going to volunteer.

I looked toward my right and caught Carlo's eye. He smiled and winked, nodding his head approvingly. He was in too.

Sergeant Burns continued: "Now, if any of you men think you have those qualifications I mentioned, report to the battery commander for an interview at ten-thirty. But remember this: It's a tough outfit that needs tough men who want action—dangerous action. I don't want to scare anybody, but they say that the Commando training is even more dangerous than their actual fighting. Now is the time for all you guys who have been griping about coming over here to police-up the matchsticks in Ireland to step out. If it's action you want, this is it."

After the formation was dismissed, the men banded together in small groups talking over the sudden news. "Volunteer? Like hell I will," one corporal was saying to several buddies grouped around him. "I learned a long time ago by bitter experience not to volunteer for anything in this man's army. What will they ask you to volunteer for next? Nobody in their right senses is going to ask for a bellyful of lead by joining up with a suicide outfit. I'll take my

16

chances by sweating out the war with the old Armored. Who knows, they might keep the First Armored here to guard against an invasion of Ireland. I'm not going to stick my neck out."

Carlo came over to me, highly elated. "This is what I've been waiting for," he said. "Now we can sign up for a real fighting outfit. I'll bet they won't waste our time by policing-up butts in the Commandos."

"I like the idea of the hard training we'll get," I said. "Before we go into action we'll know what it's all about. What do we know about war now? None of us has any idea what actual battle is like."

As I said this I wondered to myself how much I really wanted to get into action—or was I just bluffing? Anyway, I had spoken my sentiments as I thought I really felt them, and now there was nothing left for me but to follow through.

At ten-thirty we reported at battery headquarters. There were sixteen of us, and heading the line was Top Sergeant Burns—a fact that caused no little stir of comment. There were big men and little men, and all of them had the glint of expectancy in their eyes. Most of the volunteers were noncoms who held key posts in the battery. I thought to myself, "The old man isn't going to like this too well." Most of them had been with the battery since it was first activated and had undergone months of hard, detailed training at their specialties.

The heavy, oak-paneled door of the orderly room swung open and we filed smartly in until we were abreast of the C.O.'s desk, then halting, we did a sharp left face, saluted and stood at attention stiffly.

"At ease," Captain Elfring, young, sincere and capable, said. Then he added: "The information we have received about this new Commando-type unit is not too specific. We know that all volunteers, both officers and enlisted men, will be under the supervision of the British for training purposes. After a hardening and weeding-out process at an American Army camp somewhere in Ireland, those who have passed all qualifications will be sent as a unit to a Commando depot in Scotland for more intensive training. After that the American contingent *may* operate as a Commando unit."

17

Captain Elfring paused to let his words sink in, then clearing his throat he continued: "It's rather hard for me to lose some of my top men to another outfit. But if you can qualify I wish you all the luck in the world—and with that wish goes my admiration, because I think it will be a topnotch outfit composed of the best from every outfit. . . . Now I want to ask each one individually why you would like to join—and I want truthful answers."

Sergeant Burns was the first to answer, and we all stretched our necks as he stammered out: "Sir, I really couldn't give you any specific reasons except to say, I like a challenge."

The next man in line, a usually garrulous fellow who was particularly handy with his dukes, said he felt the same way. The third man spoke out slowly in a Kentuckian drawl: "I figger it this way, Cap'n. When I'm up there facin' those Krautheads I wanna make sure I got some good support on my left and on my right. It appears to me that when the trainin' is over every man who pulls through will be a darned good man who can be depended on in a tight spot. That's the kinda people I like to be with when the shootin' starts."

The captain smiled broadly and said, "Next."

Carlo, who was fidgeting with his cap in his hands, looked first to his left and then to his right before answering. "Well, sir," he said, "it's like this. . . . I've been in this outfit for six months. I work hard, I don't get into any trouble—I mean real trouble—and yet I'm still a Pfc. Now, I don't mind being a Pfc. if there's a future ahead. But the trouble is that over seventy per cent of the people in the battery are noncoms and the rest privates whose only future seems to be in the police detail. So I think it would be better for me if I got in a new outfit. But don't get me wrong, sir," he added respectfully, "it's a pretty good outfit, but not enough room for advancement." Sergeant Burns was glowering with knitted eyebrows as Carlo spoke.

When it came my turn, though it seemed I had a million reasons why I wanted to join, I had difficulty in condensing my thoughts. After hesitating, I said simply, "I like the way the Commandos operate in small groups with light weapons. That type of fighting appeals to me because more emphasis is placed on personal initiative."

18

I wondered if I sounded a little foolish talking about warfare that appeals, as though I were a grizzled veteran of many battles.

Sergeant Smith was next. Besides being one of the best-looking men in the battery, Smith was trim and well-built, the result of a vigorous athletic life during his high school days at West Catholic in Philly. He was modest, sincere and a good mixer, and what he told the battery commander was in keeping with his character.

"Captain," he said in a soft voice, "I like this outfit very well. I am happy with my job and with my friends here—but I feel it is my duty to volunteer. I don't wish to appear overly patriotic, but I feel that the sooner we meet the enemy the quicker we'll defeat him, and I would like to be among the first of the American forces under fire on this side."

That was all he said, but that was enough. His statement had a stimulating, uplifting effect on all present. The captain seemed greatly impressed. I wondered how many other Sergeant Smiths were volunteering for the new outfit, and I also wondered if I would be able to keep up with real men like Sergeant Smith.

One by one the other men voiced their reasons, while the captain made some markings on a paper slanted across his desk. Most of the reasons were original, but a few put the thoughts of others who had spoken before them into different words. Several really didn't seem to know why they were volunteering except that it seemed the popular thing to do; some, because they felt that others expected them to and they wanted to keep their stock high among their battery mates.

After the last man had given his reasons, the captain surveyed the group, looking us over individually as though he were already deciding who would and who would not be eligible. Then he spoke clearly:

"There are several steps to be taken before the eligibles will actually be assigned to the new unit. First, there is a stiff physical by the battalion medic tomorrow at two. Those who pass that will then be interviewed by especially selected officers who are to lead the new unit. If you pass them, you go on to the preliminary tests at a camp somewhere near Belfast. Those who survive will go on to Scotland, and you won't really be a bona fide member of the new unit until you pass the toughest of all the tests under the Commandos." He added: "You will find on the bulletin board tomorrow the names of those who are eligible to take the medical exams. I wish you all luck."

At two o'clock the next day the volunteers whose names were posted on the bulletin board reported to the battalion medic for the first physical examination. As we queued up on the outside of a low barnlike building, green-molded with age, I noticed that two men had already been eliminated from the list by Captain Elfring. Soon a sergeant came out and told us to strip down to the waist, then we filed into a large room furnished with cabinets of medical equipment and several scales. One by one they called our names and examined us in assembly-line style. It was the most thorough physical examination I had ever had. When it was all over, three men had been eliminated.

That night I turned in feeling tremendously exuberant—but the really important thing was the interview with the officers who would personally select the volunteers the next day. I wondered if I would impress them as the type of man they would want in their outfit. I knew that all those who were to be interviewed with me were wondering the same thing.

It was eleven o'clock the next morning when Top Kick Burns blew his whistle with a ferocity seldom heard by the men of Battery A. When we lined up at formation, he looked very serious and he spoke his words deliberately: "The following men will fall in double ranks in front of the company as I call out your names. Altieri . . . Contrera . . . Smith . . . Rucco . . . Yardborough . . . Munge . . . Thomason . . . Kepler . . . Keberdle . . . Stuart . . ."

We all answered, "Here," then stepped into ranks in front of the battery. The men in the battery ranks behind us stared hard as Sergeant Burns turned them over to another sergeant for close-order drill, took his place beside our small detail and marched us off to meet the Commando officers. My heart was beating double-time, and I felt as if the whole world depended on whether or not I was accepted. The others, too, had set lines on their faces. And even Carlo's usual wiseacre smile was missing.

20

Sergeant Burns marched us into the courtyard of an impressive vine-covered castle, which served as battalion headquarters and housed the officers. There volunteers from other batteries in the battalion had already assembled. Ten minutes later the officer in charge of the volunteer detachment called us to attention as a group of officers walked briskly to the front of our detachment, accepted the salute from our officer in charge, spoke a few words and then proceeded to look us over.

We looked them over also. They were all well built and had an assuredness I seldom before had seen. One of them, a large broad-shouldered captain who looked like a wrestler in top condition, seemed to be the leader. Another captain, who was lithe, slender and extremely light on his feet, was on his right. After scrutinizing our volunteer group in almost the same manner a rancher might appraise a prize herd of cattle, they walked into the castle. Each one was given a separate room in which to conduct the interviews.

Gradually the line moved forward, and then I was through the door. I must have looked very grim as I saluted because the big, broad-shouldered captain broke out with an amused smile as I babbled out my name. "Technician Fifth Grade James Altieri, sir!"

"Have a seat, Corporal," he commanded. "I'm Captain Miller. Why do you want to join this outfit?"

I told him what I had read concerning the Commandos and added the same reasons I had given my battery commander.

"Do you realize the dangers of being in such an outfit? All training will be with live ammunition and a certain percentage of men are wounded or hurt during training."

I replied I fully realized the dangerous possibilities of training and thought that the rugged training should fully condition a man for real warfare. By this time all traces of my former nervousness had left completely, and I was beginning to talk easily.

"Are you of Italian descent?" he asked.

"Yes, sir. Both my mother and father were born in Italy, but they have lived in the States for over forty years."

"What would be your attitude about fighting hand-to-hand with the Italians? There is every possibility that our actions might bring us into contact with them. Do you feel you would give your best against your own blood?"

"Well, Captain," I returned, "naturally I would much prefer to fight the Germans or the Japs. I would feel bad about fighting the same people my father came from—but I feel that when the time comes, that factor won't interfere with my duty as an American soldier."

There were a large number of fellows of Italian extraction in the Army, and I wondered how many of them felt as I did. We were at war, the line was drawn and personal feelings about the matter must give precedence to duty.

"Have you ever been court-martialed?"

"No, sir."

"What sports have you been active in?"

"I've played baseball a lot," I said, "and I used to do a lot of boxing in my teens. But football was my favorite sport. I used to play halfback on a sand-lot semipro team in Philly. I like swimming and tennis, too," I added.

"How far can you swim?"

"Two miles was the longest I ever tried," I lied. The longest I ever swam was about a mile, but I had heard through rumors that only good swimmers would be accepted, so I added another mile.

"Have you ever been in any brawls, barroom fights, gang fights where people have been hurt bad?"

I could answer him truthfully on that score. "Yes, sir, I grew up in a tough neighborhood. You either fought or you didn't live."

The captain raised his eyebrows slightly, rubbed his right hand over his forehead, then he stared straight through me and said, "Did you ever kill a man? You may answer truthfully without fear —anything you say here will be held in strict confidence."

That question startled me. What type of men were they looking for? Do you have to be a killer to get into this outfit? I wasn't going to lie about killing.

"No, sir," I yammered out very emphatically. "I never went quite that far. Nothing worse than a brawl."

"Have you ever seen anyone killed?"

22

My thoughts went back to my childhood in South Philly during the reign of the beer barons and the Tommy-gun-toting racketeers. When I was only six years old I had narrowly escaped death when a long black touring car screamed down the narrow street where I was playing marbles. A hail of machine-gun bullets splattered around me as the occupants of the car cut down two men walking just ten yards from me. I told the captain about it.

"Do you think you would have guts enough to stick a knife in a man's back and twist it?"

"I guess a fellow can do anything in the heat of battle," I replied. "Sure, if it had to be done, I think I could do it." I was lying. The mere thought of using a knife on someone repelled me. I even hated to see chickens killed. But if knife-twisting was what these people specialized in, then I would be a knife-twister. What's the difference if you kill someone with a bullet or a knife? A dead man is a dead man regardless of how he is killed.

All the time the captain did not reveal in any manner whether I was answering his questions satisfactorily or not. While I was answering he doodled on a sheet of paper with his pencil.

"Have you ever had any experience in navigation?"

"No, sir. The closest I ever navigated was when I went canoeing and I didn't navigate long before I turned over."

If I made any impression on him, he did not show it. And, after he dismissed me curtly, I began to doubt that I had measured up to the requirements.

A bright sun pierced the dark-shrouded sky for the first time in two weeks as we volunteers said good-by to our battery mates and were whisked away by motor convoy to the town of Carrickfergus, north of Belfast on the coast. Carlo, Munge, Smith, Yardborough, Rucco, Winsor, Keberdle, Stuart, myself and two others had been accepted. As I sat in the bouncing, crowded truck next to Sergeant Smith, my thoughts went back to the last words Captain Elring said as he shook hands with each of us before we boarded the vehicle.

"Give it your very best," he said. "But remember if you don't like the new outfit or can't make the grade, you can always find your place waiting for you in Battery A. I don't want any of you to feel that your return will be considered a failure. There may be a thousand reasons why you may not like the life you are about to enter—and it is a man's privilege to change his mind."

That was all he said. With these words he had given us a pathway of retreat without embarrassment. I hoped I would not have to take that pathway.

CHAPTER 2

THE training camp, one mile north of the outskirts of Carrickfergus, was a beehive of bustling activity when our convoy swung onto a narrow macadam road between neatly spaced rows of large Nissen huts. There was a peculiar briskness about the place. Men were occupied in cleaning greasy cosmolene off newly issued weapons; some were playing football in the large playing field; others were busy cleaning out their new quarters. There were lines of men waiting in front of a building for another physical examination, the first step for the newly initiated, we were told. Most of them looked rugged and sturdy and as our convoy made its way to the headquarters building, we got a lot of heckling and jibing.

After we dismounted and swung our heavy barracks bags and gear onto the ground beside the trucks, we were surprised to see the trucks being mounted by a group of dejected-looking men who had been waiting for our arrival. "Where are those guys going?" I asked the burly sergeant detailed to assign us our quarters.

"Right back where they started from," he said. "They've been here for three days. Most of them don't like the new outfit, and some are being sent back because they aren't qualified. At the rate people are going back to their old outfits, I don't think we'll have enough men to organize one company before we leave this place. You'll understand what I mean after you've been here for a few days."

"Boy, this doesn't look so good to me," Carlo said after we had been temporarily assigned to a bunk side by side. "Those guys were

25

here only three days and they're going back already. Now what the hell can they do to a man in three days?"

"It looks like the weeding-out process is designed to get the dead-heads out in a hurry," I answered. "That sergeant didn't seem too optimistic about our possibilities, did he?"

"Sergeants are never optimistic about anything but getting another stripe," Carlo answered.

The next morning we were assigned to our new companies, and after reporting to the acting first sergeant I received another physical examination, a new issue of clothing and an orientation lecture, all in the same morning. Carlo was placed in Company D, and I had drawn Company F. The acting first sergeant of Company F, a loud-talking, self-assured three-striper from the Thirteenth Armored Regiment, First Division, told us in no uncertain terms what he expected of us. First call was at six, chow at seven and formation at eight. And we'd better not be late for any formation, the sergeant bellowed. His name was Donald Torbett, and he walked with his chest fully inflated and his chin tilted at a defiant angle. One of the fellows who had been there a few days told me he was a tough stickler and a hard guy to put anything over on. "He's buckin' for the first sergeancy of this company, and, brother, he's going to make it or else!"

The men in our company were from almost every branch of the service: Artillery, Infantry, Tankers, Signal, Antiaircraft, Ordnance, and even a few from the Quartermaster—to everyone's surprise. Not that the Quartermaster doesn't have good men, but we thought they would hardly be the type to go in for Commando work. I found out later that some of the very best men came from the rear-echelon outfits.

The afternoon of that first day was devoted entirely to sports. Some fellows played baseball, some wrestled, some put on boxing gloves, while the rest played football. I joined the group playing football and got a good opportunity to study the slim, trim captain who was commanding our company. He was on the same team with me and was distinctive even without his bars. He was as fast as a deer and as tough as nails. I guessed him about thirty years old, but he moved with the agility of a nineteen-year-old. What

26

impressed me most was that he made no effort to dominate the team's strategy. His name was Roy Murray.

The next morning we received our first introduction to the speed march, which was to become one of our outfit's secret weapons. With Captain Murray and a small, wiry lieutenant at the head of our double column, we started off at a brisk pace down the narrow macadam road. Each man looked fresh and vigorous; each man looked confident. Already I could sense the difference in spirit between this outfit and the one I had just left. As we marched past the camp gate and swung up a steep road which wound its way northward through green-velveted fields, Private Gomez, a stocky, light-skinned Mexican lad, broke out into song:

> "The Infantry, the Infantry,
> With dirt behind their ears,
> They can lick their weight in wildcats
> And drink their weight in beers.
> The Cavalry, the Artillery,
> The lousy Engineers,
> They couldn't lick the Infantry
> In a hundred thousand years."

Almost as soon as he finished the first line, a strong chorus of voices picked up the song and the deafening result drowned out the sound of our hard-heeled shoes striking the road. The men from Artillery, Engineer and Cavalry units joined in the singing as enthusiastically as the men from the Infantry. But the singing was interrupted abruptly when the captain yelled back to us, "Double-time. . . . March!" We ran in step for three hundred yards before we got the command to quick-time again. I was breathless. The captain stepped up his pace, taking a good thirty-six-inch step. We were now beginning to sweat heavily, and I was thankful I had cut down my leggings to half their usual size so that they fitted snugly below the calf.

Gomez had registered well among his new company mates with his vocal contribution to company spirit. We decided to follow through by picking on the poor Quartermaster Corps. As no one

27

else in the company knew the words, Gomez sang alone as we sped along the highway:

> "Oh, where do the broken majors go,
> Kicked out of the Infantry,
> The Engineer captain whose bridge collapsed
> Who went on a two month's spree;
> The 4-F brass that nobody wants,
> The cream of incompetency?
> Why, the buzzards are all colonels now,
> In the fighting QMC."

The company roared in laughter when he finished. Even Captain Murray turned back and smiled. Fellows like Gomez are essential to every outfit. They are priceless in their contribution to company morale. Without them, life in the Army would be drab and dull, without color or humor. When we returned to camp at the finish of a five-mile hike which we made with full pack and equipment in one hour, the company seemed as high in spirit as when we first started out—even though five men had dropped out.

Before we were dismissed for chow, the short, wiry lieutenant, a Louisianian named Loustalot, gave us a short talk—more or less a briefing on what to expect in the new outfit. He spoke slowly and deliberately with a faint suggestion of a drawl:

"Men, I want to welcome you all to Company F. We are all here for the same purpose—to prove ourselves qualified for the new American Commando outfit. We may be here for two or three weeks before leaving for Scotland, and during that time our training will be stepped up each day. Any man who can't keep up with us will be sent back to his old outfit immediately, as well as anyone who proves troublesome. Discipline in this outfit rests with the individual himself—it's up to you, as we don't intend to waste any time on foul-ups. And remember, you are free to request return to your old outfit at any time."

He was a sincere talker and the type of man who did not waste words. That he had the qualities of leadership demanded in an outfit of that nature could be plainly seen even before he spoke.

The first hike proved a snap compared to the two weeks of stren-

28

uous marching, drilling and training that followed. Every morning was spent on a long speed march or mountain climb. We were driven relentlessly until it seemed our aching bodies could take no more. The sight of men dropping out on the marches, broken and beaten, was disheartening. Each day the distance of our marches would be lengthened until we were doing twelve miles in two hours, which included a five-minute break. At the breaks men would drop like sacks of beans, tired and exhausted.

Each day I thought would surely be the last for me—I felt I couldn't take it. Then I would think of returning to the battery as a failure, a would-be Commando. No guts, nothing but a lot of talk. I remembered how I had spoken to Carlo about initiative and gumption. When I thought about those things I would close my eyes and clench my fists until the palms bled from my fingernails digging deep, and I would resolve to die rather than go back. I would look at the captain who was setting the marching pace and curse him under my breath. Then I would look at the small lieutenant who was also having a hard time, more so than the rest of us because of his shorter legs. *Dammit,* I would say half aloud, *if they can do it, so can I!* And I would dig in.

I would look at the faces of the men around me who were suffering as much as I was and I would admire them and feel proud to be one of them—if I could only last. There was Private Howard Andre, who also was from Philly. He had sandy-brown hair, a well-chiseled face with a prominent but not sharp nose, and a habit of whistling while he marched. He always whistled regardless of how tired he was, and he never seemed to look as exhausted as the rest when the marches were over. With broad shoulders and erect carriage, Andre fired me with ambition to keep up with him. Occasionally he would look over at me when he noticed me faltering and say, "Come on, Altieri, show these guys what kind of men Philly produces." And then I would feel ashamed of myself and try harder.

Then there was Sergeant Harris, a modest, thin, frail-looking man who had great difficulty in speaking without stuttering. Sergeant Harris did not look like a Commando. He was the type you would visualize as a clerk behind a typewriter. If a vote had been taken among the men in Company F at the beginning of our training as to who would be the first to be eliminated, Sergeant Harris would have been unanimously elected. But Sergeant Harris, besides being one of the smartest in the company, was proving that he had more guts and stamina than most. I was beginning to learn that what counted in this outfit was what a man had within him.

Every day new volunteers arrived at camp to find lines of men awaiting truck transportation to return to their old outfits. Sergeant Torbett told the company at formation one morning that over two thousand men had volunteered—and slightly over five hundred were still at camp. That was at the beginning of our second week. After that, the number leaving diminished to a mere handful every other day.

The third week found the battalion actually organized into sections, platoons and companies, with each man given a specific assignment in his organization. Unlike a regular Infantry battalion, our outfit had small companies, consisting of three officers and sixty-four enlisted men. The Commandos had found that for short, decisive encounters, such as night raids, establishing beachheads or seizing points behind enemy lines—operations that depended much on contact and control—smaller units were preferable.

Each company had two platoons and a small headquarters section comprised of the C.O., a runner, a supply sergeant and a sniper. Each of the platoons consisted of two assault sections composed of twelve men and a mortar section with five men. There were six line companies—A, B, C, D, E, F—and a headquarters company of eighty men. The Headquarters Company was responsible for services such as supply, communications, personnel, transportation, the S-1, S-2, S-3 and S-4 sections, and the all-important kitchen force.

30

CHAPTER 3

JUNE the nineteenth was a big day for our outfit. We were to be officially activated as a combat unit. All would-be Rangers diligently polished and spruced for a ceremonial parade and inspection. It was rumored that a big British general of the Special Services Brigade would speak to us about the Commandos.

At ten in the morning, a bright sun beating down on us, we lined up by company on the large playing field, each man attired in his best uniform change and trying to look serious and soldierly. A large olive-drab touring car loaded with British officials swung up the macadam road and discharged its passengers. They were met by Major William O. Darby, our C.O., and his executive officer, Captain Herman Dammer, and escorted to the reviewing stand. A band, borrowed from a nearby Signal Corps detachment, struck up a martial tune, and one by one the companies led by their respective commanders paraded smartly past the reviewing stand.

Standing beside the British general, erect and confident, was our young commander, Major Darby. He had a bright ruddy complexion that harmonized well with his steel-blue eyes. He looked the part of a man singled out by destiny to lead a group of men who required leadership of the highest caliber. His arms were folded firmly against his chest, and a scar on the left side of his face seemed to glow a brilliant red as he proudly surveyed his men passing before him.

Major Darby had been an aide to Major General Russell P. Hartle, commanding general of the Thirty-fourth Infantry Division, the first American unit to go overseas to Great Britain. In late May Brigadier General Lucien K. Truscott, the man who conceived and initiated the idea for the American Rangers, came to General Hartle with special orders from General Marshall to organize the Ranger unit and select an appropriate well-qualified commander. General Truscott at first wanted to select the leader personally. But General Hartle said that inasmuch as the troops would come from his command it was appropriate for him to name the leader of this daring band. "And who might that be?" asked General Truscott. "You are looking at him right now," said General Hartle pointing to the pleased Major Darby.

Despite the fact that Darby had an excellent position handling appointments for the general, attending social functions and other miscellaneous duties, he immediately accepted the challenge to lead the roughest, toughest collection of individualists in the entire army. Thus the Darby story was basically the story of every Ranger. This outfit was a challenge—a stern challenge to measure up to the highest standards and demands that modern war can impose on the individual, an opportunity to show ourselves what we were truly made of and what limits we could endure.

Darby was of medium height with a slender waist but broad chest and shoulders. There was a magnetic quality about him that defied description. His expressions were lively and he seemed to possess a dynamic energy. It was rumored he was a West Pointer and a stickler for discipline, but was a just man who knew the true psychology of leadership.

Captain Dammer standing on his left seemed to complement him. Dammer was tall, angular, taciturn and terribly efficient.

After the ceremonies were over all companies massed in front of the reviewing stand to hear the general and Major Darby speak.

Major Darby spoke first: "Men, we are honored by the presence here today of Brigadier General Laycock, who is commander of the British Special Services Brigade, which we will be under when we leave Ireland for Scotland. For three weeks I have watched you train, observed your spirit and noted your appearance as soldiers. For three weeks I have received daily reports on each individual's progress. Men have come and men have gone until now the chosen few remain. You few are now officially known as the

32

First American Ranger Battalion, a name honored in American military-history annals, since it first was used by Rogers' Rangers of Indian war fame. And now General Laycock. . . ."

The general—iron-gray hair, slight of build, dapper, with riding crop in hand—stepped to the fore of the reviewing stand and spoke slowly but crisply.

"American Rangers, when you arrive in Scotland you will be under my command for training purposes. It is our responsibility to condition and train you in all aspects of Commando warfare, and to that effect our best instructors will be assigned to each of your companies at the training depot. This, the formation of the American Rangers, is an experiment, novel in modern American military history. The outcome of this experiment may determine the type of training your Infantry divisions will receive; may determine new battle tactics to be employed in amphibious landings and will undoubtedly result in the saving of countless lives. You are pioneering in a daring field of warfare at a critical time when our fighting forces, reeling from early defeats, must rebound and assume the offensive. In the British Army the Commandos have provided the spark for that offensive spirit; you men are destined to provide that offensive spark for the American forces in Europe."

After a few more words about our future with the Commandos the general remarked about the fine, sturdy appearance of the troops and added that he felt the Rangers would in the near future make history. But he also cautioned that the road ahead was a trying and exacting one that would require each individual's stoic and enduring determination for perseverance. His effect upon the Rangers was like a charge of electricity. His words were to stand out vividly in our minds for many long months to come.

CHAPTER 4

IT WAS raining lightly when our troop train pulled into the railroad station at Fort William, Scotland, after a twenty-six hour ride from a small port on the Irish Sea where our battalion had disembarked from Ireland. First sergeants were roaring orders to their respective companies as we crawled, staggered and limped from the rickety cars with our ponderous barracks bags draped on our shoulders.

A short ride on a British train, cramped into small compartments like sardines, is real torture. I consoled myself with the thought that no training could outdo the rigors and discomforts of that train ride.

First Sergeant Torbett's lusty voice cracked loud above the sounds of confusion as the men of Company F wrestled with their equipment outside the car.

"F Company . . . fall . . . in!" he roared. The sergeant had by now become well liked by most of his company mates. Although firm, he was a good-natured fellow full of yeasty humor. He had plenty of color about him in everything he did, and he drank and gambled with the best of the sharp boys in the company after duty hours—even though it was against regulations for noncoms to gamble with privates. But he still sounded off the loudest when the officers were present, especially when Loustalot was around, because Loustalot was strictly all Army.

"Let's go! Let's go!" he raved. "We're holding back the war. Just because we're the last company alphabetically in the battalion doesn't mean that we're supposed to be last in falling in. The way

34

some of you guys fuss with equipment every time we make a short move, you'd think we were a ladies' auxiliary group." After receiving the report from his platoon sergeants, Torbett turned smartly on his heels and saluted Lieutenant Loustalot, saying, "All present and accounted for, sir."

Like everything else he did, Sergeant Torbett gave an emphatically vigorous salute—so vigorous that we wondered why the velocity of his right arm swinging forward didn't carry him along with it. Lieutenant Loustalot returned the salute just as vigorously. The lieutenant liked things to be done snappily, and it was easy to see that Torbett was registering well with him. When the lieutenant was around, the company could always depend on Torbett to perform in his best and most truculent manner—and the company enjoyed every bit of the show.

With Major Darby and a Commando officer on Captain Murray's left at the head of the column, we started our trek with our packs and rifles. The seven miles felt like seventy when we reached the outskirts of the Commando camp. The road from Inverness to Achna Carry twisted uphill through richly tufted fields, dotted with quaint, picturesque farmhouses and flanked by steep hills. The Scottish countryside, now basking in sunlight after a mild rain, was a beautiful sight, and I wondered if it would still look that attractive after a few days of Commando routine.

As we turned a sharp bend beside a towering hill mass on the left of the road we saw a level clearing stretching for almost a quarter of a mile. A huge ivy-covered castle replete with ancient battlements towered high over rows of uniformly spaced Nissen huts and small canvas tents that looked like Indian wigwams. Far to the right raced a swift river barely visible from the road. The scene looked almost too tranquil for a Commando training camp.

As we swung off the road, we marched by a small graveyard where a number of crosses over freshly dug mounds caught our attention. A Commando officer standing by bellowed out: "Take a good look, lads! This is where the lax and the dead rest."

We looked—and I wondered if joining this outfit wasn't the biggest mistake of my life. I'm sure others felt the same way.

The British Commando officer led the battalion out onto the flat field where the unit assumed its regular battalion formation. A group of British officers came over to Major Darby and introduced themselves. In the center of the compound to our right, between two rows of Nissen huts, a detachment of British troops was undergoing the rigors of close-order drill.

"Holy smoke!" Andre said to me. "This is one place I never expected to see close-order drill. Just look at them go through their paces."

The conversation was cut short when Major Darby called the battalion to attention and introduced the commandant of the depot, a chunky, ruddy-faced colonel armed with the inevitable swagger stick. He spoke slowly and clearly. He reiterated all the things that General Laycock had told us and added that the Rangers were on the threshold of a glorious adventure; that our outfit would have the unique honor of being among the first American troops in action, in that part of the world. He also told us that his Commando instructors would have complete supervision over each company, and that much depended on our readiness to comply with their instructions which would mold us into the type of outfit ideal for Commando-type warfare.

What stood out in my mind in a comforting way was his statement about the dangers of training. "I know," he said, "that you have heard all sorts of rumors about the high risks in Commando training; that some men are killed and wounded, the result of using live ammunition in our training. Unfortunately, we have had a few accidents, some through carelessness and some through circumstances which are the fault of no one. But more often it has been as a result of carelessness on the part of the individual. Remember to listen to instructions intently and try to keep a cool head at all times. Every accident we do have is more than compensated for in the field of battle.

"The lessons learned here will adapt you both physically and mentally for the dangerous work ahead. You become used to danger, you become confident, then when battle comes, it is just like another maneuver. You are cool, you know what it is all about and your chances for fatal blunders are much less than if you had received no realistic training.

"Initiative and resourcefulness are two characteristics that can come only with strenuous, realistic combat training. This has been

36

proved time and again by our own Commandos. It has enabled them to accomplish feats deemed impossible by military strategists. They could not possibly have accomplished such feats if they were not first thoroughly indoctrinated with fundamentals of modern warfare provided by training in Commando depots scattered throughout the British Isles. I am proud to say that this school is noted for being the toughest of all the Commando schools. I am sure you Rangers will prove as good as the best this school has produced. . . . It is up to you!"

After he had spoken, one officer and two noncoms were assigned to each company as instructors. A tall, powerfully built lieutenant with massive shoulders and broad weather-lined face, sporting the latest in Highlander kilt fashions—accompanied by two sprightly legged noncoms wearing woolly tams cocked jauntily on one side— briskly presented himself to Captain Murray with a salute very proper and very precise, as only the British can deliver.

"Lieutenant Cowerson, sir," the leader said. "I will show Company F to their quarters, and after they are settled I would have a word with them to outline our schedule."

Our quarters turned out to be in the wigwam-like canvas tents we had first noticed coming into the clearing. They were spaced six feet apart, and each company was given an entire row. Company F was assigned the row paralleling the road. We wondered how many men would be quartered in each tent; it seemed that no more than four could possibly squeeze in. The tall Commando lieutenant told us that eight men would be housed in each tent and that we could sleep very comfortably if we would lie with our feet toward the central supporting post, much like the spokes of a wagon wheel. He warned us to build circular ditches around the tent to take care of heavy rains and added that rain in the Scotch Highlands was habitual. After each section was assigned respective tents, Sergeant Torbett blew his whistle and the company lined up to hear what the Commando lieutenant had to say.

I have seen few men who looked more sure of themselves, more forceful and who spoke more candidly than Lieutenant Cowerson of Mountbatten's Special Services Brigade as he stood in front of the company, flanked by his two sergeant assistants. This was for most of us our first real contact with British troops. Up to now,

37

our opinions of them, good or bad, had been formed from hearsay. We realized that the caliber of the Commandos must be higher than that of the regular British troops, but how high we did not know. We all received a good idea of what to expect from our instructors when Lieutenant Cowerson spoke:

"I don't know too much about you Yanks," he started off, "but I'll bloody well know before the month is up. You are supposed to be the best the American troops have—so they say. The training will soon prove how right they are. Before this month is over many of you will hate me; you will curse me under your breath every time I take you through an obstacle course. On every road march some of you will hope that I meet with an accident. Some of you will spit on the ground every time you see me. You will curse yourselves for joining this outfit and you will want to quit— but most of you will still go on regardless of how much you come to hate me. The real men will stay on, the weak will fall out." He paused to inhale a deep breath before concluding.

Most of the Rangers of Company F were staring with fixed eyes, hardly believing their ears. He sounded like a blood-and-thunder man. Already his words had a challenging effect.

"Supposed to be the best," he had taunted. Why did he start out with us like that? Then I wondered if that was not part of the psychology of instilling the competitive spirit—a challenge that naturally must be accepted. If it was, Lieutenant Cowerson was a great actor.

He continued: "Every time the company moves in formation it will be on the double-time; everything here at the Commando depot is done on the double. You will march to chow on the double, you will march to your parade formation on the double, you will even march to sick call on the double; and let me warn you in advance that only the half-dead will be accepted for sick call. You will learn to treat yourselves for any minor hurts or illnesses. This is no place for the weak sisters. And the fakers will be quickly sifted.

"Assisting me in the instruction of Company F are Sarn't Blimt—" he gestured toward a small, squat, neatly uniformed sergeant who smiled genially as he clicked his heels to attention and with his left hand twirled the end of his walrus-like mustache— "and Sarn't Brown," a slender, upright sergeant who seemed the

38

sterner of the two. "Their orders will be followed explicitly, and their reports on your progress will be the determining factor to your successful completion of this training."

After laying down the law in no uncertain terms, the lieutenant briefly outlined the coming schedule, which would start the next morning, July 2. He said that the training would start off rather mildly and gradually increase in tempo. After one month we would be sent to a naval station in northern Scotland for further training.

"And keep this in mind," he ended his talk, "I will make men out of you—or kill you in the attempt."

CHAPTER 5

THE next four weeks found Lieutenant Cowerson living ruthlessly up to his promise. He wasn't satisfied that the men in Company F were keeping up with the other companies in the battalion. Everything we undertook had to be *better* than the others.

When Company E made a seven-mile speed march with packs and rifles in under one hour, he insisted that F Company should better the record by five minutes—and we did. When A Company went through the obstacle course—a laborious grind through slushy mud, over dangerous cliffs and gigantic tree-logged walls rimmed with barbed wire—in ten minutes, he exhorted F Company to make it in eight! When men straggled during the grueling road marches, he would grab them by the seat of their pants and rush them back to their place in the company. If they fell out again, he would taunt them unmercifully, chiding them that they lacked the necessary substance in their stomachs. When men keeled over from sheer fatigue, no longer able to keep up the maddening pace, he would order them to make the speed march after duty hours.

He was cursed, vilified and spoken of as an inhuman monster who had no regard for flesh and blood. The things he led us to do were almost impossible, but he would say, "Nothing is impossible. It is all in the heart and in the mind." It was that simple to him.

At the end of each speed march he would look at his watch, then glance over the entire company and say, "Only fair; you did it in three minutes less than E Company," or it would be four minutes

40

less than B Company or it might be one minute less than the Commando record. He was a fanatical perfectionist.

His favorite training course was the amphibious landings which were made under live fire. When Company F made the landings, machine-gun bullets, fired from shore positions manned by Commando marksmen, would splatter rowing paddles to splinters in the hands of the men that held them as our collapsible boats neared shore for the assault landings. As we hit the beach, charges of dynamite would explode almost in our faces as we dashed madly for cover to evade the snapping Bren-gun bullets which kicked up dirt between our strides. We would return fire at designated targets on the sloping hillside as our company, a section at a time, would advance up the slopes to take our imaginary enemy gun batteries. Our mortar sections, generally wedged in a ravine at the base of the hill, would support us by laying down barrages as we advanced. Co-ordination and control were the essential factors. If one section got a little ahead, it could easily become the target of our own mortars. Several times sections got crossed up on signals and almost got under heavy mortar barrages. The Commandos pulled no punches.

On one particular landing a Commando tossed a live grenade into a boatload of Rangers. A grenade has only seven seconds to explode after the pin is pulled, and the boat was still out in deep water. Luckily, a quick-thinking lad picked it up after it had bounced off another's head and threw it far out into the lake where it exploded harmlessly. The man who was hit on the head was admonished later by the lieutenant for being unobservant.

Lieutenant Cowerson had complete charge of the company from eight in the morning until five-thirty in the evening. Our officers, although consulted, naturally had to take it like the rest of us. They were not accorded any special consideration, other than courtesy between officers. In a way, their lot was a little worse than ours because they were always the first to be initiated into the hellish training devices that Cowerson concocted for Company F.

"A company is as strong as its weakest man," Cowerson would say. "It is just like a chain—one link can bring disaster if it is not as strong as the others."

He seemed a man without emotion. For a man to get a "bloody

41

good" out of him was like drawing blood from a stone. He was cruelly direct in his admonishments. To be singled out by him for failing to do something exactly the way he wanted it done was an embarrassment long to be remembered.

Junior Fronk was the youngest volunteer in the battalion. He had just passed his eighteenth birthday and had never used a razor. Although Fronk had a sharp tongue that was always getting him in hot water with Sergeant Torbett, he was a good soldier and despite his small body was keeping up with the best of the men in Company F. He had plenty of spunk and was greatly admired by his older mates. But Fronk had a habit that Lieutenant Cowerson did not like. When the company was not in formation, Fronk would put his hands in his pockets.

Cowerson had repeatedly warned the company that he did not want to see anyone with hands in their pockets at any time, whether they were on duty or not. "Commandos never put their hands in their pockets," he would say.

One day after a long road march Fronk inadvertently put his hands in his pockets. Lieutenant Cowerson, ever watchful, caught him and as punishment ordered him to take a swim in the ice-cold river with all his clothes and equipment. Fronk never again put his hands in his pockets.

To the elation of the men in Company F, Lieutenant Cowerson was not always with us. All the companies worked on a rigid schedule that included unarmed combat, physical training, bayonet drill, scouting and patrolling, small-unit tactics, assault landings, cliff climbing, river crossings with ropes, weapons training, map and compass reading, street fighting and combat problems fired with live ammunition. In a way, the training schedule resembled a well-co-ordinated assembly line. While one company was being put through the paces of an obstacle course, another would be going through the assault landings, while the remaining companies would be taking part in the other phases of Commando training. Although our own instructors handled most of the subjects, many of the courses were supervised by specialists who did nothing but receive companies for instruction on their particular speciality. And on these occasions Lieutenant Cowerson would repair to his

42

quarters to prepare his plans for the next period when he would have us again.

However, the agony imposed upon the men of Company F by Lieutenant Cowerson was more than compensated for by Sarn't Blimt and Sarn't Brown.

Sarn't Blimt, with his enormous mustache, was a great morale factor to the company. He had a way of giving orders that was amusing and yet got results. He was also a very patient man and would take great pains to explain small details during instructions so that everyone clearly understood exactly what he meant. If a man blundered he would amiably say, "Now, look here, laddie, sure you can do better than that. And what would the bloody Hun be doing if you did that way in battle? We must train to destroy him—not to help him." And on the grueling road marches when the company was not doing so well, he would bellow, "Get off your bloody knees, you people!" Then he would suddenly burst from behind the company, running hard until he was about thirty yards ahead and turn around and wave to us in a challenge to catch up to him. He was chipper and cocky all the way, and just the sight of him full of vigorous energy spurred us to keep up with him.

CHAPTER 6

KEEN competition was the theme in all our training. The First Ranger Battalion was striving hard to outdo all previous Commando records. Each company in turn was trying to exceed the others within the battalion, and each platoon within the company was seeking top honors. Among the sections rivalry was as intense as between the companies. Each individual thought he was in the best section, the best platoon, the best company and quite naturally the best damned outfit in the American Army.

The assault section is the basic unit in the army, and consequently the efficiency and caliber of each section determines the over-all quality of an army. In the Rangers unusually heavy emphasis was placed on the importance of the section because in Commando-type warfare sections were frequently given missions completely on their own. They were expected to be self-subsistent, yet able to work in unison with the company. They were trained to be able to operate miles behind enemy lines for long periods, to assault strongly fortified coast positions without support, to attack enemy front-line strongpoints and withdraw in order. If their mission was connected with street fighting, a section could be expected to clean out an entire city block of houses, depending upon the scope of the operation.

Like all other sections in the battalion, the men of Second Section, First Platoon, F Company, felt that their group was the greatest bunch of fellows that ever lived, whether Lieutenant Cowerson thought so or not.

Our section leader, whom I will call Sergeant Jack Mulvaney, at

44

the time he was selected, seemed to us the ideal choice. He was twenty-one years old, a former boxer and rowing enthusiast and an all-around outdoor man. He had the best-developed physique in the company, large full chest, broad shoulders and narrow hips. Like more than two-thirds of the Rangers he was a former member of the Thirty-fourth Infantry Division, which was composed mostly of National Guardsmen. Although brusque in manner and not too congenial, Mulvaney by virtue of his aggressiveness and aptitude for leadership enjoyed the confidence of his men.

One of the most colorful men in our section was our first scout, Pete Preston, a small wiry coal miner from West Virginia. Pete chewed tobacco constantly and was full of original stories about his coal-mine experiences. He had a sharp, keen mind, a sharper tongue and a vocabulary of cuss words that flowed in torrents when his short temper became aroused. Pete was tough and as cocksure as they make them. He had the spit and fire of a bantam rooster and was one of the best marksmen in the company. No one enjoyed the training like Pete. At the end of the day he would corner Sarn't Blimt and chide him about his Commando training being a snap that was an insult to a hardy coal miner who was used to far more rugged work in the West Virginia coal mines. Sarn't Blimt liked Pete and often the two of them would spend the evening at the Naafi tent, drinking beer and trying to outdo each other's tales.

Ray Rodriguez was our second scout, a dark-skinned Mexican lad with black hair, nimble and willowy, who could run like a jack rabbit. "Rod," as everyone called him, was the neatest soldier in the section, his weapons the cleanest and his clothes the sharpest. He was always smiling, and although somewhat shy he was an avid audience whenever the section indulged in bull sessions.

As a scout Rod had few peers in Company F, and together he and Pete made a first class team. His proudest possession was the Tommy gun all scouts carried. He took care of it as though it were made of diamonds; at night he would wrap it carefully with oily rags as insurance against rusting and tuck it under the covers with him when he turned in. Rod could see in the dark as keenly as a night owl; could find his way to any point by the stars at night and could creep noiselessly through thick underbrush. Everything about

45

Rod reminded me of the lithe Indian Hiawatha. During training he seemed to take everything with calm, unprepossessing courage.

It is said that almost every outfit has a poet laureate. The second section did not lack for representation in the literary field, for Pfc. Robert C. Dunn was endowed with prolific talents in verse.

Dunn, tall, sinewy, blond, with sharp clean-cut features, whose home was in the Arkansas foothills of the Ozarks, was the outstanding rifleman of our section. He was moody, temperamental and had a marvelous command of the English language which he used profusely. As an efficient soldier Dunn had few equals. His markmanship was uncannily accurate, his knowledge of soldiering as thorough as an old-line Army sergeant's, and his poise and bearing as exact and precise as a Prussian general. He quoted poetry, especially Kipling, beautifully, and almost every day he made up verses which he recited at night to his tentmates after turning in.

He did not gamble or drink, and he frequently lectured the lost souls of the Second Section on the merits of a chaste, moderate life. If anyone showed the slightest doubt of what he said, he would pull out an old worn Bible and refer immediately to the exact passage that substantiated his preachings.

Dunn wrote long, backbreaking letters and would proudly show off a letter to some of his comrades as a masterpiece in prose before mailing. He was particularly adept with descriptive passages about the countryside, the sky, the budding flowers and countless other details that the average soldier doesn't include in letters back home. The officer who censored Dunn's mail was in for a real grind, and I imagine that lots were drawn to see who would undergo the tiring task. But, aside from frowning on Dunn's making each letter a work of art, the officers and noncommissioned officers could find no shortcomings in Dunn as a Ranger. He was exact, punctual, quick-thinking, resourceful and could boast that he was one of the very few men in Company F who was never gigged by Sergeant Torbett.

Only one other man in F Company, whom I will call George Fuller, could rival Pete Preston's cusswords. He was also in the Second Section. But even more chronic than Fuller's use of cusswords was his addiction to griping. Nothing was ever right. He was always getting a raw deal. The sergeants were against

46

him; Lieutenant Cowerson had singled him out as a scapegoat; the food, the weather, the weapons, the clothing—everything to George was constantly ailing. One day he would have severe pains in his stomach which he attributed to the chow. The next day he would be moaning about blisters on his feet which he blamed on the shoes not fitting properly. But for all his griping, George managed to keep up with the rest of the section, although he swore it was killing him.

Though Company C proudly boasted that it had the best guitar player in the battalion in the form of the popular Corporal Stradyuski, our assault section rightfully contended that Pfc. Vernor Lodge, of Pittsburgh, Pennsylvania, was the most distinguished and talented all-around musician of all American forces then in Great Britain. Lodge, a rifleman, volunteered for the Rangers from an antiaircraft unit stationed near Belfast. Tall and lean of build, handsome, with light brown hair, Lodge had studied music at Carnegie Tech and had been a member of Benny Strong's popular dance band when he enlisted. Lodge could play a variety of musical instruments, but his favorite was the clarinet on which he belted out the swingiest tunes then in popularity.

Vernon's descriptions of life with the big name bands helped fill the evening gab sessions. Occasionally the members of the Scottish military band would cluster around him for musical pointers. Not only did he give them pointers; he wound up as honorary leader of their band and taught them the swing version of the "Bagpipe Blues."

He was an extremely sincere and likable fellow and he put his whole heart and soul into everything he did. A highly articulate conversationalist who could discuss a wide variety of subjects, Vernon earned the respect and esteem of all Fox Company members, and we became the best of friends.

The entire company came to regard George much as an engineer might regard a safety valve on a boiler. If we became particularly irked on a matter, we had simply to refer it to George and he would at once launch into the subject using his choicest invectives. We would listen to him and feel better because we knew he was giving it far better treatment than any other person could. At the end of a road march or an obstacle course it was not unusual for the members of the second section to turn to him and say, "All right, George, let's have it. Tell 'em how p----d off we are."

George would tell 'em—but not loud enough for Lieutenant Cowerson to hear.

Although we thought our bunch was the greatest that had ever lived, we magnanimously conceded that the other squads in our company were certainly qualified to be "next to the greatest." And later, after we'd got a few battles under our belts we even went so far as to include them as "the greatest too." But regardless of what bunch was the greatest, everyone would agree that the First Platoon of Fox Company's mortar squad was certainly the most colorful, the most talked about, the drinkingest, singiest, most swashbuckling, most closely knit bunch in the entire Ranger unit.

This squad boasted Sergeant Walter S. Sieg, better known as El Siego, an ex-Merchant Mariner who had been all over the world, knew all the angles and considered himself the rival of Morton Downey, Bing Crosby and Russ Columbo. His canteen was seldom known to carry a drop of water, but whatever liquid refreshments were most easily available in whatever country we were in at the time. Sarn't Siego and his rollicking crew added a great deal of zest and dash to the company.

Among this sanguine crew were Corporal Thomas Ryan, a tall athletically built lad from Iowa, amiable, intelligent and with a keen sense of pixie humor; Corporal Wilbur R. Gallup, also from Iowa, a fine-looking fellow, probably the quietest and most conservative of the group, who was always showing his girl's beautiful picture around the camp, and kept showing it even after we had seen it a dozen times. Gallup and Ryan were inseparable, and they did their best to restrain the more irrepressible members of their famous band.

Private Robert K. Chesher, of Sioux City, Iowa, a tall, burly, rock-jawed, black-haired fellow, had the loudest and lustiest voice in the company, and there were those who averred that he gave El Siego a close second for being the thirstiest. Chesher was as rugged a man as could be found in the Rangers.

Private John B. Woodall of St. Louis, known as John B., a short, perky fellow who would fight anyone if he was at least six feet tall,

48

would team up with Sarn't Sieg in songfest, slugfest or drinkfest, whatever the occasion called for.

This merry crew never gave us a chance to complain that things were dull around camp. Later, in battle, we could never complain about the splendid mortar support they gave us when we needed them.

CHAPTER 7

BY THE end of two weeks' training, Lieutenant Cowerson had become a legendary figure throughout the entire battalion. Other companies had instructors who were also strict and exacting, but no other company was blessed or cursed with a martinet as merciless as our broad-faced, peak-nosed, unrelenting Cowerson. His reputation spread swiftly and with such exaggerations that the men in the other companies would not have been the least bit surprised if F Company had failed to come back after the day's training. They would have naturally assumed that Lieutenant Cowerson had calmly decided to march the company off a cliff or perhaps blow them to smithereens by the devilish dynamite charges he had hidden along the obstacle course. But if Lieutenant Cowerson was a blood-minded, almost fiendish tyrant, the men in Company F were all the more fortunate in having such a person direct our training.

His favorite bellow: "It is all in the mind and in the heart," became a popular standby for each man in Company F. Often when I would be on the verge of keeling over during a road march, I would think of that statement and what it really meant. He had told us many times that the reason for the speed marches was to improve our endurance and stamina so that in battle we would be able to march for long periods at breakneck pace in lightning-like raids far behind enemy forward lines. But we knew that besides conditioning us physically, the speed march was another means of determining guts and perseverance. With lungs bursting and joints aching, we found the temptation to fall out of ranks and drop down on the cool grass beside the road was very strong. But to drop out meant to fail. It meant that all the weeks of training thus far undergone would be lost. It meant going back to the old outfit in ignominy.

To me, who had a strong physique and good wind, it would have meant no guts. But there were fellows who dropped out because their physical constitution simply could not stand the pace. They had plenty of guts, but their bodies were not quite up to the strenuous requirements. For them it was not failure—although of necessity they would be returned to their units. They had given it all they had, and they could therefore return with honor. We respected those men and realized that it was only their physical handicaps that prevented them from making the grade. But for people like me, who were not so handicapped, it was a test of courage. Sometimes the line between courage and cowardice is very thin. Several times during training I came close to crossing that line.

One day our company was on a fifteen-mile speed march with full packs and rifles. It was particularly hot and Lieutenant Cowerson was particularly exacting. Before we started he told us that he expected us to make it well under two hours, which meant double-timing half the way. I was in a bad humor because they had served us a slab of fish and a cup of rotten tea for breakfast. I hated fish, and to see it for breakfast disgusted me almost as much as it did George Fuller, who let go with his entire vocabulary of invectives.

"How in the hell do they expect us to make these damned marches on a breakfast of fish?" I asked Sergeant Torbett.

"Fish gives you iodine. Iodine gives you iron and iron gives you strength," he said, laughing.

"Yeh, I wonder what Cowerson had for breakfast," I returned. "I'd like to give him some iodine—in large doses."

Before the march was half over I found myself weakening. It wasn't so much from lack of food as it was the depressing frame of mind I was in. My legs were getting heavy, like a ton of bricks; the pace was furious; all around me men were panting hard, sweating profusely. Even Andre, who was always on my left, was having a hard time. To hell with it, I thought to myself. I can't go any

51

further. How can I with no breakfast? I was trying to rationalize, to put the blame on lack of food instead of lack of courage. Within myself I was paving the way so that I could drop out and not feel guilty about it because of breakfast.

It was a good device. I might never get the excuse to fall out as I had now. Of course, the alibi I was building for myself was a figment of my imagination. But it seemed a good excuse to soften my compunctions about having failed.

Just as I was ready to call it quits I noticed Junior Fronk, two men ahead of me and on the right column, staggering blindly but fighting hard to keep up. Before I realized what was happening, a tremendous reservoir of energy seemed to cut loose within me. I was no longer tired. I felt strong; strong enough to grab hold of Junior with my right arm around his waist, supporting his sagging body and continuing to march. For three miles I marched with Fronk's left arm around my neck, and then Andre supported him the rest of the way in. I felt very much ashamed of myself. Fronk had saved me from falling out.

The part of Commando training I feared most was cliff climbing. There were few men in Company F who welcomed it. I have seen men who were not the least bit fazed by bullets twanging close to their heads, by grenades exploding several feet from where they lay, by swimming in the racing, ice-cold river with full equipment and by all other dangerous Commando courses, become taut and worried and unsteady when it was their turn at the cliffs. The Commandos told us that cliff climbing was one of the most important parts of our training because much of the enemy-occupied coastline, especially France, was rimmed by steep, perpendicular cliffs. And because the enemy would hardly expect a major landing against easily defended heights, they seldom kept heavy garrisons along the cliffs. Therefore, Commandos and Rangers, by becoming adept in cliff climbing, by scaling such points along the coast at night, could easily effect a surprise landing. "We must learn to hit the enemy at the least-expected places," was another of Cowerson's favorite axioms. I hoped I would never have to climb or descend any cliffs so precipitous as the one we practiced on, situated on the northward face of the large hill mass just a few hundred yards from the Commando depot.

52

The evening before the day our company was to have its first lesson in cliff climbing, I was overcome with fear. The thought of climbing and descending the jagged rock cliff made me tremble. My imagination ran riot and my mind entertained all sorts of gruesome possibilities that might befall me. What if I should slip and come bouncing down off the sharp protruding slabs of rock jutting out from the cliff walls? It would mean sure death. I foolishly visualized myself lying at the base of the cliff in a bloody inert heap. What if suddenly at the top of the cliff I refused to go down with the others? The thought of the resulting contempt from the other men was depressing and soul-wrenching.

There was only one way to prove to myself that I would not falter the next day. And that was to try it by myself that very evening! With a fast-pounding heart I slipped out of camp and headed for the ominous hill mass.

Panting hard, I climbed to the top of the cliff by way of a goat-path that twisted narrowly through underbrush on the slopeward side of the cliff. Once at the top, I got down on my stomach and peered cautiously over the rim. It was just twilight, and I could barely discern the bottom at the base where I knew were huge boulders of jagged rock. My insides seemed to be turning over and over as sweat broke out on my forehead. I couldn't do it! It was no use. I decided to call it off. But then something from within me started to taunt and ridicule me. Perhaps it was my conscience; perhaps it was a voice of determination that sometimes is alive even within the weak-willed. If I didn't do it now, I knew I wouldn't do it tomorrow! And if I didn't do it then, I could never live with myself. I would either make it or get killed trying.

It seemed like a nightmare when I wrapped the rope around my leg and cautiously began to descend. I dared not look down because I knew if I did I might be so overcome with fear that the rope would slip from my grip and I would go hurtling down to the bottom. Halfway down I paused for breath on a slight ledge, holding firmly to both ropes for dear life. So far so good, but I was still scared stiff. With a final burst of determination I continued my descent a foot at a time. When my feet finally touched the bottom I felt as if I had conquered the world. It was a strange, exalted feeling such as I had seldom before experienced. It was now dark, and as I made my way back to camp I began to whistle lightheart-edly and when I turned in for the night it was with eager anticipation of the cliff climb the next morning.

But when it came my turn to go down the rope the next morning, I found myself just as frightened as I had been the night before. I was still cautious as I wrapped the rope around my leg and pushed off. I lived over the fears and anxieties of the night before but overcoming that fear was the knowledge that I could do it—and I did.

After I reached the ground Sarn't Blimt told me that I had taken the cliff like an old hand. If he only knew what I had gone through the night before! When I saw the others slide and lurch down the straight-faced cliff, I experienced a guilty feeling because I had had two tries at it while they had only one.

Each man came down with an exalted expression, as though he had overcome fears similar to mine. Cliff climbing and descending is a very serious thing because in few courses of our training was the individual's life so entirely in his own hands, his own judgment so essential. Dangling high above the ground a man can depend on no one to help him, and if he slips he has only the jagged rocks to soften his fall.

CHAPTER 8

ALTHOUGH discipline and military courtesy were expected and received by the officers from the enlisted men, they were not given reluctantly. Our officers had the respect and confidence of their men. They were young, aggressive, intelligent, but not overbearing. They instilled spirit and morale in us by their leadership, encouragement and understanding of each individual. The officers in Company F supervised the men, not by unlimited and arbitrary power, but by developing a spirit of mutual helpfulness and co-operation in which all ranks seemed to strive to assist their leaders with their responsibilities. And in this respect, discipline became more or less voluntary and willing. In turn, the sergeants and corporals enjoyed the same consideration from those under them. We all seemed to realize that discipline was necessary to morale and efficiency, and that in our type of outfit it was all the more important. We came to regard our outfit as a co-operative and mutually military business in the success of which every man was personally interested as a shareholder. I found out later that such discipline paid off in large dividends on the battlefield.

Major Darby set the pace for his officers. Despite his complex responsibilities in supervising the administrative problems of an entirely new organization, developing a streamlined personnel section and adapting British innovations to American Army standards of tactics and organization, Major Darby was constantly in the field with his troops. One day he would go out with A Company as they went through the assault landings, the next day he would be with B Company on an overnight problem, the next day with C on a forced march, and so on. Full of energy, purpose and amazing endurance, he cut a rugged well-poised figure that exuded confidence. Nothing escaped his attention, not the slightest detail. At the end of the day's training he would call his company commanders together and make remarks as to what he had observed. He called them all by their first name.

"Roy, your company could stand a little goosing on their rifle range," he might prod.

"Max—" Lieutenant Max Schneider, C.O. of E Company— "your fellows are getting careless on the assault landings. That man who got hurt today had no business being so far out in front of his section. These people have to learn to combine cautiousness with recklessness. A good medium, not too brash. We need better control of these firing problems. If not, we'll be leaving this camp far under strength."

Darby was keen on making quick decisions. There was nothing vacillating about him. He could size up a situation, tactical or administrative, and have a solution in a matter of seconds. He was direct, forceful and sometimes explosive, and both officers and men when called down by him could probably remember the incident for the rest of their lives, he was so cutting.

It was common knowledge among the men in the battalion that Major Darby had been an aide to Major General Hartle who commanded the Thirty-fourth Division, before he organized the Rangers. It was also known that before coming across with the Thirty-fourth he had been a captain, commanding an Artillery battery at Edgewood Arsenal, Maryland. To look at him it was hard to visualize him as a one-time, pencil-pushing aide-de-camp. The assignment he was now faced with required the qualities of a rugged, brilliant and determined leader; a man who would have to set the pace for those he would lead, a pace that would often tax the farthest limits that mind, flesh and blood could endure. Major Darby seemed to his men just that type of leader.

In contrast to Darby's fissionable characteristics, his executive officer, Major Dammer, was a leavening influence. Dammer, whose ancestors were German, was by nature reserved, taciturn and ingeniously keen on detailed planning. With blond hair combed

56

straight back and well-chiseled aristocratic features, "Herm," as Darby called him, came to the Rangers from Vernon Lodge's ack-ack outfit, where he had been an adjutant. He spoke seldom to the battalion, but when he did, every word was precise and appropriate. He had the happy faculty of saying a tremendous amount in a very few words. Like Darby, he too accompanied different companies in various phases of the training.

Darby and Dammer made a well-synchronized team, and each added to the other's stature. I have seen few men balance their characteristics and talents so effectively to the benefit of their men as Darby and Dammer did.

One week after we arrived at Achna Carry our company was joined by a tall, lanky, dark-haired lieutenant. All of six-feet-four-inches, with long loping strides that seemed to eat up the ground, Lieutenant Nye, a native of Lincoln, Nebraska, was readily accepted by the men. Whereas Loustalot, who commanded the Second Platoon, was volatile and conclusively assertive, Nye seemed the easy-going, quiet type. He was thorough and painstakingly conscientious in everything he did. Seldom did he reprimand, and when he did he seemed to do so only with great effort. Before we undertook any field problems or any instructions that he was responsible for, he would carefully explain every detail and then he would have us ask questions. If a man had a worthy suggestion to offer, he could do so; and if it had merit, it would be readily accepted by Nye. There was nothing officious about him. On the field there were few men who could equal him in efficiency, guts and stamina. It was not hard to respect a man like Nye, and the men of the First Platoon came to look upon him as a man they would happily follow into battle.

CHAPTER 9

THE month passed swiftly. Although the training was furious and dangerous, our casualties were few. One man had drowned in the racing river when he lost his grip while crossing a toggle-rope bridge, and was carried away by a swift current before help could reach him. Several had been wounded during the assault landings, one of them our own First Sergeant Torbett.

Before the company started on the assault course that day, Torbett had warned the men to move fast when they hit the beach: "This is the last time we'll make the assault landing," he said. "Now let's give Cowerson a bloody good show, as he would say. When you hit that beach, spread out fast and fly across it to the nearest cover—and remember to keep those butts down. Some of those Commandos are anxious for a little blood. Let's not give them any of Company F's. They're getting closer and closer each day with those Bren-guns."

I knew what he meant when he said closer and closer. Two days before, my bayonet had been neatly plunked from my rifle by a Bren-gun burst as I charged up the steep slopes. I was so scared I couldn't talk coherently for several minutes. When the problem was over I felt like a veteran who had already seen battle. But when Lieutenant Cowerson saw what had happened to my bayonet, he gave me hell for not being in my proper position during the mock attack. "It's people like you who give the Commando instructors gray hairs," he scolded.

Heeding Sergeant Torbett's advice, F Company made an unusually good landing, and each section quickly cleared the beach in record time. Every phase of the problem was smoothly enacted; not a man was out of place. Not once did Lieutenant Cowerson have cause to criticize. After accomplishing our mission—which was to blow up imaginary coast guns located on the top of the hill with bangalore torpedoes—long pipes stuffed with dynamite—each section withdrew back to the beach, where we loaded into our boats and pushed out into the lake. This was known as the assault withdrawal often used by the Commandos on their raids against enemy coast installations.

Before our boats had cleared fifty feet from shore, the Bren-guns opened up again, splattering bullets close to our dipping paddles. Suddenly Sergeant Torbett, who was at the stern end of our collapsible craft, winced in pain. A bullet had struck him neatly in the buttocks, piercing through his hindquarters from the left side. At once we raised white handkerchiefs to warn them to stop firing; then rowing hard we headed back toward shore. Lieutenant Cowerson was there to meet us when we lifted the sergeant out of the boat into a waiting ambulance, which was always on hand during firing problems. Looking over the wound—an ugly gaping hole—Cowerson merely remarked, "It's nothing but a scratch, a small scratch."

Sergeant Torbett earned himself a good two-week rest. He joined the outfit later at the naval training-station and was none the worse for his experience. After that he became known as Sergeant "Butt" Torbett.

Company F, at the end of the month, had not fared badly in performance. Under the goading, pronging Cowerson we had managed to pull through with only three eliminations—and all three went back to their old outfits because of ailing feet.

Our bodies were now trim and muscular; our confidence and spirit high. And far from hating Lieutenant Cowerson, the men looked upon him with great admiration and respect. He and his sergeant assistants had molded us into a closely knit, sturdy and aggressive unit. His challenging taunts, his unwavering demands and his example of leadership had instilled a tremendous urge in each man to survive the grind. Each man had high confidence in himself and his company mates. We were attuned mentally and

59

physically for the battle missions we knew we would be called upon to perform. The Commandos had given us the best of their hard-earned experience. They had taught us in one month what they had learned through a year of trial and error and high casualties.

On the last day of our stay at Achna Carry each man was interviewed personally by Lieutenant Cowerson. He wanted to know how the men reacted to the training, and if they still wished to continue with the Rangers. The interviews were held in a small tent that served as the company orderly room.

When it came my turn I stepped into the tent, faced the lieutenant and saluted, saying: "Corporal Altieri, sir."

"How did you like the training, Corporal?"

"I think I am twice the man I was before I came here," I said.

"Do you wish to continue with the Rangers?"

"Yes, sir. I wouldn't think of quitting now."

"Bloody good," he said. "Bloody good. Always remember this—it is all in the mind and in the heart."

I walked out of the tent on clouds. For the first time in my life I felt that I had accomplished something significant. I thought of the letters I would write home telling all about making a great outfit. I thought about my old buddies back at Battery A, and the fact that I need no longer dread being sent back, lifted a tremendous load off my mind. To me, being with the Rangers meant being with the greatest group of men ever to be assembled as a fighting unit. We had a long way to go yet—our fighting had not yet started—but within me was the feeling that when the time came for action, the group I was a part of would give a good account of itself.

CHAPTER 10

THE early Scottish morning was brisk and sunny for the first time in weeks as we lined up in battalion formation in the parade ground meadow. Colonel Vaughn, flanked by Major Darby and Captain Murray, spoke briefly. He thanked us for our spirited co-operation and our zest in accepting the most foreboding challenges. He effusively congratulated both officers and men for their perseverance and dedication to the new outfit. As Major Darby beamed proudly, the colonel ended his talk by saying: "You Yanks bloody well surprised us. We expected to grind you to bits. Instead, some of my best Commando instructors have been hard put to keep up with you. A cracking good bunch, you Rangers."

The colonel's sparse but effective tribute seemed to stir each Ranger with unbounded *esprit de corps*. Marching to the stirring strains of the kilted bagpipe band, company after company swept by the reviewing stand, lines straight, rifles smartly angled, arms swinging precisely, legs measuring off long strident paces. Each man looked buoyant, assured, rugged. From the sideline Commandos looked on with approving smiles. Their work had not been in vain.

Back in the company areas after the parade, Sarn't Blimt and Sarn't Brown came by to say their farewells. Every Ranger of Company F stopped packing to shake hands with them.

Suddenly a voice thundered, "Company F . . . fall in!"

Sarn't Blimt and Sarn't Brown immediately backstepped from the group. In unison they both came to attention and threw us a salute. "Happy hunting, Rangers," said Sarn't Brown. "Good luck and God bless," said Sarn't Blimt. Before we could answer they did an abrupt about-face and marched briskly away toward their quarters.

Captain Roy Murray, Lieutenant Walter Nye and Lieutenant Loustalot appeared before the company formation. Murray spoke: "Fellows, the battalion is going to be split up for further amphibious training in the Scottish Hebrides with the Royal Navy. E and F Company will be camped on an island called Van Crippsdale. The other Ranger companies will be camped on nearby islands. All units will engage in assault landings and withdrawals and additional toughening up. Meanwhile, a group of forty-five enlisted men and six officers will leave the battalion for advanced training in demolitions with the Commandos in the south of England. The men whose names I call out, and myself, will be with that group. In my place, at Van Crippsdale, Lieutenant Nye will be in command of F Company."

This was a surprise! Nothing had ever been said about demolition training.

Murray continued, reading a list of names. After he finished, George Fuller raised his hand for permission to speak. The captain nodded. "Captain," said George, "we've been on a hard grind all month without any passes. We forgot what a shot of whisky tastes like, and the only women we've seen are those spinster Naafi girls—and the Commandos had them sewed up. Are we gonna get a chance to go to town before we start this here amphibious training?"

The whole company roared.

"That's up to Major Darby if and when he thinks it can be arranged," answered Murray. "But there's nothing on the schedule that includes town passes. And, for your information, Van Crippsdale is one of the most remote and inaccessible islands in Scotland—forty miles from anything that looks like a town."

Loud groans echoed through the camp. This Spartan life was getting just a little too much to take. Once again George uttered our feelings. "No passes, no women, no beer. They must think we're a battalion of Trappist Monks."

"Yeah," spoke up Junior Fronk, "we're lusty Rangers and we got lusty appetites, but we just have no food—if you know what I mean."

62

CHAPTER 11

VERY little Ranger spirit was in evidence when the Royal Navy's fat-bellied, faded gray, transport launch eased into the rickety pier at Van Crippsdale. The island was all that Captain Murray had said, only worse. Mountainous, with steep cliffs rising perpendicular from the water's edge, it seemed to us the most forlorn, forsaken, dismal piece of real estate in the United Kingdom. A gauze-like mist completely enshrouded it, making the high summits barely discernible.

We were met at the pier by a dapper-looking Royal Navy officer armed with a cocky smile and the inevitable swagger stick. Glumly we picked up our bedrolls and weapons and followed Lieutenant Nye and the officer in single file up a muddy slippery trail to a large stone house, nestled in a small meadow between two mountains. We parked our bags and equipment and wearily stood by, waiting for someone to tell us where to pitch our pup tents.

The naval officer seemed to be enjoying our dispirited discomfort. He bounded up the steps of the stone house and faced us with a cocky smile. As he spoke, he waved his swagger stick somewhat grandiloquently toward the mountains.

"Welcome to Van Crippsdale, Rangers. This is not the most lavish training site, but you will find the solitude of the mountains most conducive to keen concentration on the training chores. You will be completely on your own, under the supervision of your own officers except when the Navy beckons for amphibious problems. . . . I trust you will make yourselves comfortable, and I trust too that you will not shoot the King's deer—they are the only inhabitants of this island besides yourselves. The King is very touchy about his favorite deer preserve, and the penalty for the assassination of one deer is forty pounds!"

"What kind of rations will we have up here?" Junior Fronk asked. "British or American?"

The British officer looked at Fronk with a condescending smile: "Your rations will be furnished by His Majesty's Royal Navy. You won't find our fare quite as elaborate as yours, but I'm sure you will survive."

That did it! A loud howl erupted from the tired, weary and hungry dispirited soldiers. "Not quite as elaborate! The understatement of all history," yelled Fuller.

"You're damned right we'll survive," mumbled Fronk, "if we have to assassinate the King's whole herd of deer."

Lieutenant Nye immediately put down the near-rebellion by reminding us that the way of a Ranger was rigorous and promised that there would be happier days ahead. His statements were punctuated by earsplitting thunderclaps and followed by wind-driven sheets of rain. Our welcome to Van Crippsdale was a foretaste of what was to come.

The following weeks proved the most miserable stretch of training we had endured. It rained every day and, even thought it was summer, the nights were bitterly cold. When it did not rain, we were plagued by the most vicious mosquitoes that ever harassed flesh and blood. Our pup tents were repeatedly blown down by the cruel winds, and it got so bad that some of the Rangers dug themselves hillside caves to protect themselves from the unkind elements.

Our daily training schedule was even more exacting than at the Commando depot. Lieutenant Nye and Lieutenant Schneider of F Company contrived the most grueling obstacle course ever devised by man. It led through swamps, up steep-slanted rocks, across canyons, through forests and down cliffs.

Lieutenant Schneider, the C.O. of E Company, was a good-natured, hell-raising officer who was well liked by his men, but he seemed to feel that now that we were on our own, it was his destiny to take the place of Cowerson. He set the pace for the over-all

The commanding officer of the U.S. Ranger unit,
Lt. Col. William Orlando Darby, on a motorcycle
before the City Hall of Arzew, Algeria.

Lieutenant Colonel Vaughan and Major Darby.

Rangers conducting bayonet drills under the watchful
eye of their British instructors in Scotland.

Darby and Rangers inspecting an enemy vehicle
after a successful ambush.

French prisoners of war, 1942.

The Rangers in a speed march across enemy terrain in Tunisia.

Phil Stern

Ranger spatial scouts search out the enemy at El Guettar.

U.S. Army Signal Corps

Prisoners of the German Afrika Korps.

Phil Stern

Congratulations to 1st Sgt. Donald (Butt) Torbett on the destruction of an enemy tank by Fox Company in Tunisia.

training program of both E and F Companies. A rugged individual- ist, he insisted on training problems that would tax the individual's powers of endurance and persistence.

About twice a week His Majesty's Royal Navy called to pay their respects in the form of a flotilla of Higgins' assault craft. These craft would take us down the firth to rendezvous with the rest of the First Ranger Battalion for amphibious landings along the coast. At times we would make an opposed landing, coming into a beach where Commandos would be in position with Bren-guns and mor- tars. With bullets cracking inches above and live mortar rounds landing as close as six yards from our craft, we would zoom into the beach, tumble out of the boats, then streak for our beach objec- tives. After blowing up imaginary coast guns, we would withdraw, still under fire. We often made landings at night against rocky cliffs from boats lashing about precariously in huge swells, and often a Ranger would miscalculate his leap from the boat and fall into the waves, narrowly missing being dashed to bits against the rocks.

Opposed landings, cliff assaults, silent reconnaissance landings— every type of landing the Commandos had experienced was re- hearsed over and over with unrelenting persistence. Often during these exercises I would get an opportunity to see Carlo Contrera and compare notes. Each time Carlo would come up with a new problem. His arches were falling, he was starving from the British rations, his girl in Brooklyn wasn't writing often enough, his rela- tions with his first sergeant were deteriorating.

All this was harrowing enough to Carlo. But his most humili- ating misfortune was to be fined forty pounds for being caught red- handed killing one of the King's deer. He wasn't a very good shot with a rifle. He had fired ten rounds and missed, he complained. So he and another Ranger had crept up on the deer and stalked it into a mountain defile, trapping it in a narrow cleft. Then, being out of ammunition, they went after the deer swinging their rifle butts. Carlo had managed to hit the deer on the head, felling it, but breaking his rifle. Being hungry, they had immediately set upon the hapless deer, skinned it and were preparing to put it on the fire, when the King's deer warden made his appearance and apprehended them in the name of His Majesty.

65

Since the matter was reported to Major Darby, Carlo was now worried that he might even lose his coveted Pfc. rating.

Despite the fact that our training was very important, despite the promise that sunnier weather would be ahead, we were all very unhappy at Van Crippsdale—that is all except that demon for punishment, Sergeant Harris. This frail-looking, scholarly-speaking man was unperturbed by it all and at times seemed actually to enjoy it. During the evening, after the regular training was through, Sergeant Harris would often go over the obstacle course alone, at night, just to keep active. Gradually the men in Company F came to look up to him as a source of strength and encouragement. He was always available to give counsel to anyone, whether it was a military problem or trouble on the home front. He was calm and easygoing and had nothing but kind words even for the worst of the Rangers.

One night, sitting around a large campfire, we entertained ourselves by telling why we volunteered for the Rangers. Harris was the first to be asked to give his reasons. Without flinching an eye he said, "I wanted to be an officer because my brother and my cousin are officers and my family doesn't expect it of me. Seven times I put in for a commission back in the States—passed the exams for O.C.S. but was refused entry. I think the reason was they didn't think I looked the way a leader should look—and I don't think my stuttering helped any. So when I came to Ireland and heard about this Ranger outfit, I felt that if I couldn't be an officer, I would try to be one of the best noncommissioned officers in the best outfit in the American Army, and that's why I volunteered."

Spurred by Harris' frank revelations, the rest of our group revealed for the first time their true motives for joining the Rangers.

Howard Fuller said he joined because he wanted to get away from his "chicken outfit" where everybody and his brother was buckin'. Fronk admitted that he wanted to prove that little guys are just as tough as big guys.

Pfc. Dunn said he joined for two reasons, one, because he wanted to make the Army his lifetime career, and action with the Rangers would look good on his military records, and, two, he wanted to get in a rugged outfit destined for great things, so that he would have something worthy to devote his literary efforts to.

Vernon Lodge was equally frank. Aside from his peregrinations with the big bands as clarinetist and arranger, he had never been exposed to anything rugged enough to test his mettle. The Rangers gave him the opportunity to find out what he was made of.

The irrepressible Gomez, to the amazement of no one, also contributed to the why-I-joined-up quiz. He was out to prove that Mexicans can fight for their country as hard as anyone else. The Rangers would prove that.

One morning, still groggy from the preceding evening's shenanigans, the men of Company F were awakened by the windiest, shrillest whistle blasts we ever heard at Van Crippsdale. In a daze we stumbled out of our pup tents to gaze in awe at a once familiar figure. Sergeant "Butt" Torbett, resplendent with his new shiny first-sergeant chevrons greeted us with his familiar bellow: "All right, Fox Company, hit the line, get off your flabby rear and pack your gear!"

Loud cries of mock agony erupted from the men. Sergeant Torbett was back from his vacation in a British hospital, a little flabbier, but still the same ebullient whipcracker.

"Oh, my achin' back!" shouted George, rubbing his eyes as if seeing a mirage. "I thought we got rid of that bucking sergeant for good. Ol' Cowerson didn't do too good a job with that Bren-gun."

"Yeah," yelled Fronk, "he's been livin' it up in a nice comfortable hospital, while we been breakin' our rears on this lousy island! Now that he's rested and got those new stripes, he's gonna really throw his weight around."

We put on our shoes and leggings in a hurry and ran to reveille formation as Torbett stood there with hands on hips, holding a piece of paper. The section leaders counted heads and Torbett took the morning report.

It was then that Junior Fronk came running down the mushy field, pulling and tugging on his pants. The company roared, enjoying the drama that was about to unfold between Torbett and his favorite whipping boy. Torbett stood glaring until Fronk had taken his place beside me.

"Junior Fronk," roared Torbett, "you are always late for everything except chow call. All the time I was in the hospital I kept thinking how nice it would be to come back and find Junior Fronk a reformed man. I had great faith in you, Fronk, but what do I find on the first formation I call? Junior Fronk has let me down. . . ."

Fronk's face turned purple. "I couldn't help it. I was at the latrine—I was only following the call of nature," he blurted.

"When I blow that whistle nature's call can go to hell," returned Torbett. "Now get with it, man."

After the laughter subsided Torbett fingered the paper and spoke: "Men, I really felt sorry for you when I was in that swell hospital getting my rear massaged by those pretty nurses. I kept thinking of you guys sleeping in those pup tents and playing tag with the King's deer for amusement. Being such a soft-hearted guy, I went to see Major Darby and I got on my knees and begged him to give you guys a break."

Loud guffaws broke out again.

"I told Major Darby you guys needed some diversion—a chance to relax and live it up, a chance to meet some broads, down a few nips as the British say. Well, Darby asked me—as he usually does, he asked me—what did I suggest . . .?"

"You probably suggested a seventy-five-mile speed march," shouted Fronk.

"Shut up, Junior, and let me finish," growled Torbett. "So I suggested that the whole company should spend two whole days in a town called Oban. It's a real live town, full of bars and lonesome gals. They've never seen any Yanks before, and they've already got the news and are waitin' to welcome us."

Before he could continue, the air was rent with frenzied shouts of joy.

"All right, calm down," roared Torbett. "Let me finish. . . . The rest of the day will be spent in clothes rehabilitation. Every Ranger will have clean Class A uniform, trousers pressed, haircuts and clean fingernails. I don't want any of you Rangers spoiling the good reputation of Company F by looking like a crumbum!

"And further, when we go to town tomorrow, I expect every Ranger to behave himself like a gentleman. Be courteous to the local gentry, and please, fellows, take it easy on the broads."

For the first time in two months we had pay call. We were going into Oban loaded for bear—or deer. We were paid off in pounds sterling, the rate of exchange at that time being around four dollars to the pound. Sergeant Torbett had that old "money gleam" in his eyes as he watched us pick up our pound notes. We knew what was coming next.

As soon as the officers departed, Torbett yelled out, "All right, you guys—crap call! Down by the pier. . . ." As Deacon Dunn watched us with a hangdog look of disapproval, we literally fled toward the pier, anxious to win a fortune to spend in Oban.

CHAPTER 12

His Majesty's Royal Naval vessel, the happy ship *Alicia,* was bobbing with merry excitement as it sailed into the small harbor of Oban. Its deck was crammed with rollicking Rangers, our pockets bulging with coin of the realm, His Royal Majesty's realm. I was particularly happy because my spirits were tangibly bolstered by sixty pounds I had won in the crap game. Gomez too had fared rather handsomely to the tune of thirty pounds. The only sour puss aboard the good ship *Alicia* was Sergeant Butt Torbett. Not only had he lost his entire pay, but his next month's pay as well. Several of the Rangers were deputized to keep an eye on Torbett to see that he didn't get shot again—at least until he paid up his debts.

The ship docked flush alongside the cobbled quay and even before the hawser lines were made fast, we started leaping ashore. Several of the Rangers, carried away by their first encounter with Scottish maidens, ran right up to a group of terrified girls and, in full view of the townspeople, embraced them with bear hugs. Loud shrieks rent the air, as the terrified girls huddled together for protection. One buxom lass actually fainted!

Sergeant Torbett immediately blew his brass whistle and roared out above the sound of the ship's idling Diesel engine, "F Company fall in! You're not dismissed yet."

We quickly took our places at the dockside, wondering what was coming next, as the startled townsfolk gibbered excitedly about this contingent of strange soldiers. By their faces I could sense that they thought we were at least a third order of barbarians.

70

Torbett looked deadly serious as he glared up and down our ranks. "Now listen, you fellows: If we have any more shenanigans like that, we're gonna load on that boat and turn right back to Van Crippsdale. I want everybody in F Company to remember one thing: you're representing not only F Company—you're representing not only the First Ranger Battalion—you are representing the entire United States Army. In fact the reputation of our country may stand or fall on how you behave here. Now for the record, nobody gets drunk, I mean real stinking drunk. Nobody fights—you'll have plenty fighting when you meet the enemy—which will be damned soon—and everybody stays in proper uniform."

We fidgeted uneasily, hoping he would get it over with so we could get on our way.

"Now, to see that you guys keep order and see that you don't start any trouble, on orders from Lieutenant Nye I am hereby appointing two Rangers to pull MP duty. These fellows will have full authority to clout you on the head and pull you into the town brig, if you get out of hand. And if they don't do their job, they'll find themselves in the brig."

We all looked around wondering who the two unlucky Rangers would be. Torbett soon set us straight.

"Corporal Eastwood from the Second Platoon and Corporal Altieri of the First Platoon are duly appointed military policemen during our forty-eight hour stay in Oban. They will conduct themselves in military manner, keeping law and order among all Rangers, and—get this—they will not in any manner go into bars for the purpose of imbibing and neither will they lose themselves in the company of young ladies, however inviting these maidens may be. F Company . . . dismissed!" he concluded.

In a wild yelling surge, the Rangers tore out of the dock area, leaving Corporal Eastwood, myself and Gomez standing stupefied. As Torbett walked over to us I fought hard to control my temper. To me MP duty was the most ignoble assignment a soldier could draw. It didn't matter so much that I was deprived of the opportunity to raise hell in Oban like the others. What really infuriated me was that I, who hated MPs, was now going to be a watchdog and policeman over my own buddies. This was a stigma I could never erase.

71

"Don't take it so bad, fellows." Torbett smiled as he came up to us. "After that talk I gave, these fellows won't make any trouble. It'll be a snap for you!"

"You should have stayed in that damned hospital," I rasped out. "Just what do you have against me, Torbett?"

"Take it easy, Altieri, don't play martyr with me," he came back with. "I picked you fellows because I know you can handle the job, the boys'll listen to you. If I picked a couple guys that aren't well liked, there'd be hell to pay." Torbett was no fool. Whether he knew it or not he was a master of applied psychology. It was not unflattering to the ego to know that the top kick considered you capable and well liked.

"Do a good job, fellows, and I promise you it'll be a long time before you get such a lousy detail again. Okay?"

"Yeah," cracked Gomez. "Don't take it so hard. Think of the money you won't have to spend—and the headaches you won't have."

Resigned to our fate, Corporal Eastwood and I, with Gomez in tow, sauntered into the town square, determined to make the best out of a sorry situation. I consoled myself that at least I would see the town as a bona fide tourist, who sees but does not touch.

Walking leisurely up the main street we found Oban to be a quaint, picturesque village lined with charming shops and pubs. The inhabitants looked hearty and cheerful and we were greeted with extremely friendly smiles. Occasionally an attractive lass would pass and we would stop and accord her our most charming smiles, accompanied by our most appreciative stares.

Occasionally we would duck our heads into the pubs to see how our Ranger comrades were faring. Invariably we would see Rangers lined up five-deep, guzzling Scotch whisky and acting as though the day of reckoning was at hand. Harried bartenders would dash to and from their liquor storerooms, trying frantically to keep pace with the fearful onslaught. Several bars we entered were empty of Rangers—simply because the bar was bone-dry!

But the most amazing social phenomenon of Oban was to see the streets full of Rangers walking around blithely with girls on their arms as though they had been there for years. In the two

72

hours since our arrival in Oban, the Rangers had completely established their beachhead.

We had just come out of a coffee shop when a huge strapping Scotchman in Kilts stopped us. "Welcome to Oban, you bloody Yanks!" he bellowed. "Welcome to the best town in the whole of Scotland." Somewhat startled by this exuberant outburst, I took his proffered hand and said: "We're pleased to be here, laddie, indeed we are."

"Well, now," said he, "if we're happy to have you and you're happy to be here, then that calls for a bloody nip." Sadly I had to inform him that there was nothing I'd like better than to take a bloody nip with him but, regretfully, I could do no nipping while on MP duty. This made him very sad, and he allowed as how it was a "piping shame" that we were so restricted, but he was not to be put off.

"You know, lad, we must be about doing something to show our esteem for you Yanks," he said. "If we cannot cheer each other with a few nips, then we must take our pictures together, shaking our bloody hands."

"Great," yelled Gomez. "We'll title it 'Our Day In Oban.' It's a real tourist gimmick—'Rangers pose with local inhabitant.' Oh, how exciting our trip to Oban has become."

The Scotchman, evidently mellowed by several previous nips, was carried away by Gomez's satire. "A smashing idea," he roared, "a right smashing idea!"

With that he took us both by the arms and literally dragged us up the street to a tiny photographer's shop. Barging into the shop he bellowed to the shopkeeper to take the best bloody pictures he ever took of him with his bloody Ranger comrades.

We took a dozen or so different poses. We took poses shaking hands, arms around one another's shoulders, sitting on the floor cross-legged. We took poses laughing boisterously, smiling lightly, looking grimly serious as though recording an historic moment. We took poses without hats, without jackets, with one another's hats, and we even took poses with Scotch whisky bottles in our hands as though we were on a tearing binge.

And each time, when I thought we were finished, the Scotchman

73

would yell, "Now how about this position, laddy? I think it would make a cracking good show." This went on interminably until Gomez came up with a brainstorm. "Hey, Al," he said, "how about you and the jolly Scotchman exchanging clothes? Boy! The folks back home would get a big charge seeing you in kilts, with leopard skin around your shoulders and a big staff—you know, Al, just like that Scotchman on the labels."

Before I could answer the exuberant Scotchman leaped into the air and clicked his heels with glee. "A corker! A bloody corker! I always wanted to put one of these fuzzy Yank uniforms on. My lass will truly like such a picture. Indeed she will!" That settled it. Without saying a word I proceeded to disrobe, wondering when this picture-taking madness would let up.

With the help of Gomez and the shutter-crazy Scotchman, I finally stood before the mirror resplendent in my kilts and leopard skin. Standing there imperiously, I must confess I was not completely unimpressed with myself. I got so carried away that I even tilted my chin upward, just like the labels, and I imagined that I looked like a very noble warrior Scotchman whom the Black Watch would be proud to have.

As I stood there in front of the mirror making final adjustments on my skirts, which seemed a bit too long, we were startled by a yelling Ranger outside the shop shouting "MP . . . MP!" I immediately ran to the door—staff in hand—to see what was up. About six Rangers and a group of townsfolk were milling outside a pub which had been most peaceful just a half hour before.

Immediately I dashed out of the door, with Gomez close behind, leaving the Scotchman standing in front of the camera—in my uniform!

The crowd parted as Gomez and I fought our way into the pub—just in time to be knocked down by a body that came hurtling through the entrance seemingly propelled by some unseen force. Getting up, I stood completely stupefied as I watched the most ferocious barroom fight I have ever witnessed. Lined up against the bar were four E Company noncoms, all swinging away at four British sailors and two Royal Marines. A burly Ranger sergeant was grappling with a huge giant around six-feet-five, who was trying to get a headlock on him. The sergeants were flailing wildly at the

74

sailors and marines. On the floor were three Rangers and five sailors—out cold.

Gomez and I were so fascinated by this wonderful fight, we just stood there and enjoyed it. There was something very inspiring about this fight and I didn't feel like I should be a spoilsport and try to stop them.

Suddenly, just when the Ranger sergeant had belted his giant with a log-felling left uppercut, I heard Sergeant Torbett's voice yelling outside the pub. "Where's the MPs?" he was roaring. "That's me," I said to Gomez. "I better do something." With that I lunged into the melee, Scotch kilts, leopard skin, biff staff and all. "All right, fellows, break it up," I said, trying to sound as though I really meant business. I said it real loud because I wanted Torbett to hear me and know I was doing my duty.

But that was all I said because the next instant a huge fist—a Ranger's fist no less—came hurtling toward my jaw and the next thing I knew total darkness had completely and thoroughly enveloped me.

I woke up to find Sergeant Butt Torbett standing over me with the most contemptuous look I have ever seen worn on the face of mortal man. Gomez, with woebegone face, was kneeling beside me, patching up a cut on my cheekbone. Shakily I got up on my knees and surveyed myself. My kilts were ripped, my leopard skin was on the floor, blood-spattered and my noble biff staff was splintered to bits. I didn't mind getting knocked around, myself, but I felt real bad about my poor Scotch friend who had loaned me his outfit.

As Torbett just glared at me, I looked at Gomez and said, "Who hit me?"

Gomez sadly shook his head. "One of our gang lowered the boom on you, Al—but he didn't know it was you. He thought you were a Scotchman helping out the sailors. They took five of 'em to the hospital."

Torbett spoke up for the first time: "You're the sorriest MP I ever saw—going around town masquerading as a big-shot Scotchman. You're nothing but a damned tourist, Altieri, a damned kilt-wearing tourist."

"Get off my ear, Torbett," I said. "So I dress up for a gag. I

75

was still on duty and I came in here as soon as I heard about the fight and I tried to break it up . . ."

"The only thing you broke up was your jaw—and, I thought you could handle any situation."

Before I could answer, my Scotchman friend barged into the pub, took one look at his once lovely skirts and blood-spattered leopard skin and yelled a blood-curdling battle call. He started toward me with murder in his eyes. "A fine way to treat a chap. I loan you my very best garb and you tear it and bespatter it with cruddy blood!" Fortunately he was restrained by two bobbies before he could get at me.

The Scotchman—though restrained from breaking my neck—was not restrained in the least in claiming reimbursement for his ruined outfit. In thundering tones he threatened to sue me, the Rangers, the Army and in fact, if necessary, the government of their lost colony, the United States. By this time a rather large crowd had gathered, voicing their sympathy for the outraged Scotchman in no uncertain terms. The incident was jet-balling into the stature of an international *cause célèbre*.

"Let's get the hell out of here," Gomez pleaded, "before they lynch us."

Torbett came to my rescue with a suggestion that was entirely at my expense. "Look, Altieri, you got all us Rangers on the spot with these people. You better pay up right now and show them we Yanks are really generous."

"All right," I said to the Scotchman. "How much do you want for the damages?" Still restrained by the huge bobbies holding his arms, he shouted at me. "It cost me ten pound and five shillings, but I'll settle the bloody mess for ten pounds."

Gomez was holding my money. Without saying a word he handed me the roll and I peeled off ten pounds and tossed it magnanimously into the Scotchman's out-thrust hand.

A murmur of approval rippled through the curious crowd: "Bloody generous!" "Bloody good bloke!"

Somewhat carried away by the crowd's approval, I peeled off ten more pounds and threw them on the bar. "All right, everybody," I shouted. "Let's drink up—it's all on the Rangers."

The crowd yelled its delight and streamed into and around the bar, lead by the once-irate Scotchman. My back was pounded until I was black and blue. "You Yanks are a bit of all right, indeed you are," they chorused.

Torbett, his chest inflated, turned to me. "See that! What the hell would you guys do without me around? You just gotta learn how to be a diplomat when you're in foreign lands. All it cost was a few pounds to restore international harmony!"

Suddenly Junior Fronk came running into the bar, shouting at the top of his lungs and carrying a newspaper with ten-inch headlines.

"Hey, fellows," Fronk yelled: "Our guys have been on a raid— some place in France called Dieppe." He thrust the paper under our noses as the crowd surged around us.

We read in stunned silence the bold black headlines: ALLIED FORCE INVADES FRANCE. CANADIANS, COMMANDOS AND AMERICAN RANGERS MAKE DARING ASSAULT ON DIEPPE.

The article continued to tell about the first combined operations attack on Dieppe, involving thousands of Allied troops, the Royal Navy and an Allied air umbrella.

Torbett whistled. "Those are the fellows who went down to South England for demolitions under Captain Murray. Wonder how many got out of it?"

My thoughts immediately went to Pete Preston and Mulvaney and Howard Andre. I remembered how puzzled they were about being picked for specialized demolitions training. I thought of Sergeant Smith of A Company, whose main purpose in joining the Rangers was to get a chance to be the first to fight against the enemy. Sergeant Smith had got his wish. And then I wondered to myself why I had not been among that group that went, why other soldiers —far better than I—had not been selected. It was a selfish thought, but I knew many of the Rangers would be thinking the same.

Very soberly Torbett handed the paper back to Fronk. "Well, fellows, I knew we were going to make history fast, but I didn't think it would be this quick. We Rangers now have a battle history. Let's drink to the guys who went on the Dieppe Raid."

Fishing out the rest of the forty pounds I had won in the crap game, I flung it on the bar dramatically and challenged the whole crowd to: "Drink up! Drink to the Dieppe Rangers!" They "drank up" all right.

The day after we returned from Oban, Captain Murray and the Dieppe contingent of Rangers came back. We met them at the pier without fanfare. They all looked weary, much older and deadly serious. Howard Andre, Mulvaney and Pete Preston barely spoke to anyone as we picked up their bags and escorted them to their quarters. Sergeant Ed Thompson, leader of the First Section, Second Platoon, was the only one of the returning warriors who had anything to say when we pressed them for information.

"It was murder, pure murder," he said. "The Jerries were waiting for us; they had us zeroed in the artillery, mortars, machine-gun fire. They couldn't land our launch, so we just took it like a sitting duck. Then this Jerry trawler came in for the kill, raking our deck with HE. . . . Twenty Commandos and sailors were killed, and the boat commander had his leg shot from under him right next to me."

"How did Lieutenant Loustalot get it?" I asked Thompson.

He hesitated a long second, then looked toward the ground. "The lieutenant was with a group of Commandos that tried to take out the gun batteries on the cliffs of Bernaval. Halfway up the cliffs the Commando captain, Richard Wills, got killed. . . . Loustalot took over, got to the top, then he got it with crisscross machine-gun fire. . . ."

As I listened I recalled the first words I had heard Loustalot speak back in Carrickfergus, Ireland: "We are all here for the same purpose—to prove ourselves qualified for this new American Commando unit." The lieutenant had certainly proved himself.

Spurred by Darby's stinging verbal lashes concerning Oban and sobbered by the experiences of our buddies at Dieppe, the Rangers of Easy and Fox Companies plunged into the remainder of the training at Van Crippsdale with renewed vigor and purpose.

As our training progressed the men who had gone to Dieppe loosened up and spoke more freely of their bitter experiences. Andre, we learned, had taken over a pom-pom gun when the gunner was killed. He had helped stop the onslaught of a deadly German trawler. Pete Preston had his first taste of combat, operating a Bren-gun against low-flying dive bombers. Private Bush, caught on

78

the open deck by a strafing plane, had been hit in the leg and was now in a base hospital. Sergeant Smith, one of the few men to land at Dieppe, was one of the last men to withdraw into a waiting boat when the attack was called off. Corporal Franklin Coons, we learned, was credited with killing a number of Germans while attacking a gun battery with Lord Lovett's Commando group.

Most of the Rangers who went to Dieppe seemed very bitter that the over-all plan had met with failure. They had seen wave after wave of fine Canadian troops decimated as they hit the main fire-swept beaches of Dieppe. They had seen the full impact and horror of a large-scale landing gone wrong. Their baptism of fire under the worst possible conditions brought home to us the deadly career we had chosen voluntarily for ourselves. We resolved to make every minute of our training count.

By the end of the month the British Royal Navy informed Major Darby that the Rangers were ready. They had mastered all the landing techniques then known by the Commandos. We were now set for detailed tactics preparatory to an impending invasion or raid. The Navy was well pleased with our amphibious know-how. They were also happy to see us leave, for, since our arrival in the Scottish Hebrides, the King's prize herds had been mysteriously disappearing.

CHAPTER 13

IT WAS early morning when our special troop train pulled into the large, dark, cavern-shaped terminal at Dundee, Scotland. Staggering under our heavy loads, we swiftly emptied the train, then stood at attention as Captain Roy Murray and Lieutenant Nye, with a burly Commando officer, came forward to brief the troops. We had been told on the train by Lieutenant Nye that we were in Dundee for three weeks of specialized training on coastal defenses. We were to operate against the massive gun batteries protecting Dundee.

For the first and only time in our careers as Rangers we were also to be given the privilege of billeting with civilians, just like the Commandos. Murray was smiling genially as he said, "Fellows, Lieutenant Macrin here has given me F Company's billeting slips. Each man will take his own slip to the house listed and present it to his host or hostess. You will start right now learning your way around by finding the house yourself. You will be paid four pounds a week extra for subsistence money."

A loud cheer rang out. Four pounds a week! That was sixteen bucks. "Boy," said Fuller, "I sure hope my landlord or landlady doesn't charge that much for board—I need some go-to-town lettuce."

"Needless to say," Murray continued, "I know you fellows will conduct yourselves like gentlemen. . . . I hope I will not have any reports of misconduct either in the homes or in the public. I will expect each and every one of you to use discretion and self-discipline. The first man who does foul up will be sent packing to his old outfit."

We all nodded our heads in agreement with the Captain. No one had any intention of getting out of line and being deprived of the wonderful privileges and experiences that were ahead.

Murray continued: "Parade formation will be at 0800 in the Dundee Park Grounds. You will get there on your own steam and you will return to your quarters on your own after the training day ends at 1700 hours. The rest of the time is your own except when the battalion or company has night problems."

His talk concluded, Murray took Torbett's salute and disappeared with the Commando officer and Nye. Torbett yelled out, "All right, my gentlemen of Fox Company—my nice Lord Fauntleroy Foxes— pick up your billet slips and get moving to your destination as I call out your names. . . . Altieri, Runyon . . ." Swiftly I moved up, took my billet slip and read: Mrs. N. Gibson, 104 Granston Way.

Runyon had drawn the same address. Corporal Runyon was a small, wiry BAR-gunner of the Second Section, from Sioux City, Iowa.

As Torbett roared out the names of the other Rangers, Runyon and I decided the best way to get there was to get a taxi. We hailed one cruising by, threw our gear into the back, waved good-by to our buddies and gleefully settled back to enjoy the local scenery.

Like all cab drivers, be they in New York or Dundee, our cab driver was persistently loquacious. Dundee, he told us, was a mighty jute-milling center and a once great port. The people of Dundee were the most hospitable in the world. Dundee, he said, was not lacking in entertainment and other divertisements. Downtown boasted the largest cinema houses in Scotland, with daily showings of the best American flickers. There were numerous night clubs and two large dance halls, featuring excellent bands. . . . And further, although the rationing system had somewhat dented their reputation, Dundee was well represented with fine teashops and restaurants.

This was all very stimulating. At last we were on our own in a big city, living the life we had envisioned. Surely, I thought, joining the Rangers was the best thing I ever did. Gone was the rigorous Spartan life in the Highlands; gone were the days of sleeping in pup tents in the rain, living on skeleton rations. Now we would be fed and boarded by the town's own citizens. Oh, what a wonderful war we were fighting!

Soon the cab pulled up to a modest-looking stone house fronted by a small stone fence and grilled gate. We jumped out, unloaded our gear, paid the driver, opened the gate, knocked on the door and stood there, the both of us with the most naïve, innocent smiles we could muster, determined to assure our hostess that we were indeed the most splendid gentlemen the United States Army could send to her lovely home.

The door opened and a smiling, blond woman, around thirty years old, with sparkling blue eyes and a ruddy complexion, stood there looking us over. Mrs. Gibson was a lady of dignity and charm, and I immediately felt I was going to like her. In that fleeting moment of mutual appraisals, I wondered how she was going to like us.

"Good day, ma'am," I said cheerfully, handing her the billeting slip. "Corporal Runyon and myself, Corporal Altieri, have the good fortune of drawing your home for quarters. . . ."

Before I could say more she stepped aside, saying, "Oh, yes, the American Rangers! Do come in. You must be so tired from that horrible train ride."

Runyon and I—our faces beaming—scooped up our luggage with alacrity and brushed past her into the anteroom where we set our belongings down and looked around. The house seemed small but comfortably furnished, in a late Victorian style. China and silver dominated the small dining room and the living room was crammed with antiques and knickknacks. A large brick fireplace fronted by a brass screen occupied a corner. On the wall a huge picture of a handsome British major dominated the room.

Still smiling, Mrs. Gibson led us into the living room and bade us sit down while she went to fetch some tea and crumpets. Runyon and I, still a bit overwhelmed with it all, sat down gingerly on a large chaise lounge, exchanging appreciative glances as she left us.

I was admiring the fine-looking major's picture when Mrs. Gibson returned with the tea and crumpets, set them down on a small end table and started to pour. "That's my husband," she said. "He is serving with our force in Egypt. He's a medical officer."

"A very fine-looking man," I said. "How long has he been away?"

"Two years," replied Mrs. Gibson, "but it seems like a lifetime."

I felt very sorry for her. She said it rather stoically. I wanted to say something that would lift her spirits. "Well, it won't be long before the war will be over," I said, "then he will come back."

Mrs. Gibson proved her sense of humor when she laughed. "Aha, now that you Yanks are here the war will soon be won?"

Runyon, amused by it all, spoke up for the first time: "Well, we wouldn't exactly put it that way, Mrs. Gibson, but we're very anxious to get this thing over with, aren't we, Al?"

As I nodded approval and took a sip of tea, Mrs. Gibson excused herself and left the room. She came back shortly with a little blond, blue-eyed boy around three years old. He was sucking his thumb and looking very shy as Mrs. Gibson introduced us. "This is Robert, Rangers. He is the little man of the house. He has done a fine job looking after me."

We both shook hands with little Robert and soon I had him sitting on my knee sharing a crumpet. It was a good feeling. At once we felt right at home, part of this wonderful Scottish family. I knew that fate had been very kind indeed, to provide me with a temporary home with such a lovely lady and delightful child. And I knew Runyon felt the same way.

Later that evening Runyon and I were introduced to our first meal in a Scottish household. Mrs. Gibson had prepared a fine rabbit stew and an excellent pudding. It was delicious, and we complimented her profusely. Very modestly she told us that the rationing had somewhat dulled her daily menus, but with our additional ration allowance she would try to improve culinary matters. Sugar in particular was very scarce and coffee and candy were almost unheard of. Very gallantly Runyon and I assured her that we would see that her food stocks were vastly improved—we would bring her our own weekly PX rations.

Mrs. Gibson told us why she and the other families of Dundee had accepted the Yanks into their homes: "The Commandos had often been billeted among the people of Dundee. We admire and

83

love the Commandos—they conduct themselves so well. . . . So when the Lord Mayor appealed to the citizens to volunteer living quarters for the American Rangers who had been trained by the Commandos, we readily responded."

I asked Mrs. Gibson if having two Rangers in the house would not create too much of a burden for her, what with the cooking, cleaning and so forth. Without hesitation she crinkled her lovely blue eyes and answered: "Everyone must share some burden to help in this war. If I can help make two soldiers feel at home for a short while, this is but a small contribution compared to what you Rangers will be making when you see action. I know my husband George would want me to do something like that. . . ."

Her answer moved me deeply. My admiration for Mrs. Gibson and the citizens of Dundee was unbounded. I resolved that I would certainly do everything I could to show Mrs. Gibson that we Rangers were worthy and grateful for the warm hospitality she had already accorded us.

Dundee was going to be more than a second home.

CHAPTER 14

OUR training schedules at Dundee were the most varied and most interesting we had ever encountered. One day we would concentrate on street fighting in an abandoned housing project; another day we would attack the huge coastal batteries flanking Dundee. Other days we would have combat field problems, with the Commandos and Home Guard units playing the role of enemy forces. Often we would go out of town—as a unit—to a distant objective. Then each Ranger would have to make his own way back to Dundee, using his own ingenuity.

Unit contact and control, individual initiative and combat planning, were the themes most emphasized. Compared to our previous hardships and endurance tests at Achna Carry, the training in general was comparatively easy. Major Darby and Captain Dammer took turns going out with each company, and we could see by their relaxed manner that they were not displeased with our progress.

One morning, before battalion formation, a jeep roared into our company area driven by the company supply sergeant, Sergeant Perry. The back of the jeep was loaded with canvas bags—mail bags. With wild shouts we tore toward the jeep and surrounded Perry, babbling excitedly. This was the first mail call in months, and we could hardly restrain ourselves. Sergeant Torbett, who was always putting himself in the limelight whenever there was good things to distribute, at once mounted the jeep and started reading off the name on the letters Perry handed him. "Eastwood, Gomez,

85

Dunn, Altieri . . ." he thundered, as though he himself, through the gratuity of his heart, was giving us a special gift with the top kick's compliments.

As he continued to call out other names, we tore into our mail and read avidly. My first letter was from my dear friend Father Carr, the pastor of our church in Parkesburg, Pennsylvania. Father Carr, a learned, gray-thatched, scholarly priest in his late sixties, for whom I had once served as an altar boy, was keeping close tabs on me since I joined the Army. I had written him about joining the Rangers and this was his reply:

Dear Ranger Jim:

I knew you were quite a devil as a boy, but I didn't realize you were so daring. This Ranger business sounds like great stuff; been reading all about your training and exploits at Dieppe. We are all proud of you, Ranger, and we all look forward to big news about your outfit's future exploits.

I felt real good reading that letter. It was nice to know that people back home had read about our outfit. It gave me a feeling of pride and incentive. I tore into another letter, this one from Mrs. Kalber, the town's most dedicated war mother, whose son, Norman, had entered the Army with me. Mrs. Kalber made it a point to correspond with all the boys from Parkesburg, and she kept us abreast of local news and gave us a great deal of amusing patter and encouragement. She too had read about the Rangers and she expressed her admiration with unbounded enthusiasm. My morale soared skyward.

Suddenly Gomez screamed like a wild man: "Hey, fellows, I'm a father! That's right . . . I, Simon Gomez, now have a fine eight-pound boy!" Gomez's eyes were flashing proudly; he was grinning from ear to ear. "No more crap games for me, fellows. . . . From now on every pound I get goes home—I got real responsibilities."

We crowded around Gomez and pumped his hand, slapped him on the back and kicked him in the rear. Gomez had earned himself the distinction of being the first Ranger to become a father.

Before our enthusiasm for Gomez' good fortune had subsided,

Torbett let out a big roar. "Hey, you Rangers, you got a real hero among you. . . . That's right. Ol' Donald King Torbett is a real hero in West Virginia." In his hand was a local newspaper with his picture under a byline saying: SERGEANT TORBETT WOUNDED IN DIEPPE RAID.

"How do you like those apples?" spoke up Junior Fronk. "Ol' Broken Butt gets shot in the rear during training, five hundred miles from Dieppe—and he now gets a hero's rating in that backwoods state of his."

"Yeh," Sergeant Ed Thompson spoke up, "I'll bet he wrote home and told them he went to Dieppe."

Torbett, happy to be the center of attention, laughed good-naturedly. "Honest, fellows, I didn't say a word. All I told my wife was that I had gotten a dose of lead in the rear. She probably thought I had been in action when the news broke about Dieppe. . . ." He took a lot of kidding, and he loved it.

That night a good number of the Rangers of Fox Company celebrated the birth of Gomez' son in true Ranger style with a party at our favorite pub, where a number of Black Watch troops congregated to swap lies with the Rangers each evening.

CHAPTER 15

ON THE last day of our training Captain Murray started the day by leading Fox Company on a ten-mile speed march north of Dundee. Our destination was the Van Arbrith cliffs, towering perpendicularly hundreds of feet above the sea. Our last training mission at Dundee was to scale those clay cliffs without benefit of ropes, a project that filled me with terror.

I was shaking quite visibly when we reached the base of the cliffs —so much so that Gomez tried to buck up my confidence. "Don't worry, Al," he said. "You made out great back in Achna Carry. You can do it again. Hell, those cliffs ain't so high—you can go up blindfolded."

I didn't say a word. I just stood there trying to muster up my courage again. Soon Murray followed by Nye started the long ascent. One by one the Rangers of F Company followed at an interval of six paces. Watching the men go up those cliffs was an ordeal. They were slipping and sliding, clutching at weeds to keep balance, searching for crevices for their feet and finding nothing but loose dirt and thin shale. Gomez, smiling confidently, was soon climbing, and before I knew it I was moving up right behind him.

Frightened and gasping for breath I managed to follow Gomez to a narrow cleft two-thirds of the way up. Then suddenly someone shouted above us: "Rock! Rock!" I looked up to see a small boulder hurtling down on us. Quickly I pressed myself against the cliff wall and prayed.

The next instant I heard a dull thump. I looked up to see Gomez, his arms outstretched, come hurtling over my head. Frozen with horror I watched his body careen downward, strike a cliff abutment, then bounce into space again. I couldn't look any more. I heard Gomez strike the ground, a hundred or so feet below, with a resounding thump.

Swiftly the Rangers below me started scrambling and sliding down the cliff. I got to the foot of the cliff in time to see four medics carrying Gomez to the field ambulance which always accompanied us on dangerous training problems. I ran up to the ambulance just as they were putting his stretcher in. "Is he dead?" I asked, as I looked at his blood-covered, motionless body.

"He's still breathing," the medic answered. "But he's in a bad way—back of his head's caved in." By this time a large cluster of Rangers had gathered about, silent, sad and mad. Gomez was to all of us the real morale booster of Company F. There was not a man in the company who didn't love him like a brother. There were few dry eyes around that ambulance as it pulled away in a cloud of dust.

Andre threw his rifle on the ground, disgustedly. "It had to happen on our last day, to the nicest guy in the outfit."

I just stood there numbly, hoping I would wake up and find it was all nothing but a bad dream.

Captain Murray, we knew, was hit as hard as we were by the loss of Gomez. Nevertheless, he knew well enough that this tragedy could unnerve some of us for cliff climbing. Immediately Murray surveyed the cliffside and started ascending—without asking the company to do likewise.

We watched him scramble upward without hesitating once on outcroppings. He went up faster than a mountain goat. Nye and Torbett followed him. Soon one by one all the noncoms were joining in the cliff climb. I was so unnerved by Gomez' fall that I felt faint. I was ready to call it quits. To hell with the Rangers—I couldn't take it any longer!

But as I saw my closest friends—Howard Andre, Vernon Lodge, Sarn't El Siego, Ran Harris and many others take their turn at the cliff, I knew I couldn't leave them. Somehow I found the courage and the agility to tackle the cliffs again.

Without incident I made it to the top and breathed a great sigh of relief. I knew then that never again would I be afraid of the highest heights. And I believe every man in F Company felt the same way.

Downcast, depressed and silent, Company F made its way by speed march back to Dundee. We moved swiftly along a narrow macadam road paralleling the beach. Halfway to Dundee we saw a large group of Rangers clustered around two more ambulances.

As we reached the group the ambulances pulled away with sirens wailing. "What's the trouble?" asked Captain Murray.

The officer in charge was ashen white, his nearby men were grim-looking, their faces betraying deep emotion: "Three of my men stepped on land mines during beach tactics problems. One man was killed, one blinded, one emasculated."

A noncom came over to Mulvaney and opened up. "My best buddy, Murray Salkin, got a hunk of steel in his eyes. He'll never see again. The British told us that the lousy beach was de-mined. . . . They forgot to pull up a couple, and it was just our luck to hit them on the last day."

I winced when Murray Salkin's name was brought up. Murray and I went through basic training together at Fort Knox. I remembered well how proud he had been of making the Rangers. He was a shoe-leather salesman from Baltimore, and his fondest hope was to become a three-stripe sergeant. Poor Murray—he never had a chance even to get wounded in combat. . . . I felt miserable. Everyone did.

The next morning found us standing in battalion formation dressed in our Class B—OD's and cut-down leggings—ready for our departure from Dundee. An hour earlier I had said farewell to Mrs. Gibson with deep feelings of gratitude for her gracious hospitality. Runyon had already said his good-bys and had hastened out ahead of me. As I stood there at the doorway she wished me luck, and said, "I enjoyed having you lads and want you to know that this house is always yours if ever you come this way."

Our Ranger chief stood before us, looking poised and seemingly unperturbed by the previous day's disasters. On his cap was the silver leaf of a lieutenant colonel, in recognition of his work in organizing and training the First Battalion.

90

With the aid of a field loudspeaker, his words were crisp and telling: "Rangers, today we leave Dundee for our staging area near Glasgow. I am very proud of the way you all conducted yourselves as guests of Dundee. The Lord Mayor has asked us to come back whenever the fortunes of war permit—which is a good indication of the esteem you have earned from the people here.

"We leave Dundee deeply saddened by the terrible accidents that occurred yesterday. However, I want all you Rangers to remember that these men who were wounded and killed in training are as much heroes as anyone killed in battle. No one could have sacrificed more for their unit and their country. . . ."

If anyone else had been saying those words, we would have felt that we were being loaded with the usual patriotic pitch. But Darby somehow put sincerity and strength and true meaning into his words. "Remember, Rangers! Casualties in training—painful though they may be—mean saving lives in battle, through the lessons we learn. . . . You will find that out very shortly."

With those words, Darby took his place at the head of the battalion, roared out, "Forward, march," and led us out of the parade grounds, to the streets, enroute to the railroad station for our departure to Glasgow.

The railroad station was teeming with civilians when we finally arrived. Waiting to say good-by were many of the townsfolk whose houses we had shared and many of the young ladies whose affections we had shared. Colonel Darby, not unmoved by the large turnout, magnanimously allowed us a fifteen-minute break before traintime to say our good-bys in appropriate Ranger fashion.

A wild surge of females converged on the troops like a tidal wave. It was even more stirring than our departure from Oban. Elderly ladies came up to us, bearing big pots of hot tea and warm biscuits and cookies. Young ladies thronged about, excitedly offering us the choicest gifts that young soldiers could ever receive—warm, vibrant embraces, some mingled with passion and affection, others with remorse and sorrow, all with deep rapport of the many joyous experiences shared together.

It was there at the station that many Rangers, carried away, vowed to return and marry their lassies. Several, we learned later,

91

had already been secretly married. And it was then too that several Rangers who were doing double and triple duty with the local lassies finally got caught up with.

One Ranger, never at a loss for words, had no less than three young ladies to see him off. When they converged on him for a fond good-by and found him surrounded by rivals, they let him have it: "You sneaky creature!" one stormed. "You told me there was none but me." Another let fly at him: "So this is the game you Rangers play—you horrible fraud!" The last one sobbed: "You wretch! It was up the garden path you led me. . . . Never again will I let a Yank pull my leg."

The poor Ranger, unmasked, retreated into the crowd. I saw him later with a sweet elderly lady, accepting a cup of tea with a hang-dog look.

Finally we boarded our train, after pulling ourselves away from our friends with the greatest reluctance. As the train began to move, many of our well-wishers ran along the platform snatching a last kiss, clutching a hand for the last time, waving a last good-by.

For most of us this was the last time we would ever see these grand people. To some of us a great deal more than we would care to admit was left behind. To all of us Dundee and its wonderful, spirited, gracious people would never be forgotten.

CHAPTER 16

IN CONTRAST to our plush living conditions in Dundee, we found Corker Hill one of the ugliest, messiest collections of pyramidal tents we had ever seen. Sprawled out for miles in a sea of mud were lines of soot-sodden tents barely discernible through the overhanging fog.

"I knew it," shouted Howard Fuller as we clambered down from our Quartermaster trucks. "Ol' Darby figured we were being spoiled, so he wants to remind us we're just like ordinary soldiers."

We were met by some Rangers from Headquarters Company, who had been in Corker Hill several days ahead of us as part of the advance detail. They led us squashing through the black mud, up a narrow company street to a line of tents. "We're right next to the Eighteenth Infantry Regiment of the First Infantry Division," the Ranger said as he pointed to the tents we were to occupy. "General Terry Allen's boys are going with us on this deal."

We knew immediately what that meant. Our impending operation was no small-scale raid. With an entire infantry division behind us, we were scheduled for something real big—perhaps a full-scale invasion. I had heard a great deal about Terry Allen and his "Big Red One" Division. It was considered the best-spirited and best-trained division in Britain. It was very comforting to know we would fight alongside a crack outfit like our own.

Swiftly each section was assigned a tent and the Rangers soon settled down in their dreary homes. Our tent quartered eight men and was furnished with canvas cots. The floor was only partially covered with wooden slats and a small kerosene stove dominated the center.

Wearily we dropped our equipment by our bunks, tried to scrape the mud off our shoes and pants, and settled down for what we hoped would be a very short stay in this muddy meadow.

Our days at Corker Hill were mercifully short. Our training program, to our satisfaction, was very limited. In the mornings we did our PT, followed by the usual ten-mile speed march. In the afternoons we had weapons instructions, map and compass reading, bayonet drill and occasionally a spot of unarmed combat. But our main function at Corker Hill was simply to wait; wait till the ships were assembled in the Firth of Forth to take us off to our great adventure.

Evenings we would go into the city of Glasgow, make the usual rounds of the pubs and dance halls, meet the usual Scottish lassies, share the usual joys and come back to camp in time for reveille.

One morning the entire battalion was assembled to hear a colonel from G-2 who was a specialist on international law. This colonel, a mild-mannered gentleman with glasses, who looked like a college professor, was very solicitous about our fate if and when we got captured. As Darby stood by looking on the entire proceedings with unconcealed skepticism, the colonel spoke:

"Remember men, you are only required to give your name, rank and serial number. Under no circumstances will you identify your unit, your past organizations or any battle plans you are aware of. When you are captured, you will rely on the senior noncom to intercede and speak for you on any injustices perpetrated. You will be permitted to write to your relatives and receive mail and food parcels through the International Red Cross."

Before the colonel could proceed, Colonel Darby, visibly vexed, interrupted: "Thank you, Colonel," then with his chin outthrust and a flashing smile, he addressed his Rangers: "This information you have just heard is all very well for those troops who are going to be captured. But that is not for the Rangers. We have no intention of allowing ourselves the luxury of being captured. If there is any capturing done, it is the Rangers who will do it—not the enemy. Now it is up to you Rangers to prove that I am not a liar!"

To a man the entire battalion roared its approval as the embar-

94

rassed colonel returned Darby's curt salute and swiftly disappeared from the platform.

Our battalion strength was considerably enhanced during our travail at Corker Hill by the addition of some colorful characters. The first addition—officially, that is—came when Colonel Darby shanghaied the battalion cooks, who had been only loaned out to the Rangers through the courtesy of General Hartle. These cooks, led by Mess Sergeant Peer S. Buck, a huge ponderous ex-hotel detective from St. Paul, Minnesota, never volunteered for the Rangers. It was their understanding that they would only serve up their culinary masterpieces to the voracious Rangers until such time as the battalion was ready for departure.

Although handicapped considerably by British rations, our incomparable cooks had performed near-miracles in making our chow nearly bearable. Sergeant James (Slum Burner) Smiley, in particular, a former native of Tennessee, had won the esteem of the Rangers by his good nature and ability to bear up under the tirades of invective hurled at him and his associates. Sergeant Peer Buck, who supervised the mess crew, had soon found out that Darby, although not unappreciative of his prowess in the kitchen, was more interested in him as the battalion sergeant major. Darby liked Buck because he was big, rugged and knew how to deliver orders to the tough first sergeants of the battalion.

Peer Buck and his erstwhile crew were greeted one drizzly day by the following order on the battalion bulletin board:

First Ranger Infantry Battalion
APO 464

SPECIAL ORDERS NO. 104

The following men are relieved from TEMPORARY assignment with 1 Ranger Bn. and assigned PERMANENTLY to 1 Ranger Bn.

Buck, Peer S.	Master Sergeant
Smiley, James	Sergeant
Simpson, Ernest A.	Pfc.
Teague, Letch	Corporal
Montee, Elmer	Pfc.
Ziola, Frank	Sergeant

BY ORDER OF COLONEL DARBY.

95

Sergeant Buck and his crew, although stunned, proved they were qualified Rangers when they served up their fanciest chow to commemorate the occasion. Pfc. Dunn, carried away by the situation, decided to commemorate the occasion with a sample of his literary talents. Under the special orders Dunn tacked on a paper bearing this special verse:

> They also serve who ruin our chow,
> Our rascal cooks are Rangers now.

The second addition to our ranks appeared one day while we were returning from a speed march. As we approached our camp we were met by a moonfaced, stocky sergeant, loaded down with seven or eight cameras and a pack full of film. This strange-looking apparition seemed to burst with excitement as he ran alongside us, puffing heavily, snapping pictures. Sergeant Torbett, end of the column, lost no time in getting out of ranks to belabor us. "All right, Rangers, get your a——s off the ground. . . . You're movin' like a bunch of WACs."

"There he goes again," said Fronk. "Wants his picture took, the publicity hound."

"Say, Sergeant," the photographer spoke out, "that was great. . . . Would you do that again, please? Make a good layout of a tough Ranger sergeant for the *Stars and Stripes*."

"Yes, Sergeant," barbed Fuller, "show the nice Snapdragon what a real rugged top kick you are."

Suddenly Junior Fronk darted out of the column, ran abreast of the cameraman, puffed out his chest. "I eat first sergeants for dinner, and I kill lieutenants with my bare hands. I'm Junior Fronk, the hairiest Ranger in the outfit—take my picture too."

As Torbett roared for Fronk to get back in ranks, we doubled up with laughter so that we couldn't run any more. Fortunately Captain Murray called out, "Quick-time!" and we settled down to easy strides with the photographer snapping away like mad and Torbett's face redder than hell.

This moonfaced, peripatetic sergeant, we soon found out, had a most serious mission. Pfc. Presly Stroud, Colonel Darby's field clerk, who was formerly with F Company at Achna Carry, gave us

96

the lowdown on Phil Stern, who already was known throughout the battalion by Fuller's choice name, "Snapdragon." Stroud acted out the entire scene for our enjoyment.

Stroud said he had been in the tent when Stern reported to Darby. Stern presented his orders without very much military courtesy, and Darby had curtly straightened him out. Darby then asked Stern why he volunteered for the photographic assignment. Quoting Stern, Stroud recapitulated:

"I was in Headquarters in London, living in plush quarters, sitting out the war shooting pictures of generals at social events. It was good duty but I had a feeling of being nonessential to the war effort. Then I read about volunteers being wanted for the Rangers. Well, sir . . . I have belief in our war cause and want to fight it a little more concretely than taking pictures of bigshots. Also, I felt that the Rangers would be an outfit whose deeds should be recorded by pictures—a colorful outfit with a colorful commander. And without bragging, it should have its pictures took by the best cameraman in the Army."

"Which, of course, is you," cut in Darby, according to Stroud.

"Yes, sir . . . I worked for *Life* and for some movie mags in Hollywood before the war."

"That's hardly a recommendation to be a Ranger, Stern. What do you know about soldieriing? What do you know about weapons?"

"Frankly, sir, I don't know which end a bullet comes out of a gun . . . but I can learn."

"You'll also learn how to make a fifteen-mile speed march, how to kill a man with your bare hands. You'll learn how to field-strip a rifle blindfolded. . . . We don't want any dead weight around our necks in this outfit."

"Yes, sir. I'll get the hang of this Ranger stuff, Colonel," Stern had bravely ventured.

Whether Stroud had quoted Darby and Stern accurately, we didn't know. Stern, we found later, was a very genial, loquacious fellow. For some reason or other, possibly because he considered Torbett very photogenic, Stern made Fox Company his adopted outfit. All the other companies were a bit peeved because F Company got most of Stern's attention. But the men of F Company seemed

97

to feel that it was only logical for Stern to select our men for the most action-packed shots. After all, we were the very best outfit in the battalion—at least that's what we thought.

Whenever we got bored with our own tall tales we yanked Snapdragon into our tent and challenged him to give out with some colorful stories about Hollywood personalities he had taken pictures of. Stern never let us down. He either was the most sought-after photographer in Hollywood, or he was the world's best liar.

The latest addition (temporarily) to our outfit came upon us in a most embarrassing manner. Harrison, Fronk, Contrera, Vernon Lodge and I were in the huge PX tent one evening, giving forth with the most popular soldier song in Britain. Having guzzled some six or seven cans of the first American beer to arrive in Britain, we were giving the song our lustiest:

> Oh, they're saying good-by to them all,
> The long and the short and the tall,
> There'll be no promotions this side of the ocean,
> So cheer up my lads ——— them all.

The standard word after lads was "Bless." Only in this instance we were not using that word. Instead of "Bless" we were substituting a four-letter word as was the military custom. Suddenly, as we started to sing the chorus after the second stanza, a trim, natty Commando captain, of slight wiry build and medium height, wearing black horn-rimmed glasses and sporting a green beret, stepped up and joined the circle.

In a loud gusty voice, that was surprising for such a slight fellow, he came in on the chorus, drowning out our vulgar word with:

> Bless them all
> Bless them all
> The long, the short and the tall . . .

Vernon Lodge gulped, his eyes sank. I looked at his collar incredibly. The silver cross of a chaplain was shining brightly. Our lusty chorus dwindled into a hushed silence.

98

Smiling mischievously, the captain spoke: "Come, Rangers, don't let me spoil the fun. You sing right well, you know, even though you don't get all the words right."

Fronk's pale face turned crimson. "We're sorry, Chaplain, we were just knocking it around a bit . . . We really didn't mean that word like we sang it."

The chaplain continued to smile graciously. "You Rangers surely do a grand job of knocking those vulgar words about. I have been in camp only four hours and I have heard language that would make our Liverpool stevedores sound like clergymen!"

"Are we that bad, Chaplain?" asked Pete Preston, with an innocent hurt expression.

"Much worse. I had planned to give a service here tomorrow by special request of Colonel Darby. However, I see I will be spending more time here than I expected. There is lots of work for a chaplain here. . . .

"Incidentally, my name is Chaplain Albert Basil. I am with the Commando Special Services Brigade. I hope to see you all at the services tomorrow."

With that Chaplain Basil waved genially, turned and strode out of the tent, leaving us there, mortally humiliated, but nevertheless pleased to know that the chaplain would be with us for a while.

The services, held in a large mess tent, were brief and to the point. A few Bible readings, a hymn or two and a short talk— short in length but long in thought.

"Rangers, I thoroughly appreciate those of you who were thoughtful enough to attend services today. I would like to say I am not here to prate and belabor you on the need for faith at this crucial moment. Faith in God is not something to be forced upon you; it is something that must come from within, something you alone must feel.

"But I do say this: Every man in this unit must face the important decision: Do I go into battle with God at my side, or do I go into battle without Him? It is as simple as that. For those of you who wish to go with Him, I am here to help you in any way I can to bring you closer. I am not here to chastise. I am here as a friend who knows and understands soldiers, who knows that stresses and strains of military life can sometimes cause us to doubt, to weaken, to find excuses to indulge in the most profligate adventures when the opportunity presents itself.

"I came here to say service because there are not enough American chaplains available. I am deeply sorry you do not have your own unit chaplain because one is certainly needed here. With your indulgence I have elected to stay here with you until you sail. . . . Please tell your Ranger friends that I want to know them. All of you feel free to come and see me at any hour of the day. . . . Thank you, gentlemen."

Thus did Chaplain Basil win over the Rangers who braved his services that misty day.

But Chaplain Basil proved that sermons were only a small part of a chaplain's functions. The next few days found him visiting each company, getting to know each man individually. He never imposed himself on people, he merely introduced himself and chatted amiably about their families, their home towns, their civilian occupations. If a man was interested enough to seek guidance and counsel on religious matters, he would bring him to his quarters and enlighten the individual in accordance with the size and scope of his problem. Father Basil said Mass for the Catholics each morning as he was required, but the rest of the day he spent seeing all creeds.

With sharp, intelligent features, he was at times witty, amusing, satirical and at all times approachable. Before long the services in the mess hall tent became packed with his new-found friends.

CHAPTER 17

THE ORDER to break camp came September 21, 1942. Sergeant Torbett was deadly serious that morning when we lined up for formation. "We're shoving off at 0900 tomorrow morning with full battle equipment. Every Ranger turns in his barracks bag to supply with name, rank and serial number. You better leave all nonessentials in that bag. We won't be seein' 'em for a long time."

"How about passes to town tonight?" Fronk asked.

"Junior, will you keep that big yap shut just once? I'm coming to that right now. Passes for all those not on detail. And God help the poor bastards that come in tomorrow late for reveille or AWOL. . . ."

Sergeant Thompson, Pfc. Carlo Contrera, Vernon Lodge and I started the evening off with a visit to the Red Cross building in Glasgow. It was our custom to start the evening off here because we could stock up on cigarettes, look the assorted hostesses over, then decide our course for the rest of the night.

We were lined up at the cigarette counter when Ed Thompson gave out a wild yell. "Holy Gomez! Simon Gomez . . ." Ed started running toward the door as we turned our heads and stared. There, standing transfixed, a bandage wrapped around his head was Simon Gomez, a dazed expression on his face as he spotted us.

We rushed to him, threw our arms around him, shook his hand: "Gomez," I shouted. "We thought you were in bad shape at the hospital in Edinburgh. What are you doing here?"

"Fellows, I couldn't let the outfit move off without me. I heard from one of the nurses that the Rangers were near Glasgow. I figured you'd be pullin' out soon, so I stole me some clothes and went AWOL. . . ."

We led him to a large leather couch, sat him down solicitiously. Lodge ran for some coffee and sandwiches as we hovered around him like a bunch of old ladies who had suddenly found a little orphan.

"We sure miss you, Gomez," I said. "The company isn't the same without you."

"Thanks, Al, but I'm gonna stay with the outfit. . . . I'm not goin' back to that hospital."

"Whatsamatter Gomez," Contrera cut in. "Ain't those nurses treatin' you right?"

"Yeah, Gomez, aren't they massaging your rear like they did for old Broken-Butt Torbett?" enjoined Fronk.

Gomez laughed a bit weakly, put his arms around the two of us sitting closest to him. "Those limey doctors know their stuff and those nurses sure make a fuss over me. But that's for sick people. My head is as good as new."

"Ol' rockhead, Gomez." Ed Thompson laughed.

"Rockhead is right," returned Gomez looking at me. "You know, Al, my teacher once told me my skull was too thick for anything to ever penetrate. . . . I believe she was right."

Suddenly he stood up. "Hey, fellows, let's go back to camp."

"But, Gomez," I pleaded, "you're in bad shape. You need attention!"

"I'll get by." With that he stood up shakily, put on his cap and said, "Let's go, fellows. I wanna see the gang. How's ol' Darby treatin' you guys these days? And Torbett? Has he stopped any more bullets?"

There was nothing else to do but support Gomez by the arms and gingerly escort him down the steps to the street. I hailed a cab, helped him in. Then with Vernon Lodge and Ed Thompson, we settled down for the long drive back to Corker Hill, wondering what the outcome of this strange expedition would bring.

It was ten o'clock when our cab pulled up to the outskirts of our company area. We paid the driver, helped Gomez out and made

102

our way through the squashy mud to quarters. All the time Gomez kept saying how great it was to be back with the company, how he was gonna check in with the supply sergeant for a brand new rifle and Commando knife, how he was gonna sing some real zippy songs for the company aboard ship.

It was heartbreaking to hear him talk like that because we knew the battalion medic would never agree to take him along in that condition. I was real worried something might happen to him at any minute. I felt we should summon a medic at once. As Ed Thompson helped Gomez into our tent, I whispered to Lodge to run for the medic, pronto. Lodge took off.

Gomez was fooling around with my Commando knife as he always did when Lodge came back with Captain Jarret. Gomez jumped up indignantly, his face contorted with surprise and pain, pain that his friends had betrayed him.

"A helluva way to treat a pal," Gomez rasped.

"It's for your own good, Gomez. We wouldn't really be your pals if we didn't look after you," I tried to explain. Doc Jarret smiled and sat down next to Gomez. He knew full well the extent of Gomez' injury, knew that his entire back skull had been severely factured, knew that the slightest jar might cause complete paralysis or death. The doc asked Gomez how he felt.

"Great, Doc. These old ladies here are making a big deal over nothing." The doc disarmingly reached into his bag, pulled out a needle. "What you need is to get some rest, Gomez. Now just relax and let me give you something that will help you sleep."

Gomez stood up, flared. "Nothing doing, Doc. I'm okay I say. I don't like all this horsing around. I'm here to stay. Ol' Darby will let me. I know he will." Jarret was nonplussed. He just stood there trying to think what to do next.

Gomez quickly decided the issue. "I'm going right now to see Darby. Al, if you really are my pal, you'll take me to see the ol' man." Gomez meant business. He was a man with a mission—a simple mission—to be with his buddies on their first fight. His sincerity, his pathetic loyalty overwhelmed me. Maybe he was not too bad off. Maybe he would swiftly recuperate aboard ship. With his friends all around him maybe it would be much better for him to come with us. With these thoughts running through my mind I went with him toward the Command tent as the rest of our group stood there with pained expressions.

Colonel Darby was surprised when I poked my head into the tent and announced my mission. "Colonel, sir, Ranger Gomez of Fox Company has an urgent request to make."

Darby looked up from his game. "Come in, Corporal," said Darby. "I thought Gomez was still in the hospital. How did he get here?"

I parted the tent flap wide, and Gomez followed me in. We both stood at attention, but Darby put us at ease pointing to his cot. "Sit down, Gomez, relax. It's good to see you again. They can't keep a good Ranger down, can they?"

Gomez, all smiles, sat down then, his eyes clamped on Darby. "Yes, sir. That's what I've been trying to tell my buddies and Doc Jarret—that you can't keep a good Ranger down, sir. I went AWOL from the hospital when I heard our outfit was shipping out. Sir, I feel that I can make it with the rest of the boys. I'll carry my own weight."

Doc Jarret suddenly entered the tent. Darby nodded to him, then went over to Gomez and sat down beside him. "Gomez, I think you're one helluva Ranger. We need men with your spirit. I'd like to take you, but you must understand that the final decision must rest with my medical officer. No commanding officer—not even a full general—can rule against the professional counsel of the Medical Corps. The Army owes it to you to protect you with all the care possible. I'm sure you understand."

Gomez' smile vanished. The hurt, bewildered look returned.

"Perhaps we might arrange to have you catch up with the Rangers after you're fully mended, Darby suggested. "How will that be, Gomez?"

Gomez' face lighted up. "Colonel, that's okay with me. I know you would take me if you could. I just didn't want to be lost from my outfit for good."

As Gomez stood up, Darby took his hand and shook it firmly. "Let me say this, Gomez—you may not be with us physically on our first battle, but you have already made as great a contribution to our mission as any Ranger will ever make. You have given us all

104

something very personal to fight for. You have helped mold the true Ranger spirit!"

Gomez was all aglow as he accepted the colonel's tributes. His pearly teeth flashing a smile a mile long, he saluted crisply, did the most military about-face—even more military than the best Torbett could offer—and walked out of the tent, a proud, happy Ranger.

CHAPTER 18

SQUADRONS of seagulls crisscrossed the misty October sky as we trudged across the creaking gangplank into the moldy hold of the H.M.S. *Royal Ulsterman* in the harbor of Glasgow. Dock workers and sailors stopped working to stare and listen as we sounded off in lusty song:

> "Commandos said they'd make it tough,
> But they couldn't make it tough enough,
> Darby's Rangers . . . Rugged Rangers
>
> Ol' Cowerson trained us bloody well,
> Now we can fight our way through hell,
> Darby's Rangers . . . Fightin' Rangers
>
> We trained like hell to fight a war,
> We're ready for a foreign shore,
> Darby's Rangers . . . Ready Rangers."

We had good reason to be singing. After months of rigorous, exacting and sometimes repetitious training, we were anxious to "get cracking." That morning before breaking camp we had heard the crinkly-eyed, colorful General Terry Allen tell us how proud he was to have the First Ranger Battalion with his First Division on the impending first action of American troops—aside from Dieppe—in this war theater. The rugged general said he considered the Rangers as he did his very own troops. Together we would make history.

106

Our high spirits were temporarily lowered when we were introduced to our quarters by Sergeant Torbett and a petty officer of the Royal Navy. British troop ships are renowned for their cramped quarters. They are also notorious for their lack of comfort, lack of lighting and fresh-water showers. After one glimpse into the low-beamed, hammock-lined, pipe-crossed, evil-smelling hold that was destined to be our living quarters for many long weeks, we were convinced that the *Royal Ulsterman* was the flagship of all the moldy rust-ridden derelicts in the King's Navy.

After we delivered our choicest invectives against the King's Navy and the fates that ordained our assignment to the *Ulsterman*, a misnamed ship if there ever was one because there was certainly nothing royal about it, we settled down to speculate on our destination.

"We're headin' for Dieppe again," said Pete Preston. "The Limeys don't like the beatin' they took there, so we're all going back again for revenge with spades."

"You're off your rocker," spoke up Sarn't Sieg, who by now had grown a tremendous mustache. "We're gonna hit 'em somewhere up North, maybe Norway or Denmark."

Ray Rodriguez, who seldom ventured opinions, also contributed: "We're gonna land somewhere in Spain, then attack the Germans through France."

"You're all 'way off course," spoke up Mulvaney. "We're gonna sail around Africa and come up the Red Sea to Egypt and give General Montgomery's lads a hand."

"You're all a bunch of amateur strategists," remonstrated Fronk. "Actually this whole thing is a big bluff to make the Germans think we're gonna hit 'em with a second front. They'll tell their friends, the Japs. The Japs will relax because the pressure is on their Axis pals . . . and then, blooey! we sail all around the world and land in Guadalcanal to help out the Marines."

Everyone ventured an opinion and everyone was wrong. We didn't go anywhere. For three whole weeks we sailed up and down the Firth of Clyde making rehearsal landings against simulated gun positions, perfecting our night tactics, polishing our assault technique. Boat drills, load and unload, fire drills, sinking drills, aircraft attack drills, daytime, nighttime, drill, drill, drill, became our routine.

Our intrepid flotilla would sail into some remote island harbor and drop anchor. In pitch-black darkness, loaded with full battle gear, we would scramble into the assault boats, then shiver in the piercing cold as we were lowered into the choppy waves. The assault boats, manned by veteran seamen who had participated in many Commando raids, would rendezvous with the assault craft from the other ships. With perfect timing, the assault waves would form, then the swift steady dash to shore.

The terrain chosen for the rehearsals was as close as could be found for the real thing. The purpose of these rehearsals was explained over and over again by our company commanders, by our platoon leaders and by our section sergeants. Somewhere there was an important port that was needed as a base of operation for a mighty invasion. This port was protected by a massive four-gun battery on a bluff overlooking the harbor and a two-gun battery at the harbor itself. No ships could approach this harbor without coming under fire from these guns.

It was the mission of the First Ranger Battalion to make a surprise night landing, silence both batteries, occupy the water-front area and protect the landing of Infantry and armored troops. The guns had to be knocked out before dawn. If we failed to accomplish our mission, the Navy would resort to bombardment. That's all they told us. We had no idea where or when this invasion would occur. We just kept on rehearsing, night after night until finally we could go through the entire operation with blindfolds.

Then one day we returned to the harbor of Glasgow to see a sight that was awe-inspiring. The entire harbor was choked with ships, large flat battle wagons, sleek cruisers, narrow gray destroyers, tiny corvettes, ponderous carriers and bulky troopships. We found ourselves anchored in the middle of a massive, mighty armed convoy. We knew our time had come.

108

CHAPTER 19

IT WAS the morning of October 27. We were rudely awakened by a low-pitched flutelike whistle over our ship's loudspeaker: "Now hear this . . . Now hear this . . ." a crisp British voice intoned: "The *Royal Ulsterman* is now skirting the northern tip of Ireland. We are part of Combat Convoy C. Our course is due west. All ranks will conduct themselves aboard ship in accordance with the ship's at-sea regulations." Then with a breezy flair, "The Captain wishes his American passengers a fine voyage."

"Blow it out your barracks bag," shouted Fuller as the voice continued to repeat the message.

Swiftly we struggled to get out of our closely packed hammocks as First Sergeant Torbett made his appearance. "All right, you lusty Rangers, let's snap to it. Get those hammocks tied up, clean up those quarters and hit the chow line at seven-thirty. . . . I want you guys to show these Limeys what good housekeepers we Rangers are."

"Hey, Sergeant," shouted Fronk, "are you bucking to take over the ship captain's job?"

"Ol' seadog Torbett," added Pete Preston. "I thought we'd get a break from that guy once we were at sea. Now we gotta take orders from that squeaking Limey voice and him too!"

Torbett paid no attention. He just moved swiftly through the hold, dumping the stragglers out of their hammocks.

After chow we went on deck to see a spectacular sight. For miles ahead of us and around us, their funnels belching black smoke,

109

were stately lines of troopships, guarded by a strong cordon of destroyers, cruisers and battleships. Our position was in the rear of this mighty convoy. A lone corvette trailed behind us in the distance. Overhead several observation planes lazily circled the convoy, on the alert.

As Howard Andre and I stood there near the starboard bow astounded by the power of the mighty armada we were part of, we were suddenly surprised by a familiar voice in back of us. "Have you Rangers got your sea legs yet?" We turned around. There, smiling, his green beret cocked jauntily on his head was none other than Chaplain Albert E. Basil! We were both stunned. Chaplain Basil, we thought, had returned to his Commando Brigade after we embarked at Glasgow.

"Father Basil," I exclaimed, "what are you doing here?" By this time several other Rangers had come up with surprised looks.

"Well, lads," said Father Basil, "you may consider me a bona fide stowaway. . . . I simply decided that you Rangers needed me and I needed you. In fact, I was a bit jealous that you would be going on this important adventure while I was back in Scotland, so here I am!"

We were joined by Captain Murray and Lieutenant Nye. We could see by the crinkle in their eyes that they were in on the stowaway deal. Murray greeted us genially, looking sideways at the chaplain. "Fellows, now that the Padre is here, we don't have to worry about being torpedoed. We're under his wings now!"

"Sure glad you picked our ship to go AWOL on, Padre," spoke up Andre. "That goes to prove that we're the best churchgoers in the battalion."

"On the contrary," returned the Padre with his now famed mischievous look, "it only proves that Easy and Fox companies are the best cussers in the entire battalion. I may be a bit ambitious, but I have high hopes that by the time we reach our destination, your vocabularies will have improved remarkably."

We all laughed at his humor and fortitude. I knew he had a saint-sized job ahead, trying to redeem the foul-speaking souls of Easy and Fox. Of all the sins and human failings of the Rangers, cursing was to Father Basil the very worst.

Pete Preston voiced our sense of gratitude when he said: "Fa-

110

ther Basil, there ain't nobody cusses more than me in this outfit. But just to show you how I aim to improve, I'm volunteering to organize a Ranger Don't Swear Club—and each member will drop a shilling in the box every time he comes up with a foul word."

George Fuller, the second-best swearer in the outfit, was not to be outdone by George: "Padre, if this so-and-so is sincere, I'll help him organize the club. I'll be the club enforcer to make sure every-. body pays up."

Father Basil chuckled heartily: "Bully for you, fellows. Now I know my precipitate action in deserting His Majesty's Army was well justified."

For several days the invasion convoy steamed majestically westward. Junior Fronk kept telling all the fellows what a brilliant strategist he was, certain that we were going to sail through the Panama Canal and head for the Pacific. One dreamy-eyed Ranger predicted that we were going to go right back to the States and march up Broadway. His reasoning was predicated on the belief that the people back home needed their morale boosted by a big parade of overseas veterans. The fact that most of the "veterans" hadn't yet seen action made no difference to his reasoning.

Speculation on our destination grew so keen and so diverse that Sergeant Butt Torbett himself organized a company pool. Each man put up five pounds and a slip of paper with the destination point selected. The pool would be handed over to the winner on T Day (Torpedo Day), which was the day Captain Murray would officially announce where we were going. It was explained to us that Torpedo Day meant the day that it was safe to reveal secret information, notwithstanding the possibility that we might be torpedoed and survivors picked up by enemy subs. The reasoning was that even if such an event occurred and information was extracted from survivors, the enemy coudn't marshal his forces fast enough to prevent the landing.

We soon found there was no shortage of global strategists in the Rangers. I picked Bordeaux, France. Harris picked Oran. Lodge picked Dakar. Thompson listed Marseilles. Torbett, who had smuggled aboard—from God knows where—a gigantic geography book, picked Palermo, Sicily. Fronk, Mulvaney and Sieg still held fast to their previous predictions.

111

We were only three days at sea when our convoy was joined by another large convoy from the States—at a point some eight hundred miles west of Ireland. The gigantic armada then swung around on a due-south course, headed for balmier weather. The additional force, plus the new course, created a new flurry of speculation about out probable destination. Junior Fronk still insisted we were going to the Pacific, only this time we were going there by way of South Africa instead of the Panama Canal. Another Ranger insisted it was all a big bluff. He said it was a show of strength to scare the Germans into surrendering.

Some of our Rangers were so unsportsmanlike that they had the temerity to ask for their slips back so they could record a new destination. But Sergeant Torbett, flexible though he was, turned them down cold: "Rangers don't renege," he admonished with a pained expression.

CHAPTER 20

MONDAY, November 2, was Revelation or T day. At nine-thirty the entire company was summoned to the lower stern deck for our first briefing on our exact mission and destination. We gathered informally around a long sand table covered by a canvas tarpaulin. Captain Murray, flanked by the ship's captain and our two platoon lieutenants, stood alongside the table facing us. He seemed relaxed and congenial. It was not at all as we expected a commander to announce such momentous information. In fact, I felt a bit disappointed. I had thought surely he would be very grim-faced and dramatic. After all, we Rangers were going to make history. That's what General Terry Allen said we were going to do.

Sergeant Butt Torbett, however, contributed his best to make the situation appear dramatic. He was clutching the pile of destination slips in his hand, and his face was set in grim lines. With Captain Murray's announcement would also come Torbett's announcement of the winner of the pool. Torbett was today a man of destiny. At least he tried to make it appear that way, and that's the way we liked it.

Murray started out easily: "Fellows, the port we are going to take is a place few of you have ever heard of. It's in French Algeria, thirty miles east of Oran, the French Naval Base. It is called Arzew."

A murmur of voices greeted this news. No one had won the pool! The closest had been Harris, who had selected Oran. We all seemed more concerned with what would happen to our money than with the announcement of our destination.

As two noncoms unfolded a huge map of the North African coastline, Murray placed his pointer at Oran, Algeria, and continued

"The general plan is for the Americans to take over the whole of French North Africa from Morocco to Tunis. The attacks on Morocco and Algeria will be undertaken by American forces, backed up by the British Navy and Air Force. The British Army will land in Tunisia. The entire force is under the Command of General Eisenhower.

"Our mission is to spearhead the attack of the Center Task Force commanded by General Fredendall against the great Naval Base of Oran. We will be followed ashore by the Eighteenth Infantry Regiment of the First Division and Combat Command B of the First Armored Division."

I immediately thought of my old comrades in Battery A of the First Armored. I wondered if they would be in combat Command B on the same deal.

Murray continued: "Other troops will land on the coast west of Oran and move east in an encirclement. At this time we don't know what degree of resistance to expect from the French. For this reason it is necessary that we achieve complete surprise and a fast victory to prevent bloodshed."

"The rest of the morning will be spent by each section studying this sand table of Arzew."

With that, Captain Murray, followed by the ship's captain, made an exit, leaving Nye and Young, our two lieutenants, in charge. As the noncoms pulled back the tarpaulin revealing a perfect replica of the port of Arzew, a flurry of opinions broke out concerning our impending invasion. "We train like hell to fight the Germans and they send us to fight the French . . . a helluva war this is turning out to be," complained George.

"Maybe they won't fight at all.. Maybe they'll just lay down their arms and welcome us with wine and women," hopefully suggested an eager Ranger.

"Hey, Vernon," shouted Sarn't Sieg, "better get that ol' clarinet ready. You ought to really make out in those harems with that flute—those Arab women really go for flutes. Maybe you'll get a chance to charm some snakes, too."

All in all there was no particular enthusiasm among the Rangers

114

about fighting the French. Personally, I was let down. I didn't relish the idea of slaughtering people who were not really our enemies, regardless of the military gains achieved. Further, I felt that North Africa was an indirect approach that would only prolong the war. Not knowing or understanding the strategic aims involved, I felt we could accomplish much more in shortening the war by a direct assault on the continent. A number of Rangers voiced their approval of this opinion, including Randall Harris.

Sergeant Mulvaney soon led us around the sand table where Nye stood with pointer in hand. It was an exact, detailed replica of the town and harbor defenses of Arzew.

Dominating the town directly above the harbor was a huge Foreign Legion fort. About five hundred yards to the right of the fort on a high bluff was the main four-gun battery. This was the main objective.

"These guns are four inchers," Nye said. "They cover the port from every direction. Unless we capture them, they'll raise hell with our convoys and support troops. We may be outnumbered by the French, but we have a definite advantage—the element of shock and surprise."

His pointer moved from the battery, down the ravine, down to the beach on which we would land. Plainly marked were the pillboxes defending the battery.

"We've got a tough nut to crack, but A and B Companies have the real dilly." He pointed to the harbor defenses. Two long concrete jetties converged at right angles to form a narrow entrance to the man-made harbor. Two huge piers capable of accommodating a dozen ships protruded from shore. A small fort, situated on a ground rise alongside the base of a jetty, dominated the harbor.

"While we're attacking the gun battery from the rear, A and B will zoom through the narrow entrance, then head for the fort, where they make a direct assault on the two-gun battery there. They've got to get over the boom stretched across the entrance, then they're exposed to machine-gun positions on the jetties and piers."

"Sure glad they didn't pick F Company for that deal," spoke up one Ranger. "That looks like a no-return operation."

Nye looked up. "This whole operation has been carefully planned

115

by Colonel Darby and the Navy with two things in mind: co-ordination and suprise. These are the two greatest weapons any troop can have. Darby convinced the high command that the Rangers can move in and accomplish our mission, using all the techniques the Commandos taught us. Frankly, they were at first doubtful. But Darby won them over. So actually this operation is the big test for the Rangers. It may determine whether or not the Rangers will continue as a unit or be disbanded."

"What happens if something goes wrong and we don't capture the guns by dawn?" another Ranger asked.

Nye looked at us with steady eyes. "If those guns aren't captured by dawn . . . the Navy will lay down a heavy bombardment."

We all knew well the significance of that statement. The Rangers were being used on this mission in the hope of silencing the guns by speed and surprise, thereby inflicting a minimum of casualties on the French. However, if we failed, there was no alternative but to lay down destructive shell fire from the warships at sea. This shell fire might also fall on the town itself, and on all those in the immediate area, including the Rangers.

With painstaking care Lieutenant Nye proceeded to point out every phase of the operation. We knew from him the exact spot where D Company would set up its mortars. He traced the exact route we would take up the winding ravine to the rear of the gun battery. He pointed out the commandant's quarters, the barbed wire encircling the battery, the French Foreign Legion fort with its medieval-like moat. He even pointed out the areas in the town where the brothels were located.

"That's for me," said one Ranger notorious for his addiction to such places. "I'd like to go down in history as the first Ranger brothel-taker."

"That's all you would do—take it. You wouldn't know how to do anything else after that," another Ranger chided.

Sergeant Mulvaney handed us our pamphlets on North Africa when Nye completed his briefing. The pamphlet to my surprise did a good job of answering many troubling questions. It started out with:

They, the French, will ask you why you have come. The answer is straightforward and simple. We have come to drive out the

116

common enemy. We seek no gains, material or territorial. The people of this area are our traditional friends. We want to keep them as friends. We come not to oppress them but to help them. It was the wish of the President that the first blow in this assault should be primarily American. The name of the U.S. will stand for freedom to millions of Frenchmen as it does to all the people of Europe. It was the President's request that we should lead off this operation to make the issue as clear as possible. We are determined to do our fullest share in liberating the people of oppression.

Reading further I found the pamphlet did not overlook some important characteristics of the Moslem people we would encounter. It was particularly welcome news to learn that the Moslems had a good sense of humor as this paragraph informed:

North Africans, by and large, have an excellent sense of humor. You will not find it difficult to joke with them because they see the humor in situations easily. If they laugh at you, take it; don't get angry. Above all, never strike them.

I couldn't help wondering how their humor would hold up when we invaded their land on Sunday morning, the ninth of November.

After the briefing session ended, we swarmed around Sergeant Torbett, demanding our money before he got involved in a crap game. Torbett, who had never before had in his possession such a large sum, was clutching the money as though he was ready to send it home. "Just a minute, fellows," he begged, "let's keep the pool going. Let's place bets what the exact time will be when we accomplish our mission."

"Okay," said Junior Fronk, "but only under one condition—that we keep the money in the ship's safe."

"Wait a minute," I cut in. "Harris was the closest. Hell, Oran is the main objective and is only thirty miles from where we land— by rights, he won the pool."

A number of voices supported this proposal. Torbett could hardly disapprove because Harris was held in high esteem by every Ranger aboard. "It's okay with me if it's okay with you fellows," said Torbett, as though he was actually giving the money out of his own pocket.

But Harris had other ideas about the money. "Thanks, fellows," he said modestly. "I really don't think I'm entitled to it, but I do have a good suggestion how to put it to good use."

"We'll throw a party as soon as we clean up the town," spoke up the ever-ready Sarn't Sieg.

"No, let's use it to bribe these Limey cooks for some decent chow," ventured Thompson.

"How about greasing the ship's steward's palm for a handout of the King's rum," was Preston's idea.

Harris smiled. "I think my idea is a bit better. We have a fine chaplain aboard, and he doesn't have any special funds to take care of the little things a Padre will need when we get organized ashore. Let's give Father Basil the money. He'll put it to good use."

No one, not even the lustiest, drinkingest Ranger dared veto this idea. Thus was initiated Father Basil's fund for the uplifting of lost souls in the First Ranger Battalion.

CHAPTER 21

OUR CONVOY plowed steadily forward, and the weather got progressively warmer. Then one morning, we woke up to be greeted with the announcement that we had slipped through the Straits of Gibraltar. D day, November 8, was at hand.

The day started with a burst of feverish activity. Each assault section was briefed again and again on our mission. Each man recited his exact role, his exact position at the precise time. Aerial photos and map sketches were reviewed with magnifying glasses until the marked fortifications and pillboxes were indelibly photographed in our minds. Each man knew not only his own battle assignment, he knew the platoon's, the company's, the battalion's and, in fact, the entire Army's mission.

The day passed swiftly. Father Basil held brief services for the entire ship's complement at 2:00 P.M., then heard confessions and gave communion to the Catholics at three. For the last time the company went through a half hour's calisthenics to limber us up for the grueling trek over the hills with full equipment. Keeping in physical condition had been one of our biggest problems on the ship because of the lack of space. Many Rangers, like Thompson had voluntarily kept their muscles trim by climbing the lines on the foremast hand-over-hand each day. For most of us, running in single file around the poop deck, doing pushups, boxing and wrestling had been our daily routine. We felt fit.

We felt fit inwardly, too. We were assured and confident. Despite some of our personal reservations about fighting the French, we

119

knew we were well equipped to accomplish our mission. We knew we were led by the best officers in the Army. We knew we were surrounded by men who had proved themselves again and again through grueling tests of courage, endurance and ability. We knew that the man on our right and the man on our left would be right there when the lead started flying.

At ten o'clock, under a pitch-black sky, the *Royal Ulsterman's* valiant engines came to an abrupt stop some six miles off the coast of Arzew, Algeria. The loud grinding of anchor chains reverberated throughout the ship as we sat down for a late hamburger steak, our last meal aboard ship.

"Good ol' hamburger," said Sarn't Sieg. "At least we get something American in our stomachs before we die."

"There's nothing better than hamburger and coffee," spoke up Fronk. "What I wouldn't do for a cup of good ol' GI Java!"

"Come now, Fronk," cut in Lodge, "you wouldn't be ungrateful to our Limey friends the last night by suggesting coffee. A fine way to act toward our nice hosts."

It was 2300 when Captain Murray followed by Father Basil, Lieutenant Nye and Torbett appeared in our hold for a final few words. Father Basil was dressed in his British battle garb, his only weapons the inevitable swagger stick and a worn Bible. We knew he would be coming in on the second assault wave with Headquarters Company, and it made us feel real good to know that we had a chaplain who shared every danger.

As usual Captain Murray was smiling and assured. As usual he didn't have too much to say: "Fellows I know you have been taking this coming battle in good Ranger stride. Your spirit has been darned high and there's nothing I can say that would add to it . . . I do know I can depend on each one of you to go in and do the best job he knows how. Good luck; fellows!"

That was all he said. Nothing elaborate, just straightforward and simple. As laconic as it was, it stirred every man with a firm resolve to do his best.

Father Basil was also very brief. "Gentlemen, I just want you to know how grateful I am to be with my adopted outfit on its first major operation. I know you are going to put on a great show. Each and every one of you has my blessings, and please, gentlemen,

120

if any of you gets in a position to do some pilfering, please pilfer me an organ I can use for services."

We couldn't see ten feet ahead of us when we lined up on the decks at 2330 and started crowding into the assault boats. Everyone moved quietly, swiftly and orderly. Sergeant Harris and Sergeant Sieg had their mortar sections in first, to be at the rear. Our platoon's two assault sections moved in next, a file on each side of the boat. Last to move in were Captain Murray, Fronk, his runner, the top kick and Lieutenant Nye. One boat for each platoon.

We were loaded to the gills. Besides his own ammunition and weapons, each man carried a stick of dynamite for gun demolitions, two mortar shells, a Commando toggle rope, a deadly sharp Commando knife and a Mae West life preserver twined around his waist.

Suddenly a British voice cracked through the still night: "Lower away all boats! Lower away all boats!" In unison the ships' winches controlling the davits began turning with eerie, grinding noises—noises so loud I thought surely the French could hear them six miles away. Jerking spasmodically, our boat hit the water with a terrific splash, slamming us into one another with crushing force.

"I take back what I said about them being good Joes," moaned Fuller. "They like to broke my back."

"I hope they do a lot better on the landing," added Captain Murray.

The boat next to us was coming down with loud creaking and groaning of the winches. It was halfway down when a loud whip-like crack rent the night. The forward davit line had broken, hurtling the bow of the assault craft into the water and leaving the stern upended. "Men overboard! Men overboard!" A dozen or so Rangers were floundering in the water, weighted down with heavy gear. Immediately lines were thrown down by alert British seamen. Rangers in the upended boat helped pull the shivering unlucky ones aboard. Men were roaring curses that must have made Father Basil blanch.

One of the Rangers fished out was none other than our destiny-minded photographer, Phil Stern, who kept wailing about his precious film being ruined at this historic moment. Another doused Ranger was Lieutenant Samm, the battalion's mustache champion,

121

who cut loose a horrendous barrage of unkind epithets at the British Navy. "Mind your tongue, Jock," a British seaman retaliated. "Be bloody thankful our lads dipped you out of the deep."

Although the incident was near-tragic, it caused a great deal of laughter in our boat. "Poor Samm," roared Pete Preston, "he wanted to make this landing with that handlebar mustache flying in all its glory."

"Well, those guys won't have to worry about making a dry landing," added Fuller.

Aside from the discomfort of the wet Rangers, a more serious consequence was the loss of the two-way high-frequency radio set that was our only communication with the fleet. Now we would have to rely on green flares to signify success and red flares to signify failure to capture the gun batteries. We knew Colonel Darby would have a roaring fit when he learned of this minor disaster.

The engine sputtered and coughed, caught and our low-slung assault craft glided away from the *Royal Ulsterman,* then swung in a gentle arc toward our rendezvous point where we would join up with the assault flotilla. I looked over the gunwale trying to probe the darkness ahead. I could see nothing except the luminous backwash spray of the assault craft ahead.

Silently we crouched as our boat skimmed over the calm sea. It seemed as if we had covered a hundred miles when we finally reached a dozen or so other assault boats, idling their motors. The coxswain roared out into his megaphone: *"Ulsterman One."* A voice from another craft roared back: "Take your course from *Red Six,* departure 2400 hours."

By this time the craft bearing the Second Platoon eased up a few paces alongside us, then rolled with the waves as its motor idled. One by one, additional assault craft lined up on our boats. A short wait, then suddenly in unison, the powerful motors revved up to a thundering pitch and the line moved forward, following a guide boat with blinking red lights. Our target was Beach Red, a narrow, mountain-hemmed rocky strip of Algerian real estate.

Again I poked my head up over the gunwales. I was very curious about that lighthouse. So was every other Ranger. Thankfully I saw a flashing arc in the distance to our right. The French were

122

not alerted. I ducked down again, whispered to Dunn. "The light's on. We're in!"

Dunn was skeptical. "You can't tell for sure. Maybe it's a trick—maybe they found out about this agent and are using the light for a decoy."

As our boat plodded steadily forward, I pondered the deadly consequences if Dunn was right. I began to imagine thousands of troops, fierce Legionnaires, Black Moroccans, even a few Germans sitting there on top of that beach waiting for us to come in like sitting, shooting ducks. The more I thought the more shaky I became.

Then I thought of A and B Companies, which had the daredevil mission of slamming right through the harbor jetties. Once inside that harbor they would be exposed to machine-gun and cannon fire all the way to the fort. If they made it okay it would be a miracle.

Then I thought of Darby. We knew he was right out there in the lead boat. We knew he would be the first American soldier to set foot on French soil this historic night. I thought of Captain Murray, relaxed, assured, in the front of the boat; the quiet, never-perturbed Nye; the gregarious Torbett. I thought of little Fronk kneeling alongside Murray, an eighteen-year old kid who had yet to shave. I wondered what was going on in his mind. I wondered what his father would think if he could see his young son, Tommy gun in hand, calmly awaiting the most crucial moment in his short-lived life.

I looked at the men around me. Lodge, Dunn, Andre, Mulvaney, Rodriguez. I wondered how they felt, what they were thinking. Were their stomachs twitching like mine? I dwelt on Mulvaney, Andre and Preston, the men who had been to Dieppe. This was their second turn. They had already been baptized. Were they sweating this out as much as the first time, or was this easier? I couldn't tell—no one gave any traces of outward nervousness. I could only conclude that these guys around me were made of iron. What was I doing here?

Suddenly the black outline of the North African mountains loomed in front of us. Captain Murray and Lieutenant Nye stood up, looked around. Murray spoke a few words with the turret gunner up near the ramp, then turned back: "All right, fellows . . . on your feet . . . prepare to land!"

123

Swiftly we unwound ourselves from our crouched, aching positions and stood up. The sight around us was exhilarating. Although it was still pitch-dark, we could see the fluorescent sprays from the long line of assault craft, surging relentlessly toward Beach Red.

Before we knew it the belly of our craft scraped across a sand bar, then jarred to a sudden halt. Effortlessly the ramp eased downward and Captain Murray followed by Nye and Torbett leaped into two feet of water. As we charged out after them, Ray Rodriguez' voice could be heard: "Nice knowing you guys, good luck!" It was ironic that the one Ranger who said the least was the only Ranger who said anything as we hit the beach.

Quickly and quietly we hurtled across the narrow beach and bunched up against the side of a small cliff. Frantically we tugged and pulled at our cumbersome Mae Wests and threw them onto the sand. Then, sagging under the burden of mortar shells, we struggled up the dirt cliff.

George Fuller, in front of me, slipped and dropped one of his shells. "They train us to strike like lightning then they load us down with these no-good mortar shells. . . . We never use them, anyway!"

Lodge was slipping and sliding behind me. Several times I reached back and helped pull him up across an abutment. "Get the lead out of your rear," I goaded. He didn't say a word. Panting furiously he struggled upward, holding on to his rifle for dear life.

We cleared the cliffs, then bounded across the road and took up positions along a ditch facing toward the hills, ready for action. Lieutenant Nye came down the line, checking his platoon. He stopped at the head of our section. "You all set, Mulvaney?"

"All ready, Lieutenant."

"We'll move out as soon as the Second Platoon gets squared away. C Company is scouting ahead down the road toward town. So far it's a complete surprise."

I felt real good when I heard that. No longer was I afraid. With the element of surprise achieved, the odds were now all in our favor. Once again I was a brave Ranger.

Captain Murray with Junior Fronk stood in the center of the road, waiting impatiently for the Second Platoon. Something was

124

"snafued." The Second Platoon should have landed at the same time we did. If they didn't show up soon, there was no alternative except to go on without them.

As we waited a group of Rangers came by pushing carts loaded with 81-millimeter mortars—our own portable artillery. It was D Company. I strained my eyes, looking for Carlo. By now a thin slice of moon appeared and visibility was improving. The burly Carlo soon hove into view with his wide-angled walk, tugging and pulling a massive mortar cart with another Ranger. As he struggled by I reached out and tugged at his arm. "Hey, Carlo," I called softly, "how's it going?"

"I'm shaggin' ass like a damn mule. Did you get your feet wet?" That's all he had to say. He was soon moving off, surrounded by a collection of overburdened mortarmen struggling to get their weapons to their firing site at the foot of the ravine.

Suddenly the men from the Second Platoon took up their positions behind us. Sergeant Ed Thompson came up to Captain Murray and reported the delay. "Sir, we lost Lieutenant Young, Corporal Eastwood and the platoon runner. Our boat landed on a pile of rocks a hundred yards from shore. The lieutenant and the others jumped out, thinking it was the beach. Then the Limey coxswain gunned it back and left them stranded on the rocks. We ordered the s.o.b. to go back and pick 'em up but he wouldn't do it. Said it would take too long."

"All right," said Murray between his teeth. "Tell Sergeant Wojic to take over the Second Platoon."

Our line began to move. With rifles uncocked and at the hip-ready position, we swung in single file across an open, shrubby field and then into the rock-hewn hills. We marched for about two and a half miles up winding, tortuous draws and then stopped at the base of a wide ravine. Here we threw down our heavy mortar shells, relieved to get rid of them.

We knew this was the jumping-off point for our attack on the gun batteries high above us. We marched upward a hundred or so yards, then Murray called for a halt. Fronk moved up close to Murray with the walkie-talkie. Murray spoke in a hushed voice, "Fox to Darby . . . Fox to Darby . . . come in Darby."

Darby came in quickly and Murray reported: "We're moving up

125

to our assault positions at crest of ravine." Darby's voice could be heard, answering: "Good . . . put out your scouts and find the exact positions of the battery."

Word was passed down for Ray Rodriguez and Weazel-eye, the two best scouts in the company. They bounded up to Murray, received their instructions and disappeared into the darkness ahead as we continued our march up the ravine.

Suddenly a long burst of machine-gun fire echoed through the night. It seemed far off, from the direction of the harbor. "Sounds like A and B Companies are catching hell," ventured Andre as we struggled up the steep ravine. We were gasping for breath from the rapid ascent and sweating profusely from the humid North African air.

Between gasps I answered, "That does it! Now we can expect the whole French Army to be ready."

Finally, after three miles of tortuous climbing, we found ourselves on level terrain. The column still in single file halted and we sank to the ground like potato sacks and waited for the scouts to report. Soon Captain Murray was joined by Weazel-eye and Rodriguez, who came gliding silently out of the darkness. Those of us in the front of the column listened anxiously as they made their report.

"The gun batteries are directly ahead of us, about a hundred yards," panted Weazel-eye.

"They have four machine-gun positions on this side of the battery and two lines of double-apron barbed wire," added Rodriguez.

Murray consulted with Nye, then the word was whispered down: "Company skirmish line, fix bayonets." Swiftly we moved up to our skirmish line, each man deployed about two yards from the other, facing forward toward the position of the batteries.

Suddenly another long burst of machine-gun fire came from the direction of the harbor, followed by sporadic small-arms fire. It was now obvious that A and B Companies were having a hell of a battle down at the pier. Captain Murray ordered the scouts to advance and cut through the barbed-wire fences so we could move through to assault the battery.

Pete Preston and Rodriguez, armed with wire cutters, moved off into the darkness ahead as we crouched on our knees, ready to

126

advance. They were gone only a minute when the darkness was crisscrossed with orange and green tracer fire. The crisscross was joined by two more angles of machine-gun fire. Dirt was splattering all around us from the impact of the bullets when Colonel Darby arrived on the scene. Immediately Nye gave the command to fire, and we cut loose from our prone positions, aiming at the dabs of orange and green flames. Some Ranger fired a long raking burst at the right flank machine gun. The burst was immediately answered by the French. Angry whining bullets inched over our heads stitching into the low embankment behind us.

Strangely I wasn't scared. It was just like the Commando training. Close-landing bullets by now were a familiar experience. Also the drama of the battle was so completely absorbing that there was no time to be concerned about personal fears. The only pressing concern was "What happens next?"

Colonel Darby soon answered that question. Huddled up front with Captain Murray, the colonel rasped into his walkie-talkie. "Come in, D Company . . . come in, D Company!" Captain Miller of D Company came in. "Miller, I think they need a good shakeup job. . . . Give us a target round, then stand by for a barrage." Then turing to Murray: "Roy, pull your company back a few yards, then hit 'em when the barrage stops."

Nye passed the order down to our assault squads. Swiftly we pulled back and waited as the French machine guns continued raking up and down the line. We had now found substantial cover, and the fire was crackling harmlessly over our heads.

"What about Pete Preston and Rodriguez?" I asked Mulvaney. "They're still up there at the wire. Fronk's gone up there to pull them back."

I looked at the luminous watch on my wrist. It was 1:45. Darby was taking no chances. He was going to pulverize battery positions with heavy mortar fire before sending his Rangers in. Now that the enemy was alerted, he wasn't going to waste the lives of his men.

I prayed that Ray, Pete and Fronk would clear the area before the mortars came crashing down. I knew D company, our heavy mortar outfit, had the exact co-ordinates and were crack mortarmen —but one short round could wreck disaster on our own forces.

Suddenly we heard the loud flutter of a mortar round descending

127

directly overhead. We covered our heads in our arms and hugged the ground. It seemed destined to land right on top of us. With an earth-shaking crash, it landed up ahead.

"Hell! They're laying it down before Fronk and the guys are clear," shouted Andre.

"They ain't got a Frenchman's chance," Fuller moaned.

We could hear Darby up front with Murray radio instructions to D Company. "On target," shouted Darby. "Fire away for maximum effect."

In an instant the air overhead was filled with loud swishing, fluttering mortar shells speeding earthward on their mission of destruction. The entire hillside shuddered as the shells came crashing down, their flaming bursts illuminating the area in eerie shadows. For two minutes the mortar bombardment continued, then the order was passed down: "Prepare to assault."

There was still no sign of Fronk, Rodriguez and Preston. I assumed the worst had happened.

We stood up, picked up an interval from the men on our left and right, readied our weapons for hip firing and waited for the final order—to advance. The French machine guns were now silent. Ahead we could barely discern the contours of the huge gun emplacements.

A last thundering round of mortar fire crashed directly behind us, showering us with rocks and dirt. A silly thought ran through my mind: "Boy, will I razz Carlo about what lousy mortarmen he's with!"

Lieutenant Nye's strong voice rang out: "Assault!"

In a solid wave the entire company moved forward, screaming at the top of our lungs. We hit the barbed wire with running strides. I found Fronk, Preston and Rodriguez squatting down beside a big gaping hole in the barbed wire, waiting calmly for us to come up.

Preston was grinning like a bear. " 'Bout time you guys came up. We cut through the wire just when the mortar rounds started hitting."

"Those damn mortar shells hit less than twenty yards from us," added Fronk.

They joined our section as we surged through the gaping hole in the barbed wire and tore across the thirty yards to the gun battery.

128

Phil Stern

Rangers marching over the Tunisian hills. Often a hard route like
this achieved the best results, for the Rangers could
surprise the enemy, who failed to anticipate
attack from such unlikely directions.

Phil Stern

Rangers in North Africa.

Phil Stern

Sergeant Thompson before the Sened Raid.

Phil Stern

D Company of the Rangers.

Phil Stern

An Italian gun destroyed by Rangers in Tunisia.

Phil Stern

Father Basil leads service for the Rangers in North Africa.

Phil Stern

Night training at Arzew.

Phil Stern

Prisoners of War.

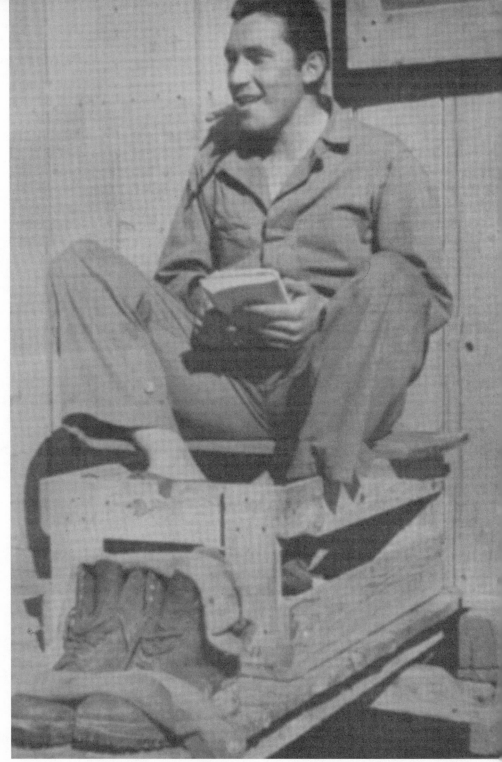

Phil Stern

Carlo Contrera at Arzew.

Capt. Charles M. "Chuck" Shunstrom.

Acrid smoke from the mortar shelling was still swirling around the emplacement as we reached the first gun. The gun crews were nowhere to be seen. Lodge and I jumped over a low concrete parapet and darted into a dugout. There huddled together in mortal fear were seven whimpering Frenchmen, dazed by the mortar barrage. Lodge prodded them with his gun as I uttered the historic words: *"Nous Americans."*

The dugout was quickly emptied. They came out with hands over their heads and even in the night we could see they were only half-dressed, the surprise had been so complete.

Meanwhile the other assault sections of Fox Company had taken over their respective gun positions without incident. From a dozen or so dugouts nearby some thirty French soldiers were rounded up. Only four had been wounded. Quickly we attached our demolition charges to each gun, ready to blow it up should we be forced to withdraw.

Lieutenant Nye then ordered our section to move up the hill and scour around for more dugouts and quarters. Fuller left Lodge and Dunn at the gun and led us out into the night, guns at the ready. Our expedition brought us an additional forty prisoners, all shell-shocked and anxious to surrender. We pulled three French soldiers out of a dugout they had been sharing with an Algerian whore. These fellows were very indignant and cussed us out roundly in French for being such cads.

We were still rounding up stray prisoners when the blue-black Algerian sky was suddenly pierced by a green star flare, signifying to the convoys waiting offshore that both batteries were in American hands. I looked at my watch. It was exactly 4:30 A.M. Right on schedule. Down by the waterfront sporadic gunfire was heard. A and B Companies were still exchanging fire with the French.

"Right on the nose," exclaimed Andre.

"We got us a port in three and a half hours," added Dunn. "Nice goin' for a first deal."

"Don't let's go wavin' flags yet," cautioned George Fuller. "We got the guns all right but we still gotta worry about a counterattack. Remember, there's supposed to be sixteen thousand troops around here, and don't forget that Foreign Legion fort—Fort du something . . ."

"Fort du Nord," corrected Lodge.

"All right, guys, let's get back to the battery with these prisoners and see what comes next," commanded Mulvaney.

We prodded the prisoners ahead of us. When we returned to the gun battery we found nearly a hundred and fifty assorted French soldiers, most of them partially dressed, all of them deeply humiliated to be captured in such an undignified manner. Father Basil and Private Roy Anctil, a Ranger of French descent who spoke the language fluently, had their hands full interrogating prisoners and assuring them that we were truly their friends. Still visibly shaken from the horrendous mortar barrage, the Frenchmen appeared dubious that such was the case.

Lieutenant Nye greeted us with encouraging news. "Major Dammer's force captured the fort in the harbor and the two-gun battery with only one casualty. They had a helluva lot of machine-gun fire on them on their way into the harbor, but they knocked them out and crashed the fort before the French could get organized."

"What's the pitch now?" Mulvaney asked.

"A and B Companies are cleaning out the warehouses down by the water front and C Company is helping them. D Company is set up for a mortar barrage on the French Legion fort. E Company is in position for a dawn attack on the fort. We'll hold these guns till further orders."

Suddenly Colonel Darby, followed by Murray and a French officer who was hitching up his trousers, made their appearance where the prisoners were huddled. "Anctil!" shouted Murray. Anctil stopped talking to a group of prisoners and bounded over to Darby and Murray.

Darby spoke: "This is the commandant of the Foreign Legion garrison. Tell him I want the surrender of the fort without any nonsense or I will lay down the walls of Fort du Nord with mortar fire."

Anctil interpreted the colonel's words to the French commandant, whose face was torn with bitter emotion. The commandant, gesticulating wildly, cut loose with a staccato barrage of French. Anctil translated for Darby: "He says he cannot ask his men to surrender without at least a token show of resistance. He says the French can only surrender after they have displayed valor."

Darby pondered a long moment. "All right, tell him we'll let

130.

him stage his token resistance. Tell him his troops can fire their rifles in the air just once, then I want them to march out of the fort and surrender at 0800 . . . or they'll be dead pigeons."

Anctil repeated this to the French officer, who immediately beamed. *"Oui! Oui!"* Darby and the Frenchman shook hands, and the officer, his chest fully inflated, handed over to Darby his pistol, sealing the surrender for history to record.

It was shortly before the break of dawn when our company was joined by our three missing Rangers. Soaking wet, shivering with cold, Lieutenant Young, the Second Platoon officer, and two Rangers made their appearance as we were preparing defensive positions.

"Where were you guys when the action was going on?" quipped Junior Fronk.

"Nuts," said a sergeant. "Our British coxswain dumped us off on a pile of rocks a hundred yards from shore. Then the s.o.b. backed up the boat and left us high and dry . . . we had to swim for it."

"Yeah," said the runner, "when we finally hit the shore, you guys were already up here fightin'. We tramped all over the hills."

"A good excuse," roared Fuller. "You guys probably paid the coxswain to dump you there so you could keep out of the fight. Fine bunch of Rangers you are. . . ."

The entire company ribbed hell out of the three embarrassed Rangers.

CHAPTER 22

THE Algerian dawn splashed across the horizon with a dazzling mixture of purplish and red hues revealing our mighty invasion forces surging toward the harbor of Arzew. From our vantage point astride the gun battery we could see the dark outlines of the Sixteenth Infantry assault craft coming in on the Beach Green, beyond the harbor. Sporadic machine-gun fire could be heard in the distance and scattered rifle shots in the water-front area, directly beneath our battery.

Although we were sleepless and hungry, the nervous excitement of the fantastic scene unfolding beneath us gave us renewed energy. Our situation seemed incredible. Here we were sitting a half-mile above the harbor watching the drama of the first American invasion unfold beneath us. In one swift stroke we had secured as a base of operations a port with all its facilities intact and with a minimum of casualties. We had opened the way to Oran.

Of all the Rangers the men of Fox Company had the choicest assignment that morning. Our mission was simply to put up a perimeter of defense around the gun battery and stand by for a counterattack. The responsibility of holding those guns was ours alone. Each man was dug in, in positions once held by the French, barricaded with barbed wire and sandbags. We felt confident we could hold off an entire division.

Vernon Lodge and I were in position facing the French Foreign Legion fort. We could look down the side of our hill where Easy Company was preparing to assault the fort, if the surrender did not come off as planned. We were anxious to witness the "token resistance" of the French Legion.

At 0800 hours we heard the sounds of gunfire coming from the fort. "This is getting to be a real comic-opera war," I said. "I never thought the French would cave in that easy—they didn't do it like this in *Beau Geste*."

"Hell, they're glad we're here. They're anxious to join us against the Germans," said Lodge as though delivering a lecture to a history class.

But something went wrong. We knew it when bullets started twanging into our positions, coming from the fort. We knew it when we saw the men of Easy Company, deployed in skirmish lines below us, open fire at the fort. And we were certain the French were double-crossing us when we saw the blast of a small artillery piece perched on a parapet.

"Ol' Schneider will grind 'em to bits," I ventured.

The next instant a huge mortar shell came crashing down a dozen yards from the moat surrounding the fort. D Company was getting the range. Then four more rounds came thundering down, one landing on top of the stone parapet.

That was enough for the French. Immediately a dozen white flags appeared along the stone parapet, followed by the lowering of the massive drawbridge. With field glasses I could see a long line of French Legionnaires walking out with their hands over their heads. I picked out the Rangers of Easy Company moving forward up the hill, guns at the ready. Soon the Rangers had the French soldiers surrounded and were marching them right back into the fort. The French, having had their moment of valor, were now prisoners in their own fort.

Our attention then turned to the harbor below and the beaches beyond, where the Sixteenth Infantry troops were landing. Huge transport vessels were easing majestically toward the docks. Launches were scurrying back and forth between ship and shore, unloading the sinews of war. Tanks and armored vehicles were thundering ashore, to be swallowed up by clouds of dust as they darted inland toward Oran.

Everything seemed well in hand when suddenly the large transport ship now eased alongside the pier was bracketed by two shell

133

bursts. I trained my glasses to the east, far beyond the beaches and picked up the bright flashes of the gun as it belched out another salvo. I was horrified as I saw both bursts land right amidships, tearing a huge gaping hole. The French were evidently using a field piece because we knew the battery we occupied and the two guns down at the harbor were the only coastal defenses.

Two low-flying Spitfires also caught the gun flashes. They wheeled gracefully, then like vengeful eagles they swooped down, blasting away with cannon and machine-gun fire. The gun was silenced.

It was all quiet on the Fox Company front the rest of D day. The threatened counterattack failed to materialize. There was a slight flurry of excitement when one of our men spotted "a mounted enemy patrol" approaching from the hills. We trained our rifles at the approaching enemy and waited. The enemy turned out to be six wandering Arabs riding jackasses. They were loaded down with oranges and eggs which we glady traded for our C rations.

Smiley the cook cheered us up with a chicken dinner fresh from the commandant's own coops. Sarn't Siego provided the company with a barrel of Algerian wine he and his crew had found near one of the French dugouts. Like good Rangers we ate, drank and tried to convince ourselves that we were really pulling important duty guarding the gun battery.

Later during the day I was visited by Carlo Contrera, whose company was guarding the oil refinery a few hundred yards below the battery. Carlo was swollen with pride over his company's marksmanship. "We sure scared the hell out of those Frenchies. Ol' Darby told Captain Miller if it wasn't for D Company's mortar barrage you guys would be still fightin' to take the battery."

"Go on," I said, "you guys were lucky. You were dropping shells all over us instead of the French."

"Listen, buddy, you guys would be six feet under if us crackshot mortarmen didn't lower the boom."

"Oh, so now you're not a beast of burden. Now you're a crackshot mortarman."

Much as I hated to admit it, Carlo was dead right. The well-aimed and well-timed mortar barrage had saved the day. We would have eventually captured the guns without the mortars, but it would have cost us a lot of casualties.

134

"Tell me something, Carlo, the honest truth," I said, changing the subject. "How did you feel coming in, not knowing what to expect?"

"Well, to tell the truth, I was shaking a little."

"I was too, until I hit the beach and found we had surprised them," I confessed.

"But I wasn't scared."

"You weren't?"

"Hell, no! I was just shakin' with patriotism!"

Another visitor to our gun battery was Snapdragon Stern, who proved he was a very resourceful Ranger. Phil now had two German Leica cameras and a pack full of captured film. He bounded up and down the gun battery like an excited kid at Christmas, taking pictures of the guns, the Rangers who had captured them and the harbor below. Stern wasn't satisfied until he had Butt Torbett—his favorite model—pose with his arms possessively around a four-inch gun, as though the sergeant himself had captured the battery unaided.

"I guess that home town paper of Torbett's will now say that he captured Arzew single-handed," quipped the ever-taunting Fronk.

"Listen, fellows," said Stern dramatically, "these pictures will soon be seen by millions of people back home. These pictures will tell the story of what we Rangers accomplished in opening the gates for the attack of Oran. These pictures will establish beyond doubt that the Rangers are the hardest-hitting, toughest troops in the whole Army." Stern said it as if he really meant it; in fact, he said it so well that we were almost convinced that this was an established fact. It was nice to have a guy like Stern around. He gave us a new perspective on our profession.

That night the Rangers of Fox Company settled down in our outpost positions on the wind-swept battery hill with high spirits. Our canteens were full of vin rouge, our stomachs full of the commandant's prize chicken, our egos full of pride for our D day accomplishments and our hearts grateful that we had pulled through without a single casualty.

"I wonder what they have cooked up for us tomorrow?" asked Lodge as we peered into the inky blackness from our guard post.

135

"This whole thing went off too easy. Maybe they'll use us to spearhead into Oran."

"I don't think so," I answered. "I don't think they'll use us like shock troops. We'll probably hole up here for a couple days, then pull a raid somewhere. Remember we're a Commando-type outfit. They don't use Commandos to spearhead ground fighting."

136

CHAPTER 23

THE next morning brought news that proved how wrong I had been about the Rangers not being used as spearhead troops. Junior Fronk, who in his position as Murray's runner was close to current developments, broke the news to our group. "General Terry Allen asked Darby for two companies to help the Sixteenth Infantry. Darby sent Charlie Company to a town called St. Cloud. Easy Company went to some village called La Macta. They're havin' a helluva battle. The Frenchies are really diggin' in with heavy artillery."

"Ain't that a stinkin' shame, a dirty double-dealing trick?" roared Fuller. "We open a port and let those guys come breezin' in. . . . Now we got to go fight their battles for 'em."

Lodge looked at me with a grin. "Al, you're a fine prognosticator. They won't use us as shock troops, oh no!"

I felt very let-down. It certainly wasn't working the way I had dreamed it would. Commandos and specialized troops were used sparingly. They swooped down on the enemy with stealth and shocking surprise, knocked out the defenses, then stood by to wave the support troops onward.

Lieutenant Nye, who had been standing nearby reading a map, either. Remember he's only a lieutenant colonel, and we're still a young outfit. It'll take some time for senior field commanders to know the exact capabilities of the Rangers and how to use us effectively. Let's look at it from the brass point of view. We took a port with few casualties, we're tough and well trained.

They run up against some stiff opposition—okay, send the Rangers in, let 'em disorganize the resistance, then let the other troops follow through."

"But what happens if the Rangers get clobbered in broad daylight without benefit of a night sneak attack? What happens if the whole unit is fed piecemeal into a static battle line? What was the purpose in organizing and training Rangers for Commando-type operations if they are going to be frittered away in mass battles?" I queried Nye.

"Altieri, I can't answer that now," the lieutenant admitted. "I can only say, let's wait and see what happens. Personally I have faith that the Rangers will be used for the exact purpose we volunteered for. This St. Cloud and La Macta business may be the exception. Let's just wait and see."

For two days we stayed in position at the gun battery, isolated from the war that had swirled past us. From time to time we were filled in with the progress of the over-all battle by Lieutenant Nye during his visits to our positions. From him we learned that the Rangers of Charlie Company, led by Lieutenant Gordon Kleftman, made a bold daylight attack against the most strongly fortified positions at St. Cloud. Kleftman was killed, and Lieutenant Charles ("Chuck") Shundstrom, an aggressive Dieppe veteran, took over the company and led a daring charge against the French across an open field. The Ranger attack completely cleared the last remaining obstacle to Oran. Armor and infantry units were now fighting on the outskirts of that important city.

Easy Company, we learned, led by the ebullient Lieutenant Schneider, had also come through its engagement at La Macta with flying colors. Schneider's Rangers had arrived on the battleground to find a battery of French 75's blocking an entire regiment. Immediately the Rangers of Easy Company commandeered a squadron of half-tracks with artillery mounted and made a daring flanking attack which over-ran the entire battery. The half-tracks were manned by Rangers formerly of the First Armored Division who put to good use their armored warfare know-how. Their mission accomplished, Easy Company was on its way back to Arzew.

The news of the Ranger exploits at St. Cloud and La Macta

138

stirred every Ranger with pride. Not only had our battalion taken a port, we had also helped clear the road to Oran. Even though most of the Rangers of Fox Company felt like mere bystanders, having done nothing but sit on our butts at the fort, nevertheless, we were as proud as if our own company had won battle honors.

On the morning of the third day the news flashed throughout the battalion that the French had capitulated and signed an armistice. Without fanfare we turned over the battery to the French, who were now our Allies, and moved into the large French Foreign fort for a few days of rest and reorganization.

Fort du Nord, now flying the French tricolor alongside the American flag, was an immense, octagon-shaped stone citadel encompassing a huge courtyard where the Legionnaires performed their drills and parades. Troop barracks, spacious enough to accommodate an entire battalion, fronted the courtyard. Here Able, Baker, Fox and Headquarters Companies, minus Charlie and Easy which were en route back to Arzew, were quartered.

We threw down our gear in a large barracks room, stripped to the waist, then bolted to the large bath water barrels where we dipped our helmets. After a fast shave, Torbett lined the company up, then double-timed us down the winding dirt road to the coast road. Here we turned left and sped along without letup, until we arrived—four miles later—at Beach Red.

"Thought you guys would like a little swim where we landed on D day," Torbett laughed.

Nobody laughed. We just stripped off everything; then sixty sweating, completely naked, cursing Rangers swarmed into the waves to wash out the grime and stink of three days' accumulation.

We got back just in time for afternoon chow. An outdoor kitchen was set up in the courtyard. To Smiley the cook's despair, the French Legionnaire cooks were now in charge. They wrought true miracles with our usual C ration fare. They took our tasteless hash, flavored it generously with spices, herbs, garlic and onions and served us a repast that made our mouths water for more. This was washed down by canteen cups full of deep red wine, much stronger and much tastier than the wine El Siego had commandeered. Poor Smiley just stood at the head of the chow line, glaring at the French

139

cooks for showing him up. The French cooks ignored him. They were happy to see us hungry Rangers so appreciative.

After chow the Rangers gathered together in small knots to recount their experiences. This was the first get-together since D day and everyone was anxious to know what their buddies in the other companies had been up to. Carlo Contrera with Pfc. Windsor of A Company found me and Sarn't Sieg toasting to happy days ahead with the belles of Arzew. It was our fourth toast on the same subject.

"Hey, Altieri!" shouted Carlo. "Whaddaya doin'? Trying to outdrink the French?"

"We're drinkin' to all the sexy French broads we're gonna have fun with," laughed Sieg.

"Well, you better drink to something else. I just cased the town and all I saw was a bunch of creepy gals all covered with veils. You know what they do? They peek at you out of a little slit, then when you take a long look back, they pull that veil back and turn the other way. And that's not all—those Arab guys don't like you to look at their women. They stand there and glare at you like they want to knife you. To hell with them. I don't think I'll get mixed up with those gals, not ol' Carlo."

"Gee, that's too bad, Carlo," I kidded. "Maybe you didn't really do a good casing job. Maybe you scared all the real nice-looking gals away. Just wait'll the Fox Company Romeos get in town. They'll come running from their hideouts."

"Yeah," enjoined Sieg, "when I walk down the street with my ol' mustache a-flying, those chippies'll scream *Ooo la la . . . la moustache d'amour!* You know guys, mustaches really have a strange fascination for women. . . ."

At this point we were joined by the gregarious Snapdragon Stern stumbling toward us with a woven raffia basket loaded with assorted Algerian souvenirs. Stern, with the cameras entwined around his neck, with his helmet pushed back precariously, with one pants leg hanging down, looked like the sorriest soldier of all the armies in the world.

"Boy, what a town!" exuded Stern. "What bargains!" Excitedly he dug into his basket, proudly displaying his acquisitions. "Look, this leather pocketbook, only a hundred francs. One buck! This-here bracelet, real silver, two hundred francs. . . . Lookit these sandals, will you? I got 'em for a lousy pack of ciggies. . . ."

"That's great, Stern, real great. You're a big bargain man. But we ain't interested in bargains—not that kind anyway. While you were moseying around town did you find—er—did you come across anything else interesting?" Sieg asked hopefully.

Stern caught on real fast. "Did I find something interesting?" He looked around surreptitiously, then leaned closer. "Look, fellows, I'm not supposed to tell you this. Keep it under your hat."

Our ears opened a mile wide. Stern was really going to give us the lowdown on the most pressing subject on our minds. Stern, satisfied that he had our awed attention, went into his story dramatically.

"It was D-plus-one. You know how I operate. I make it my business to try to cover every phase of the operation. I spent some time with you guys up at the battery, I tagged along with Darby for a while, got pictures of him on his motorcycle running from one end of Arzew to the other directing the whole operation. I saw El Darbo give hell to a full colonel for not moving his men across the beach fast enough. I took pictures . . ."

"Get to the point," said the exasperated Sieg. "Where the hell do the women come into the picture?"

"Hold your water," returned Stern. "I'm getting to it." He paused a moment, then: "Well, like I said, I get around. That's my job. So when Darby calls for an assault section to clean out some stubborn snipers on the outskirts of town, I decide to tag along. I figure a good set of pictures on Rangers doing street fighting will make a helluva article for *Yank* magazine. Who knows, maybe even *Life* will snap it up. So I cock my .45 and I go along with this tough assault section."

"Hey, Stern," pleaded Contrera, "cut the crap. Give us the meat of the story."

"Well, anyway, here we are movin' up the street when *wham! wham!* two slugs tear into the wall right over my head. Plaster falls in my eyes. I'm nearly blinded. I don't know whether to aim my gun or my camera. I don't do neither. I just hit the ground and hug it real close like it was my best girl friend.

141

"Well, these guys I'm with know their business. They rake all the windows in the street with Tommy-gun and rifle fire, then three or four of the guys move up to this big house with fancy iron grilles. It looks just like one of those sultan palaces. These guys Tommy gun the door, then break in. A minute later they come to the door and they wave for the other guys. It's funny. These guys are smiling like they ain't mad at nobody. I follow these guys into the house and what do we find?"

"Just what the hell did you find?" shouted Sieg.

"We found twenty of the most gorgeous, shapeliest, sexiest-looking dolls, all dressed in flimsy gowns. They looked well fed and they all had on earrings and bracelets, and the place smelled like it was a perfume factory. About six of these dolls were French."

"What happened then?" I begged.

"Well, one of these dolls speaks a little English. She gets down on her knees and she begs this tough sergeant to spare her and her lady friends. She says the girls are afraid they are going to be slaughtered. She doesn't understand what all the fighting is about. She says the French thought the Americans were their friends.

"This sergeant is a real diplomat. He tells her that we are indeed friends. In fact, not only will he see that these girls are unharmed, he will place a guard at the door to keep out any rowdy soldiers that try to get fresh. To make a long story short, these gals are so happy that they insist on showing their appreciation. Before I know it the whole squad of Rangers disappear.

"Anyway, while I'm looking around the palace admiring the Moroccan architecture, the Rangers come out. Then the sarge tells his men: 'All right, you guys, let's finish mopping up the block, but get this, don't tell the rest of the battalion.' Then he puts a guy outside with a Tommy gun and he writes on the door with lipstick: *'Off limits to all troops.'*

"Well, I followed these guys up the block and they just kept ferreting out these snipers as if nothing had happened. And every time they got a sniper, one of 'em would say: 'War is hell, that's what Sherman said.' And another Ranger would say: 'It sure is, bub.' "

Sarn't Sieg took a swallow of wine and twirled his mustache.

142

"Very interesting, Stern, very interesting, but that's not the kind of mademoiselle I'm looking for. Didn't you see any real French dolls, not the working kind in town?"

Stern picked up his souvenirs. "You guys must think I'm a damned tourist. How do I know? I was fightin' a war."

CHAPTER 24

THE first Ranger dead were buried the next day.

With heavy hearts and serious minds the men of the First Ranger Battalion stood at attention as Father Basil, dressed in the white and black cassock of his faith, delivered the burial service in a small field a hundred yards from the harbor. Colonel Darby, as usual, stood in front of the massed battalion a scant few feet from the open graves.

With four other Rangers, I stood about thirty paces away, ready to fire the shots that would mark the final honors of a military burial. I grimly reflected as I stood there listening to Father Basil, that those cold bodies—ready to be enveloped by the arid dirt of Algeria—had been only two days before vibrant, red-blooded American youths, not one of them over twenty-five. Lieutenant Gordon Kleftman had already been recommended by Darby for a captaincy. He had been a sturdy, smiling chunky man with blond, close-cropped hair. His men, I had gathered from Sergeant Smith, were intensely loyal to him and considered him, apart from his qualities as a leader, a regular fellow whom they could talk to without formality.

The others—Nyestrom, Escola and Grisamer—I didn't know personally. But that made no difference. They were Rangers. They could have been men from my own squad. I felt as sad for them as I would have if my own brothers had been in their places. I'm sure most Rangers felt the same way.

I couldn't help thinking also that one of those bodies could have been mine, that perhaps, after a future battle, Father Basil or another chaplain would be saying services for me and someone else would be standing here, as I was, ready to fire his rifle in final gesture.

". . . Dear heavenly Father, receive the souls of thy children and give comfort to their beloved ones . . . and we pray, O Lord, that you will keep us ever mindful of their sacrifices to their country and its rightful cause. . . . We now commit their bodies to the ground for final rest. . . ."

"Present arms!" Sergeant Torbett roared. Swiftly we snapped up our rifles and thrust them smartly to the front.

"Prepare to fire arms!" We brought the rifles to our right shoulders in unison, flicked over the safety catches.

"Ready . . . fire!" Our bursts shattered the still of the morning. Twice more we fired at the given command. Then we stood at present arms as the boxes were slowly lowered into the graves. I looked out of the corner of my eye to the right at Pfc. Elmer Garrison, a quiet, scholarly-looking soldier who was in Sergeant Rensink's First Section. Garrison's face was screwed up in a painful expression. I could see he was contemplating the same kind of thoughts I was having: "There, but for the Grace of God, go I."

Soon Darby's voice could be heard: "Move out of your companies."

The firing squad smartly did an about-face and each one of us headed for his own company. Elmer and I walked side by side.

"Don't let it get you down, Elmer," I ventured.

He looked at me sadly. "Al, I feel it. I feel my number is up next. . . . I can't explain it—but I just know I'm gonna be measured for one of those pine boxes real soon."

Elmer was one of the quietest men in Fox Company and one of the easiest to get along with. He was one of those fellows who did his job and you never really knew he was around. He didn't confide his feelings about anything to anybody. Hearing him talk like this was a real shocker.

From the burial grounds the battalion moved swiftly in a double column down the narrow macadam coast road, past the outskirts of Arzew. Major Herman Dammer, the tall, long-legged, taciturn executive officer, was at the head of the column as pace setter. We

145

marched for fifteen minutes on the winding coast road past Beach Red, then into the high mountains.

Without letup, Dammer raced us up narrow winding ravines, through rock-hewn gorges, up, up, up to the very peaks of the towering mountains. Rangers slipped, stumbled and cursed as the going got rougher and rougher. The long ship voyage and the period of leisure at the fort had taken their toll. Our legs were buckling, our feet were blistering, our lungs were ready to burst. Back in Scotland we would have taken this climb without grumbling. Now we were practically washed out.

When we paused for a five-minute break, we sullenly dropped to the ground, beat, exhausted. Few Rangers even bothered to smoke. We just lay there on our backs, gulping air, trying to replenish our resources for the grueling trek back.

George Fuller took off a shoe, revealing a raw blister. He pulled out his first-aid kit, wrapped gauze around his foot, spat disgustedly. "I oughta have my head examined. I joined the Rangers to get away from a chicken outfit. Now this outfit is getting even worse."

Dunn, sitting next to me, narrowed his eyes. "Fuller, you would do us all a favor if you went back to your old outfit. Your silly whining and griping is getting monotonous."

Fuller bristled, glared at him. "If you don't like it, preacher, you just know what you can do. I'll bitch and cuss all I want. That's one privilege no takes away. Nobody!"

"On your feet," roared Torbett as the companies ahead began standing to resume the march. Dunn and Fuller stared meanly at each other as they took their places. None of us paid much attention to this outburst. It was just another skirmish in their running battle. In this instance I felt Dunn was right. Fuller, although at times amusing, was beginning to get on our nerves by overemphasizing every unfavorable aspect of the Rangers. But no one could deny that the privilege of bitching was one right soldiers considered sacred. And Fuller certainly exercised his right to the fullest.

The march back was a nightmare. Dammer and Darby at the head of the column, plunged through the mountains at breakneck pace, grimly determined to show us what bad shape we were in physically. For ten long miles we wound over the treacherous mountainsides, now climbing, now sliding downward, now running in

146

short spurts on occasional stretches of level terrain. In twos and threes men started dropping out. When we finally reached the road, at least twenty per cent of the battalion was left behind, straggling through the hills. Once on the road we thought surely they would let up, would walk us leisurely back to camp.

Our hopes were short-lived. We heard Dammer's voice at the head of the column roar out: "Double-time . . . march." Loud groans echoed throughout the column. "Darby's Dunderheads!" "What'er they tryna prove . . . ?"

It was six miles back to town, six of the most memorable, miserable, heartbreaking miles I ever experienced. Several times I was on the verge of falling out, joining the swelling ranks of the stragglers. But more than pride, fierce anger prevented me. Darby and Dammer were up there. This was killing them as much as it was the men. They were in no better physical condition than we were. If they could take it, so could I.

George Fuller, the prince of all gripers, was still in there, with his agonizing blister, although limping. Vernon Lodge and the whistling Andre showed no signs of quitting. Dunn didn't even look tired. Torbett, running behind the company, was trying vainly to encourage the stragglers.

Fronk and Rodriguez were also still with us. Through the town we raced, as Frenchmen, Arabs and assorted American troops stood gaping. Several soldiers loitering on the streets, amused at the sight of the highly touted Rangers limping and gasping, gave out with barbed catcalls:

"Here comes the lone Rangers!"

"Hi, ho, silveeeeeer—awaaaaaaaaay!"

"Hey, Rangers, where's Tonto?"

"Those guys don't look so tough. It's all publicity!"

"How'd those guys ever take Arzew?"

Although stung by these taunts, we were too tired even to reply. Andre, however, marked them down for future reference: "Those jokers belong to the Port Battalion. I'll remember those babies."

Through the town and on to Beach Green where the Sixteenth Regiment had made their D day landings, we double-timed and quick-timed. Earlier in the morning before leaving the fort, Torbett had told us that our new camp would be on the outskirts of Arzew

147

along the beach. Easy and Charlie Companies excused from the first day's activities after the burial services, were already established in the new quarters. They looked upon us with amusement as we came limping in.

Finally the column came to a much-awaited halt. Men slumped into the sand, their rifles carelessly tossed on the ground beside them. Murray came down the line, sweating, his face grim. "All right, Fox Company, on your feet! We're still in formation. . . ."

Slowly those of us who were able stood up. Some men couldn't get up. They were out cold. In the distance, limping in in small groups, came the stragglers. These fellows although exhausted hadn't given up. They were not beaten, just winded.

Darby and Dammer came barreling down the column looking the men over, appraising the total results of the harrowing march. Rangers glared sullenly as they swept by. As Darby reached our company, Murray saluted. Curtly returning the salute, Darby asked impatiently, "How many dropped out in Fox Company, Roy?"

"Ten men," Murray replied as though he was ashamed. Then looking toward the stragglers streaming across the dunes, he added hopefully, "Most of them are coming in now . . . they didn't really quit."

"Getting in late is as bad as quitting. Those men who dropped behind wouldn't do us a damned bit of good if we had a battle to fight now." Darby moved off to inspect the next company.

Darby didn't make a speech after that march. He didn't have to. Our aching bodies, our punctured egos, our miserable performance on the grueling fifteen-mile cross-country march told us all we needed to know. We knew that Darby had pulled this march to reveal to each of us the terrible physical condition we were in. We knew this was his dramatic way of saying: "You Rangers think you're pretty hot stuff. You think, because you knocked off those batteries, you should now relax and celebrate. You think you should now be treated with deference like heroes. . . . Well, Rangers, what do you think of yourselves now? Now do you think I'm unjustified in starting another cycle of training?"

I was sure that if Darby had chosen to speak that would have been the gist of his talk. But Darby had the rare intuitive sense to

148

know when to speak and when not to. His point had been hammered home to us with crushing, sobering impact. We reluctantly conceded we needed to get back in shape.

After the last of the stragglers had limped shamefacedly back to the company, Torbett roared the company to attention. For the first time we became aware of our immediate surroundings. The beach was a narrow ribbon of white sand, curving gently eastward. The sparkling blue Mediterranean, rippling with foam-crested waves, was dotted with small fishing skiffs and sailboats. Rimming the beach at intervals of a few yards was a long line of many-colored beach houses. In the distance, away from Arzew, there were gently rolling, irrigated fields, sprinkled with palm and date trees.

I couldn't help contrasting the darkness of our moods with the beauty of the landscape. In happier circumstances, to be camped on the sand alongside the Mediterranean would have been any soldier's dream. To us Rangers that day its natural beauties didn't mean a damn. We knew we would have no time to enjoy them.

Torbett took a long time to get squared away. We could see by his pained expression that the worst was yet to come. "Now I got some news for you. In addition to our training program, the Rangers are gonna pull MP duty in Arzew——"

"MP duty!" a dozen Rangers roared.

"That does it," yelled Fuller, throwing down his helmet. "I'm getting out of this no-good chicken outfit in a hurry."

"All right, you loudmouths, settle down," pleaded Torbett. "Here's the pitch. There's been a lot of trouble in Arzew. GIs been acting so bad, the regular MPs can't handle 'em. Darby is commander of this area. He's got to keep order. So each company pulls duty one day each week."

"What about passes to Oran?"

"No passes to anywhere for a long time, anyway."

Furious cries resounded along the beach. Sullen-faced Rangers angrily picked up their rifles and trudged listlessly into their new quarters.

Following Mulvaney we entered a small boxlike cottage with hard concrete floors. We slammed our equipment down on the floor and roared invectives at Torbett, Darby, the MPs who couldn't

149

handle the Arzew situation, at everybody remotely connected with our fate.

"Ain't this a sorry state of affairs! The Rangers turn out to be nothing but a no good, chicken, fun-hating, military-police outfit."

"Next thing they're gonna do is turn us into a gravediggers outfit!"

"Trainin's one thing. I can see some purpose to trainin'. But pullin' MP duty—that's about as low as you can get."

"Oh, yeah, volunteer for the Rangers, fast-movin' Commandos, shoot-'em-up, live high off the hog. . . . Look at us, a crummy bunch of MPs!"

These were some of the milder diatribes unleashed that memorable day. No one, not even Dunn, could deny that they were well justified on this particular occasion.

Remembering my unhappy experiences as an MP in Oban and my vows to quit the Rangers if I ever pulled such ignoble duty again, I was one of those who shouted the loudest.

"Hey, Al," chided Lodge. "You should be really happy. Playing MP is old stuff to you. Maybe you can give us all some pointers when we go on duty."

I was in no mood to banter. Hot, tired and disgusted, I swiftly undressed and bolted for the beach. Now all they had to do was tell me the sea was off limits. Harris, Andre and Ed Thompson were already swimming around when I dived into the first wave.

As I came up, Harris splashed his way to my side. "This is wonderful—a camp right by the sea. We can take a dip before our training begins in the morning and a good refreshing swim after it's over."

That was Harris' way of reminding me that things weren't really so bad.

CHAPTER 25

THE next few weeks found the Rangers engaged in the most strenuous, ambitious, versatile training program in Army history. Colonel Darby, ably assisted by his efficient executive officer, Major Dammer, devised an ingenious schedule designed to condition us physically and mentally for any type of combat we might be called on to perform—amphibious, mountain, field, street fighting or radio sorties.

The first phase was devoted to physical hardening. For two weeks we marched. We made speed marches up and down the coast road, ten-milers, twelve-milers, fifteen-milers, twenty-four-milers. We marched with full field equipment, without water in our canteens, without rations in our packs. We pounded the macadam road in the blistering sun until our legs felt cut off at the ankles. We made a forced speed march to Mostagenom, an Arab village twenty miles away and returned in seven hours. The rest of the day we had it easy. We did PT on the sand dunes, spent an hour on organized sports, baseball, football, volley ball, then wound up the day with a massed battalion swim—a one-mile race to a buoy and back. This was a rare day. Darby was in a good mood.

West of Arzew a towering range of jagged-tipped mountains formed a thirty-mile promontory toward Oran. The most daring mountain goats would have hesitated to climb these steep precipices. But the Rangers didn't hesitate. Every other day our battalion shoved off into these mountains and climbed and climbed until we ran out of mountains. Then we would go right back. We would see in the distance a new peak, more jagged and more forbidding than any we had explored before. We would shudder and pray that Darby and Dammer hadn't spotted the mountain too. But it would turn out to be a feeble hope. As usual, we would see Darby point out the mountain to Dammer. Then the order would come down: "On your feet, Rangers!" Then like two pointing dogs, Darby and Dammer would take off, headed for the new challenge with us dog-tired Rangers trotting to catch up.

We gave those mountains real hell. We climbed them straight up. We circled them. We crossed them from the north, from the south and from the east. We didn't cross them from the west because they dropped perpendicularly straight into the sea. We kept worrying that one day Darby would try that angle too.

Mountain climbs, cliff climbs, cross-country day marches, cross-country night marches, speed marches along macadam roads, along dirt roads, along the sandy beaches, physical training with logs, without logs; baseball, volley ball, football, boxing, swimming, track meets—yes, track meets—these were the activities Darby and Dammer dreamed up to get us in shape.

And of course we always had our one day of Military Police duty to look forward to. As much as we hated MP duty it was a welcome respite from our training. At one point, I seriously considered joining the MPs for good. At least I would know definitely what to expect in that outfit.

The first two weeks, we learned to our dismay, were only a warmup for what was to follow. At battalion formation one late November morning, El Darbo announced the opening of phase two. Flanked by Major Dammer and the huge, bulky ex-cook, Sergeant Major Peer Buck, Darby spoke:

"Now that I'm satisfied you men are hardened enough to be called Rangers, now that I know that every man here is physically equipped to endure any march over the most challenging terrain—now we can get down to real business."

I looked around me. Rangers were staring glumly ahead, wondering what this "real business" would be. Even ol' Butt Torbett's face was screwed up with foreboding grimness. After the last few agonizing weeks nothing Darby pulled would really surprise us.

152

"Beginning tomorrow the First Ranger Battalion will concentrate on two things: amphibious landings under every conceivable condition and small unit tactics. We will improve on old methods and experiment with new concepts. What we do here will be watched closely by General Lloyd Fredendall and division commanders. The entire Army may benefit from our experience—providing we do our job right.

"Now I know there is a lot of grumbling about too much training. You Rangers feel you don't need more training. You think you're ready for more action. To those of you who are griping, let me remind you, there's a war going on in Tunisia. American soldiers are getting killed because the enemy is tougher and more battle-wise. Our turn may come any time. When it does, we're going to be ready."

Darby paused a moment then continued. "You men who are griping should thank God that Headquarters has given us more time to get in shape."

We were totally stunned by the good news that followed.

Darby, smiling fully for the first time since we landed in Arzew, concluded: "To put you in the right frame of mind for the training ahead, there will be no duty the rest of the day. Company commanders will allow passes for Oran, but mind you, Rangers—I want no repetition of our Oban episode.

"Company commanders . . . move out your companies!"

Murray saluted, then led Fox Company along the beach back of our cabanas. After Torbett dismissed us we ran yelling into our respective quarters, anxious to get ready for town. Some of the Rangers appeared jubilant. Some were still glum about the training prospects ahead.

"He thinks a one-day pass is gonna make us forget how chicken he is," roared one.

"Big deal! One day off in three weeks. We better make the most of it—it'll probably be the first and last day off we'll ever get."

"He sure made sense to me," spoke up Dunn. "Some of those outfits in Tunisia are having a rough time. They're up against Rommel's crack troops. What Darby is doing is giving us battle insurance!"

153

"Battle insurance, hell," Fuller cut in. "He thinks this training will impress the brass what a top commander he is. You heard him talk about Fredendall coming down to watch us."

That was too much for Dunn. He slammed down his helmet, leaped over me and stood towering over Fuller, who was changing his shoes. "Look, Ranger, your griping and bitching I can overlook. But your mouthings about Darby and his motives are insidious. What are you trying to do—demoralize the outfit?"

Fuller, his face red, his knuckles whitening, lunged at Dunn. "You fair-haired, Bible-quotin', blue-nosed deacon!"

Dunn, swift as lightning moved in with a headlock. They crashed to the floor. Lodge and I moved in to separate them as someone yelled, "Here comes Nye."

We managed to get them apart as Lieutenant Nye walked into the cottage. Noticing Dunn's and Fuller's disheveled appearance and flushed faces, Nye smiled. "Looks like you fellows are practicing your hand-to-hand combat."

We all laughed, breaking the tension. "I just thought I'd let you fellows know before you leave for town that I'm taking a two-and-a-half ton truck into Oran to pick up some supplies. Anyone who wants a lift is welcome. I'll be ready to leave at 1000 hours."

"Count me in," a chorus of voices answered. Dunn and Fuller continued to glare at each other for a long moment, before they both sullenly turned away and resumed dressing. We knew that at best only a temporary truce had been effected.

We were putting the final touches to our go-to-town uniforms when Snapdragon Stern's croaking voice sounded off outside. "Hey, fellows, wha'd I tell you? The whole country knows about Arzew. . . . We made *Stars and Stripes*. . . . We made the *New York Times*. . . . Look, fellows, my pictures!"

Nearly every Ranger except Fuller ran outside to gather around Snapdragon, who was madly waving a handful of newspaper sheets. Sergeant Torbett, the first to reach Stern, grabbed the *Stars and Stripes* out of his hand. We craned our necks over Torbett's shoulder. On the front page were pictures of Rangers, including Torbett at the gun battery overlooking Arzew. The bold black caption read: DARING RANGERS SILENCE COASTAL GUNS. CRACK

154

NIGHTFIGHTERS TAKE ARZEW ON D DAY, THEN SMASH WAY TO ORAN.

"How about that?" exuded Torbett. "They really played us up big."

Fronk grabbed the paper out of Torbett's hands. "Where's my picture? Hey, Stern, you didn't send my picture in. Hell, the whole world is gonna think old Butt Torbett is the whole Ranger Battalion. His ugly puss is everywhere."

"I sent 'em all in, Fronk, honest," said Stern. "I guess they only print the ones that really look dramatic."

"That's me." Torbett laughed. "I got the right pose for every situation!"

Avidly we read through the various articles.

Although it was three weeks since the invasion, only now were the papers getting through to us. The *New York Times* article, which also carried pictures of our training in Scotland, went into great detail to connect the present-day Rangers with a long list of American raiding groups, including Marion's Swamp Foxes, Mosby's Confederate Rangers and, of course, the Commandos. Another article went so far as to compare our feat in the capture of Arzew with General Wolfe's night attack on Montreal during the French and Indian War.

Stern had been right. His dramatic pictures told the story better than a million words. We looked at Stern now with new esteem. His pictures had ironically fulfilled a higher purpose than even he had dared to imagine. Not only had they made the public aware of our outfit, but they had given us a new surge of pride and spirit at a crucial time when many were beginning to doubt the wisdom of joining the Rangers. Reading those writeups put us all in good spirits. Despite the training program ahead, despite our keen disappointment that we were not being used for Commando raids as we had envisioned, we were vain enough to bask momentarily in the national spot light. Even if Darby didn't let us know how good we were, the rest of the world knew it.

CHAPTER 26

CARLO CONTRERA came waddling down the beach as we were getting our passes from Torbett. He was panting heavily, and his broad, freckled face was flushed with excitement. "Hey, Altieri!" he shouted as he drew near. "Our old outfit's camped near St. Cloud!"

"No kiddin'! I thought they were fighting in Tunisia."

"Nah, they're still in reserve, gettin' some new equipment. Smith said he met one of the boys in Arzew picking up a new self-propelled gun. . . . What say we go see the gang?"

"Maybe we can see them after we give Oran a good going over. Hell, Sarn't Siego's got a special tour cooked up. We been waitin' for weeks for this chance."

"Doncha got no pride for your old outfit, Altieri? Doncha wanna see the old gang before they go into battle? Smith said they're ready to shove off any time now."

Carlo's taunts brought back a flood of memories. Faces I had almost forgotten came into my mind. An old outfit—even a bad one—always brings back nostalgic thoughts. Contrera didn't need to do any more talking to sell me.

"Okay, Carlo, we'll drop in on them. We'll get a ride in with our gang, then drop off at St. Cloud."

"Good deal," Carlo answered. "Now we'll show those guys in

156

battery what a couple of rugged Rangers look like. I'll bet they heard all about us."

"Yeh," I returned. "They probably heard all about how we been turned into Military Policemen. They'll give us a good razzing."

We found our outfit camped in an olive grove. Line after line of ponderous, deadly looking self-propelled 105's covered the area. Men were scurrying about, cleaning the tractor treads, swabbing the gun barrels. Sergeant Burns was roaring out orders as he always did.

"Hey, look who's here," a voice shouted. Men looked up from their activities to stare at us in amazement.

Then a chorus of voices rang out: "Here come the rugged Rangers."

"Contrera and Altieri, the Suicide twins."

"Look, they're still alive. . . . We thought they was knocked off at Arzew."

"All right, you guys, make way for two real soldiers," kidded Contrera, sticking his chest out.

Immediately we were surrounded with a dozen or so of our former buddies. Top kick Burns, his face a wide grin, stuck out an oily paw. "Good to see you fellows. We really did hear you got shot up pretty bad."

Pfc. Benton, one of my closest buddies, came up with the same grin. Benton, a Regular Army man, was the Junior Fronk of A Battery. He was always on Burns's black list. "I'll be damned! I never thought I'd see you guys again. How's it going in that Ranger outfit? We been hearin' all kinds of stories about you guys."

Carlo and I pumped hands till our arms ached, then over cups of steaming coffee we told of our adventures in the Rangers, exaggerating so well that we believed our tales ourselves. After the excitement was over, Pfc. Benton and two other soldiers who were carried away by our tales insisted on hearing more about our hell-raising outfit.

"Let's go to town and celebrate our reunion with a drink," I said. "We'll really give you the lowdown on the Rangers."

We found a small French bistro that served beer and cognac on the outskirts of town. We sauntered in, sat down at the checker-clothed table and whistled for the garcon. The waiter bounded over

157

and was shocked when we told him to set up three rounds of cognac apiece for each of us. This was to be our starter.

Six rounds later the three soldiers of A Battery were weaving in their chairs and Carlo and I were still telling tall tales about the Rangers. "Yes *sir*," I was saying, "we Rangers really live it up. We don't sleep in no *lousy tents*. Not us Rangers. We're the elite. In Scotland we lived like kings in civilian houses. All the women we wanted. Here in Arzew where do you think we're living? We're right on the beach like gentlemen. We're living in cabanas that used to belong to rich people. Ol' Darby sure takes care of his men."

"Sounds real good." Benton hiccupped. "Not like our chicken outfit. We get the worst camps and the lousiest chow and we never get much chance to fool around with women. . . . But I heard you Rangers got real tough trainin'. I don't know if I could take that."

"Ah, that's propaganda," said Carlo. "What trainin'? You call taking a little walk up a mountain trainin'? You call playing games in the afternoon and taking long swims in that nice sea trainin'? Yes, we do a bit of live ammo firing now and then just to make it look good, but we don't go in for that trainin' stuff. We go in for action, strictly action."

"Yeah, that's the part I don't know about—that action you fellows get. I don't like that business of going in in the first wave at night. A guy could get killed that way," John Hammond suggested.

"Did you read our casualty figures for Arzew? We took two thousand prisoners and had only one man killed—you call that dangerous? Our tactics and our surprise—they're real battle insurance. It's the guys who come in after us who get the hell kicked out of them."

"Boy, I sure would like to get in that outfit," Brooks said.

"You would? Then why don't you volunteer? We'll be glad to have you, Benton . . . and these guys too," I said looking at the other two Armored men.

They downed another cognac and looked at one another. Hammond said, "Sure, we'd like to join up too, but we can't get out of our outfit. Our C.O. would never let us go. We're ready to go to Tunisia now."

"Whatta you mean he won't let you go? Do you know who Darby is? Do you know that all Darby has to do is call up Headquarters and say 'I want these three men' and first thing you know you're Rangers. Our old man has pull in this Army, real pull—that right, Carlo?"

"You're damned right that's right. Darby is a big gun, biggern' anybody 'cept maybe General Eisenhower."

By this time I was really loaded and was completely carried away by my own bragging. Stern's newspaper clippings that morning had romanticized the Rangers far beyond reality. Forgotten was the ignoble MP duty. Forgotten were the killing marches, the scathing chewings by Darby, the gloomy prospects of our future training. Forgotten were all the disillusioning aspects of the Rangers. In front of my old Battery A buddies, the Rangers were *it,* period. Before I knew it, crazy words were coming out of my mouth, and I knew they were crazy but I couldn't stop them.

"Look, pals. You been heein' and hawin' about joining up with the Rangers. Well, if you're really serious, I'll take you right now. Just follow me." I stood up as Carlo and the others looked at me with open mouths. The A Battery men made no move to get up.

"You fellows aren't turning chicken, are you?" I challenged.

Benton was having a big debate with himself. "We're not chicken, Altieri. We just know our ol' C.O. won't let us go."

"The hell he won't! Look, I'll take you right up to see Darby right now. I'll tell Darbo you fellows are old buddies. If I ask Darbo to take you, you're in."

Contrera was so shocked he fell over backward in his chair with a loud crash. The waiter came running, thinking a brawl was about to begin.

Rubbing his head, Contrera got up. "Hey, Altieri, you're not serious?"

"You're damned right I'm serious. If these guys aren't yellow and really want to join up, I'll personally take 'em in to see Darby."

Benton weakly looked at his buddies. They looked at each other, shrugged, then stood up.

"Okay," said Hammond. "I'm fed up with that slave driver Burns. . . . I never did like the artillery anyway. Let's go, Benton."

159

Benton shook his head, then in a daze he managed to straighten himself out. "Lead on, fearless Rangers—lead us on to whatsis name. . . ."

Flicking a thousand-franc note on the table, I wove my way out the door, followed closely by the staggering volunteers. Carlo, I knew vaguely, was somewhere in the rear, shaking his head for all he was worth.

I wasn't really stinking drunk. I had that wonderful, blissful, exultant, flamboyant, slightly swaggering feeling, the kind of drunk that makes men think they're utterly invincible. The kind of drunken torpor that digs deep into our subconscious emotional vats and eggs us on to deeds we would like to do but would never dare to do when completely sober.

Outside the bistro I paused momentarily, trying to figure out how we would get to Arzew. An unattended jeep down the block caught my eye. "Let's go, fellows—we're shovin' off in style."

Contrera blinked. "Hey, buddy, you can't go around stealing jeeps. We'll all wind up in the brig."

"Listen, Carlo, we're Rangers, aren't we? Rangers go first class. We need transportation, don't we? Okay, we just borrow that jeep for a while and bring it back later. . . . That's not an offense—that's initiative."

Our strange procession weaved down to the jeep. Benton and the two A Battery men followed without saying a word, afraid that any more protests would bring down another barrage of cowardly names. I got into the front seat, the three recruits stumbled into the back. Contrera just stood there as I started the motor.

"Listen to me, Altieri. You don't know what you're doin' You'll lose your corporal stripes surer'n hell."

"Contrera, I thought you had guts. I thought you were my buddy. If you chicken out now, that's all, brother. . . ."

"Look, Altieri, I'm only a Pfc., but I'll glady give up my Pfc. rating, much as I want it, if you only change your mind."

"Move aside, Carlo. I gotta see Darby."

I gunned the motor and was starting to move off when Carlo, a pained look on his face, finally jumped in beside me. "Okay, big shot, when it's all over, don't say I didn't warn you."

160

When we pulled up to the Headquarters area at Green Beach, a handful of Rangers were around. They stared at us in surprise as we fell out of the jeep. Contrera made a final plea. "Don't do it, Altieri. Let's get the hell out of here before Darby or Dammer sees us."

I ignored him. Turning to Benton and the two silent Armored men, I said, "Follow me. We're goin' right over to Darby's quarters."

"This is where I leave you guys," moaned Carlo as we strode toward Darby's small green cabana. At the closed door I turned to Benton. "Now when I present you to the old man, I want you fellows to really look sharp. Darby likes his men to stand up real straight and look real military. Just watch how to I do it."

They just nodded their heads as though in a dream.

Pulling myself together I rapped curtly on Darby's door.

"Come in," his voice answered.

I turned around, winked at my recruits, then opened the door and strode into the room. Darby was sitting on a chair, a worn Bible in his hand, looking at me with puzzlement written all over his face.

I came to a snappy halt, slung him a wicked, full, forced salute that made me totter slightly. "Corporal Altieri reporting to the commanding officer on an urgent matter, sir." By this time Benton and the two other recruits had moved in behind me.

Darby stared at us as though not believing what he was seeing. "Well, what's the urgent mission, Altieri?"

"Sir, my old buddies from the First Armored wanna join the Rangers. They're good men, sir—I can vouch for them because I served with them. But their commanding officer won't let them transfer out."

Darby was nonplused. It was the only time I ever heard him stammer. "Well . . . er . . . you better take these men over to battalion personnel and give them all the information. I'll see what can be done."

"Yes, sir," I said, giving out with another terrific salute that nearly broke my arm. "Thank you, Colonel. We'll go right over there now."

161

Major Dammer seated at a small desk in the large personnel tent was visibly startled when he we barged in. Captain Karbel, the battalion adjutant, was also there, but having just talked to the ol' man himself, I wasn't going to bother with any lowly captains. Right up to Major Dammer's desk I marched, with the petrified recruits behind me.

I didn't even salute Major Dammer. "Sir, Colonel Darby told me to take these volunteers over here to get signed up for the Rangers." Then, before continuing, I leaned over his field desk, supporting myself with an elbow as though I was talking to an equal.

Dammer's sharp features scowled as he stood up. "Get yourself straightened out, Ranger. You should be at attention when reporting," he said crisply. I jumped up as though struck by a brutal whip. It was humiliating to be addressed that way in front of my buddies. What would they think?

Before I could say another word, two Military Policemen came into the tent. Smartly they saluted Captain Karbel, then looked at me and my recruits. "Sir, the jeep outside was stolen from St. Cloud. We traced it here. We believe these men are responsible."

Dammer's piercing cold eyes drilled through mine. "Where did you come from with these men?"

"St. Cloud, sir."

"Did you steal that jeep?"

"No, sir. I just borrowed it for a couple hours."

Dammer turned toward the MPs. "This is your man. We'll take care of him. You can take the jeep back."

"Yes, sir," said the MPs. "How about these other soldiers?"

"You can take them back to their outfits."

Poor Benton and the two recruits were in a daze. All they wanted was some information about the Rangers and instead they found themselves nearly shanghaied into the Rangers and mixed up with a stolen jeep.

As woozy as I was, I felt real contrite about their plight. I turned to the MPs. "They had nothing to do with the jeep. I told 'em it was mine. They just came along." That was the least I could do for them.

162

The MPs nodded, saluted Dammer and withdrew, taking with them my disillusioned buddies. Dammer looked at Karbel, who was standing with a bemused look. "Get the sergeant of the guard and have this Ranger put under arrest at quarters."

That's all I remembered.

CHAPTER 27

CAPTAIN ROY MURRAY tried very hard to look stern when I reported to him the next morning right after reveille. My head was still pounding like a boiler, my mind was foggy and vague. Gone was the brazen bravado of yesterday.

"Altieri, I thought you were a stable level-headed soldier. I didn't think you had it in you to swipe a jeep, and be disrespectful to Major Dammer—those are serious charges."

"I'm sorry, Captain. All I thought of was getting my buddies into the Rangers. . . . I thought I'd be doing something for the outfit." I then went on to explain to the best of my recollections all the events that led up to my charge into Darby's quarters.

Murray listened, trying hard to suppress a chuckle. "Well, I can appreciate your motives, but not the way you went about it." He looked at me a long moment. "You've got a damned good record as a Ranger. Personally, I'm willing to forget the whole thing, but it all depends on Colonel Darby's attitude. He may not see the humor in it as I do."

"I'll appreciate anything you can do, Captain." I really meant it. To be busted down to a private and kicked out of the Rangers was a severe penalty for trying to recruit one's buddies and borrowing a lousy jeep. I could just see the men in Battery A laughing at me when I returned in disgrace to my old outfit. Why hadn't I listened to ol' Carlo? He had seen it coming.

164

"Well, get back to your squad. I'll talk to Colonel Darby at chow and see what we can do."

I saluted crisply and thanked him with all the sincerity I could muster. It was gratifying to know that my company commander was an understanding man with a sense of humor who wasn't afraid to stick his neck out for one of his men. I fervently hoped that Darby would prove equally understanding.

Sergeant Torbett was the first one to jump on me when I returned to my quarters: "Ol' Ranger-Recruiter Altieri . . . Old-Outfit Altieri . . . you're as good a recruiter as you were an MP in Oban. What did Murray say? Are they gonna throw the book at you?"

"Don't know. Murray's gonna talk to Darby. Murray's willing to forget it."

Sarn't Siego swaggered over, twirling his mustache. "Well, Al, it was nice knowing you. . . . I'll come to see you when they throw you in that stockade. I told you to come along with us. What a time we had! What dolls! You sure missed the boat."

Even Fuller got into the act in his own inimitable way. "Hell, the only punishment they ought to give you is sending you to the hospital for a medical exam. Anybody tries to bring their buddies into this outfit needs his head poked into."

"That's all right, Al," spoke up Lodge. "Darby will weigh the fact that you had an altruistic motive."

"Him—altruistic motives?" Torbett laughed. "This is Altieri from the Artillery with the ulterior motives. . . . That's why he always gets snagged in a jam."

News about my adventure spread like wildfire. Good-natured jibes flew at me from every Ranger I knew. Sergeant Smith and Windsor, my old comrades from Battery A, poured it on with glee. Someone had dramatized my recruiting sortie with great embellishment. No longer was it three men. The story making the rounds was that I had marched a whole platoon—by speed march no less—right into Darby's cramped quarters.

My incident with Major Dammer was completely distorted. Instead of just leaning over his desk, I was supposed to have actually ordered the major to sign up the men.

Carlo was shaking his head grimly when he came over and sat

down in the sand beside me with his mess kit. "The whole battalion's talking about our deal. They think Darby's gonna skin ya. I told you, Altieri . . . but you wouldn't listen to your ol' buddy."

"Hey, Carlo, will you do me a favor? Quit talking about it. That's all I been hearing. You'd think I was ready to be executed, the way these guys are talking. All I did was borrow a jeep."

"Looky, buddy, if they give you the works, I'm quittin' too. We went through basic together, we came overseas together, we joined the Rangers together. If you get kicked out, I go too." Contrera said it as if he were making a historical pronouncement. And I didn't doubt him one bit.

I was washing my mess kit in the galvanized iron can when Torbett came up to me with a somber look. "Hey, Altieri, Murray said Darby wants to see you, now, in his quarters." I dropped my mess kit in the steaming hot water as my pulse quickened. He certainly wasn't losing any time. "Good luck," Torbett shouted as I made my way through the sand to the green cottage that served as Darby's quarters.

My thoughts were jumbled. Would Darby be seeing me if Murray had successfully interceded? Hardly likely. He would have just let the matter lie in Murray's hands. No . . . Darby was going to have the satisfaction of chewing me out before giving me my walking papers. I prepared myself for the worst.

"Come in," his voice commanded when I knocked respectfully. I opened the door and walked in, stood stiffly at attention and threw a precise salute. Darby was putting on his pistol harness. He returned the salute, then said mildly, "At ease, Altieri." I tried to stand easy but couldn't.

"Corporal Altieri, I want you to answer some questions."

"Yes, sir!"

"You realize that stealing a jeep is a court-martial offense?"

"Yes, sir!"

"You are aware that you had a lot of nerve to come barging in here with three staggering-drunk soldiers and yourself included?"

"Yes, sir!"

"You admit that you were disrespectful to Major Dammer by leaning over his desk and addressing him in a sloppy manner?"

166

"Yes, sir!"

"Now I'm going to ask you to put yourself in my place. You're in command of five hundred men. You must maintain discipline and order. You certainly expect your noncoms to set an example for the rest of the men. But one of them does exactly as you have done. What should you do about it?"

I was totally unprepared for this tack. Darby had maneuvered me into a position where I must pass judgment on myself. I groped vainly for some reasonable answer.

"Colonel, you have five hundred men in the Rangers—and every one of them is an individualist. If they weren't, they wouldn't be in the Rangers. I went to see my old outfit. I got carried away, I got drunk, I got enthused about getting my buddies signed up. So I borrowed the jeep and took them straight to you. Considering the circumstances and the motives, I don't think I have done anything to be ashamed of as a Ranger except being too forward with Major Dammer, which was not intentional. I think if I was the commander I would weigh all these factors with the soldier's record as a Ranger and then I would decide."

"And what would you decide?"

"Whatever his immediate superior, his company commander, wanted to do with him."

For the first time Darby broke out with a flashing smile. My answer, unpremeditated, had rung a bell.

"Altieri," he said with his eyes crinkling, "I just wanted to see if I had figured right."

I couldn't believe my ears. Darby was letting me off the hook. I had come in expecting a scalping and wound up with almost a commendation. "Thank you, Colonel," I said excitedly. "I'll make sure it doesn't happen again."

"If it does," returned Darby, "make sure you salute Major Dammer, and don't crawl all over his desk. Major Dammer doesn't like that sort of thing."

I laughed quietly, then flung him a sharp salute, which he returned, still smiling. As I was going through the door, Darby called out after me, "Say, Altieri, did you ever hear from Gomez? He should be mended by now."

"No, sir," I answered. "I wrote him two letters."

"Well, I'll get a note back to the medical command and see what the situation is."

With that I departed, with new respect for Darby and deep pride for my outfit.

CHAPTER 28

PHASE TWO began in earnest that day. Dressed in fatigues with full battle equipment, we loaded into assault boats that came right up on the beach in front of our quarters. These boats were American landing craft much larger and clumsier than the British boats. They were manned by soldier-sailors of the Thirty-sixth Engineer Amphibious Brigade, which had set up an amphibious center in Arzew.

We could tell right away that the coxswain lacked experience and good judgment. As we roared out to sea, the boat zigged and zagged and rolled precariously. Twice our craft fell behind the others, then caught up with a tremendous burst of speed. Not only did our boat catch up; we soon found ourselves so far ahead of the flotilla that we almost lost it. We knew we were in for some unusual sea tricks.

The flotilla caught up with us and we circled the harbor of Arzew, headed out for the open sea, then veered landward toward Beach Red.

Smoke from mortars was shrouding the beach as we surged in. Tracers started stitching into the water a few paces from our bow. Lieutenant Samm and his demolition crew were on the beach acting as the opposing force. We prayed he and his men would be as expert as the Commando marksmen in Scotland. Sergeant Butt Torbett prayed the loudest.

Our boat was the most temperamental boat afloat. Instead of coming in like a good assault craft should, bow first, our boat swung completely around and went into the beach ass-backward. This was very embarrassing because our company was scheduled to land first and establish a perimeter. Murray had to radio the main flotilla to hold off till we made another try.

The coxswain fretted and fumed as he gunned the engine and tried to redeem the honor of the Thirty-sixth Engineer Amphibian Brigade. After ten minutes of heroic efforts he managed to get the rear end off the beach and away we zoomed—amid rousing Ranger cheers—for another try. Keeping the boat on an even course, the engineer optimistically yelled to Murray, "We'll make a good landing this time, Cap'n."

But the boat had a different mind. Halfway in, it veered to the right and ran smack into a sand bar forty yards from shore. In disgust Murray ordered the ramps lowered and we surged into the cold water up to our armpits, holding our rifles over our heads. Junior Fronk, the smallest man in the outfit, went right under. Howard Andre scooped him up and carried him in piggyback. It was a good thing Father Basil wasn't with us. He would have never forgiven us for the profanity we unleashed at the nettled Engineers.

Once again we clambered up the dirt cliff, the very same one we climbed on D day. Across the same road we scampered, then sprang into firing positions to form what is known as a defensive perimeter. At a shouted command from Murray we fired our weapons into the heights directly above, where an imaginary enemy coastal fortification was located. As we fired, Easy Ranger Company moved through us to take up forward positions.

Machine-gun fire crackled all around us as another company moved through to establish a firing line ahead. When the two companies ahead of us, deployed into staggered positions, started firing, Murray yelled, "Cease fire." The last company to land, the assaulting company, then passed through our positions and worked their way up a side draw for a flanking assault. Our job was to hold the perimeter and permit these companies to withdraw after they accomplished their mission.

On a side hill we could see Darby and Dammer directing the operation with walkie-talkies. We knew they weren't happy. Rangers were bunching up, weren't moving fast enough. The assaulting company started to assault before the supporting fire had ceased.

They were called back to re-form the assault line. When the supporting fire finally stopped, they were slow in launching their attack. When they did get started again they went in too close together, then didn't get out fast enough. A couple of mortar shells fired by D Company down on the beach nearly got several men.

After storming the hill the assaulting company withdrew back down the ravine as the supporting companies once again opened fire on the hills to cover their withdrawal. Then squad by squad, one covering each other, we withdrew to the beach, only to find our boats were not there. They were playing ring-around-the-rosy two hundred yards off shore.

Confused, we sat down on the beach and waited. We didn't wait long. Darby and Dammer came storming down the cliffs. Murray reported to them. After a brief consultation Murray summoned Nye and all section leaders. We listened.

"The colonel said this was the most fouled-up landing problem he's ever seen. We're going to load those boats again and do it over."

We were too tired even to protest. We just sank onto the sand and waited.

That's how our first day of Phase Two started.

171

CHAPTER 29

THE next few weeks were rough, even by Commando standards. Over and over again we hit Beach Red, Beach Green and a dozen other beaches nobody bothered to name. Over and over again the much-abused Engineer Brigade dumped us on the sand, hurled us against rocks and dropped us into water over our heads. One time we would land on Beach Red, attack the heights directly overhead, then withdraw back to the waiting boats. Another time we would make a night landing down the coast, scramble up steep cliffs, stagger over a dozen mountains, then race fifteen miles to attack an Arab town. Meanwhile the boats would move up the coast for a night rendezvous some thirty miles away. Our mission completed, we would split up into small groups and make our way by compass to the waiting boats. Sometimes groups of Rangers would get lost; sometimes our boats would get lost.

On some problems the entire battalion would be used; on others only two companies; sometimes only one. Occasionally we would have platoon missions involving sabotage of an enemy radar installation or a terrorizing coastal raid. Every conceivable type of landing operation with every possible combination of troops was tried. Darby and Dammer used every technique the Commandos had worked out and threw in a dozen of their own for good measure.

A new book on amphibious landings was written at Arzew. We made day landings with opposed fire; silent night landings; opposed night landings; against cliffs, on beaches, alongside piers.

172

We made landings with high tide, with low tide, in the rain, in fog, with smoke and without smoke. At the end of Phase Two every man in our battalion could automatically fall into position and go through his particular assignment on any given problem just like a football player.

The Rangers griped and cussed. The Engineers bleated and groaned and cursed the fates that assigned them to ferry the Rangers around. But they learned more about amphibious landings than they would have in a dozen wars. At least they weren't landing us ass-backward any more.

The high brass learned a lot too. Generals galore from every command then in Africa came down to Arzew to watch the Rangers go through their paces. They brought with them staff officers and picked noncoms to study and absorb Ranger tactics so that other outfits could benefit. We didn't mind them picking up a few pointers from us, but we resented having to put on a dress parade after the maneuvers. Once General Fredendall and his contingent watched us pull a full-scale invasion at Beach Red. We shot the works for the general—tracers, live mortar rounds, wired explosions to simulate mines and artillery. It was one of our very best shows. Every company, every man, did every tactic with perfect co-ordination. Even the Engineers were on the beam that day. Everything went off without a hitch.

We withdrew down to the beach and into the waiting boats, begrimed, fatigued and pleased with ourselves. But we weren't through yet. No! We had to show General Fredendall how snappy we Rangers looked on the parade field. Back to Beach Green the boats sped. There we tumbled out of the boats and raced into quarters and changed swiftly into Class B parade uniforms. A half hour after staging the problem we were parading on an open field as General Fredendall stood by with Darby, proudly reviewing us.

Fredendall was very much impressed, and he told us so. He presented some Purple Hearts to the Rangers who had been wounded at Dieppe and Arzew. The ceremonies were concluded when he presented the first battlefield appointment to First Sergeant Bing Evans, for outstanding leadership at La Macta with Schneider's company. Max Schneider pinned the second lieutenant bars on

173

Evans, and Darby pinned the captain's bars on Schneider. We felt real good about both promotions. Schneider's hell-for-leather dash and jaunty personality made him a popular officer. And the battlefield appointment of Evans was proof that enlisted men could rise to be officers in the Rangers if they had the goods. I could see that Sergeant Harris, in particular, seemed exceptionally heartened by this.

CHAPTER 30

PHASE TWO ended with General Fredendall's inspection. Once again Darby magnanimously allowed us a whole day's leave. The next morning, once again, the Rangers descended like locusts on Oran and other nearby towns. Sarn't Siego, just to be different, collected a handful of his loyal followers and went to Mostagenum because it was untouched by GI traffic. They came back with vivid descriptions of the beauties they encountered, both French and Arab. Sieg even insisted that a local junior sultan had allowed him to spend a few hours in his harem in exchange for his Commando knife, which was highly admired by the Arab gentry. We didn't believe him, but the story at least was original.

Vernon Lodge had a field day in Mostagenum. He found what he was searching for—a long, black Arabian flute. When last seen Vernon was wearing a red fez in a dimly lighted bistro frequented by Arabs. To the wonderment of the Arabs, he held them spellbound with the "Cow Cow Boogie." According to Junior Fronk, who reported Lodge's peregrinations, he even went so far as to provide background music for a bevy of Moroccan chorus girls. Deacon Dunn, mindful of his tragic experiences in Oran, didn't go anywhere. Neither did Harris. He took a long walk in the mountains, searching for some rare rock specimens.

I didn't go anywhere either. I couldn't. Torbett made certain I'd stay out of trouble by giving me the honor of pulling charge of quarters for the day. That's why I liked Torbett so well. He was always looking after my interests.

For a few days the Rangers took it easy on Green Beach. Thinking that the worst of the training was over, that Darby was relenting and easing up a bit, our spirits improved immeasurably. Father Basil went from company to company trying to get volunteers for his new choral group. Sarn't Sieg and Sergeant Butt Torbett—of all people—eagerly offered their services. Torbett, among many other things, was renowned in the battalion for having the lustiest voice. The prospects of seeing our tough, hard-bitten first sergeant in the Sunday choir was too much for the grizzled Rangers of Fox Company.

"He thinks singing in the choir's gonna reserve a place in heaven for him," laughed Fronk.

"He wants to do penance for all his sins against us," another Ranger said.

We took advantage of these few days. We wrote letters, sat on the beach like vacationers, played baseball and caught up with the battalion scuttlebutt. Darby, it was rumored, had gone to Algiers to Headquarters. Everyone ventured to guess at the significance of his visit. We were going to Tunisia. We were going to pull a raid. We were going back to the States to train other Rangers. We were going to be disbanded. The silliest rumor was that Darby, having run out of new training schemes, was going to put us through Paratroop training.

Mail call, our biggest morale booster, brought me a letter from Gomez and one from my brother Gene, who was a master sergeant with an MP unit back in Albany, New York. Gomez' letter was heartbreaking. He was well again, but had been reclassified to limited duty, which meant assignment to a noncombatant unit. He was in a replacement depot in Liverpool. He had been fined forty dollars for going A.W.O.L. and stowing away on a cargo ship bound for Africa. He was still vainly trying to get back to the Rangers. I pinned the letter on the battalion bulletin board.

My older brother Gene was in the dumps. He couldn't get overseas. They had him pinned down with this MP battalion, whose main function was to ride trains all over New York. Of course, Gene, being the master sergeant, didn't ride these trains. Poor Gene had to sit in a nice big office in downtown Albany and make out the duty rosters. It was awfully boring. How lucky I was to be seeing the world, enjoying places I never would have seen if I were not in the Army! I felt really sorry for my brother after I finished reading that letter.

With Darby's return from Algiers a ripple of wild rumors spread through the battalion. Something was in the wind—action on the Tunisian front, or a raid. At the chow line that morning we heard that Darby had summoned the company commanders when he arrived late last night.

Later at company formation we learned what the new mission was. Captain Roy Murray announced it briefly: "Fellows, we have a mission—a night raid on an island. It's a tough one and an important one. The next two weeks will be spent in rehearsing every phase. Fox Company will be going in first, so I want every man to sharpen up and give it his best. One thing I want to impress on everyone: no mention of what we're doing must be made to anyone outside of this battalion. That includes other troops stationed in Arzew."

Wild cheers rang out after Murray finished. At long last we were getting cracking. Everyone, including Fuller, was elated. We had been in Arzew too long. We had trained too much. We were aching for action—any kind of action—to escape the monotonous yet grueling daily grind of training over and over. Pete Preston ably summed up our feeling when he roared: "Brother, it's about time we got goin'. I'm so damned browned off at this trainin' setup that I'll take on a whole battalion of Germans by myself, just to get out of it."

George Fuller was not to be outdone. "I'll be damned. Ol' Darbo really brought home the bacon. And all the time I thought he went to Algiers to get an okay to change our name to the First Perpetual Training Battalion!"

Gradually during the next few days the plan unfolded. Our mission was to make a silent landing on a small island somewhere in the Mediterranean that had a powerful radar and radio installation and was garrisoned by a battalion of Italian troops. The radar and radio beams were hindering our air operations in the Mediterranean. Our bombers couldn't get through because of intense ack-

177

ack and fighter coverage. Huge concealed shore batteries prevented warships from moving in for a shelling. The Rangers were the answer.

As Nye explained, it was a daring mission. The Rangers would land on the north side of the island against cliffs, march fourteen miles over mountains and attack the town where the troops were garrisoned, destroy the radar station and blow up the coast guns. The entire garrison was to be annihilated, with the exception of a few prisoners for information. We would not leave the island till the following night, when the ship or ships that brought us would return to pick us up. We would be exposed to enemy bombers the entire day.

We trained hard for this mission. Night after night, Fox Company would land on the coast against rocks, march over mountains and then attack a cluster of Arab houses on the outskirts of Arzew at dawn.

One squad would advance, lay down selected lanes of fire on buildings, while another squad would crawl up to the building, assault it with grenades and Tommy guns, occupy it, then lay down fire on adjacent buildings while the rest of the company advanced. This was to be a no-holds-barred deal, street fighting at its dirtiest.

This was the kind of fighting we had all been yelling for, because this was the kind of fighting we had joined the Rangers for and were trained for. Now faced with the prospects of a smashing raid, all on our own, we once again renewed our zip and *esprit de corps*. Once again the battalion poets had a field day. A couple more stanzas were added to the Ranger's fighting chant. We sang it with gusto on every speed march:

> "We're the toughest and we're the best,
> You'll find us leading all the rest,
> Darby's Rangers . . . toughest Rangers.
>
> We love our women tough and strong,
> We're weaned on booze and lusty song,
> Darby's Rangers . . . lusty Rangers."

178

CHAPTER 31

THE days sped by swiftly. Before we knew it Christmas slipped up on us. Father Basil held high mass for the Catholics early in the morning, and at eleven o'clock general services were held for the entire battalion.

A hot sun beat down on our faces as we stood bareheaded in a huge semicircle around Father Basil on the sandy beach. After a brief sermon on the meaning of Christmas, Father Basil proudly introduced his choral group, led by the intrepid Butt Torbett, with the able assistance of Sarn't El Siego and Corporal Robert Chesher, who also did duty as altar boy. From God only knows where, Father Basil had managed to come up with a small portable organ, which was played by Sergeant Crandall, our operations sergeant.

Sergeant Torbett's hard, crusted face beamed with saintly piety as he spearheaded the choral assault on "Holy, Holy, Holy." Loud, lusty voices that on other occasions had sung the bawdiest parodies in Christendom now rang out with sanctified mellifluence. Sarn't Sieg, his red mustache bristling in the sunlight, looked like a member of a gay-nineties barbershop quartet, as he tried valiantly to drown out Torbett's voice. All that was needed to make the scene complete was a platoon of angels hovering over their heads.

After a few more renditions by the elite choir, the entire battalion joined in with "O Little Town of Bethlehem." I looked around me at Junior Fronk, Lodge, Dunn and Ray Rodriguez. In thought they were three thousand miles away, at home with their families. I looked back at Father Basil, his slight, wiry figure, now dressed in a strange combination of British and American uniforms. His trousers were GI, his battle jacket British as well as his green beret, now resting on a nearby table. Father Basil's sharp-visaged, bespectacled face suddenly looked like Father Carr, my parish priest in Parkersburg. To each Ranger standing there singing, Father Basil was the closest link to home and family and God. Thanks to him, Christmas held for us its true meaning on that hot sandy ribbon of beach in Algeria.

The last note of the last hymn was still ringing in the air when Sergeant Butt Torbett—assisted by invisible wings—leaped up on a C-ration box and yelled for our attention.

"There he goes again," exclaimed Fronk. "Even on Christmas he's gotta ham it up."

"Maybe he's gonna sing us a solo—like Scotty Monroe," added Pete Preston.

"Naw," Carlo continued, "he's gonna give out with one of those how-I-was-saved testimonials—you know, like they do down in the Bowery when the Salvation Army guys come around."

main function was to ride trains all over New York. Of course,

"Fellows," Torbett roared, "thanks to Father Basil, this outfit's not hurtin' for anything this Christmas. We got us an organ, we got us a real Christmas tree, and you guys just heard with your own ears the best damned chorus in the whole army. Now I never won medals for speechmaking, but our Padre here has really put the spirit in us this Christmas, and I think we oughta show him how much we appreciate him being here with us. . . ."

Torbett stooped low to pick up a basket, a bushel basket, and held it high over his head. "This here basket I wanna see filled to the top with franc notes. Everybody digs and everybody gives." Father Basil smiled shyly as Torbett reached into his trousers, pulled out a fistful of franc notes and thrust them dramatically into the basket, then threw the basket to the front line of Rangers. Furiously the basket rotated from one group to the other as Rangers outdid themselves throwing in notes. Finally the basket came back to Torbett, bulging with money. Proudly Torbett handed the basket to Father Basil.

180

"Here, Father, this is to cover some of the incidentals Harris is always talking about."

Father Basil beamed. "My word, Sergeant, if the news about this gets back to the British Army, every chaplain will be going A.W.O.L. to join the Rangers. . . . My word, but you Yanks are a generous lot."

CHAPTER 32

IT WAS early Sunday morning when we saw for the first time the ship that was to take us on our mission. She came steaming majestically into Arzew harbor, her flags waving proudly in the morning breeze, and she looked like a true thoroughbred. Her long, slim bow was low-slung, her cutdown stack tilted backward rakishly. The *Princess Emma* of His Royal Majesty's Navy was a far cry from the wobbly, rusty *Royal Ulsterman*. Her sleek, elegant lines were designed for speed. We knew from Father Basil that the *Princess Emma* was the number-one Commando ship with a score of daring escapades notched on her battle flags.

The entire battalion thronged onto the beaches to look at her in awe. "Now that's what I call a Commando boat with class. . . . That's the way the Rangers should always travel, in class."

"They built that ship specially for us," added Fronk.

I nudged Howard Andre. "Darby really rates with the brass to swing a ship like that. Everything's workin' out just like we figured when we joined the Rangers."

Andre smiled knowingly. "This is the turning point, Al. From here on in we'll be global terrorizers."

At 1:00 P.M. after a last chow on the beach, the battalion formed up in parade formation, and Colonel Darby, followed by Major Dammer, personally inspected each Ranger. Not one man was gigged in the entire battalion, to the pride and satisfaction of Sergeant Torbett.

Colonel Darby, now wearing dark sunglasses, assumed his posi-

182

tion at the head of the battalion to roar out his **familiar command:** "Company commanders . . . move out your companies!" We moved out, headed for the docks, headed for the assault boats that would ferry us out to the sleek aristocrat of the Mediterranean, H.M.S. *Princess Emma.*

We spent three days on the *Princess Emma.* Three days of boat drills, landing rehearsals and general orientation. The chow was remarkably good for a British ship; even the tea tasted better. We had fresh water showers, and the ship had a fine amplifying system that played the most recent American swing tunes. Lodge's favorite was Harry James's recording of "The Trumpet Blues." He would take out his clarinet whenever this number played and hook on as if he were part of James's band.

On the fourth day the *Princess Emma* pulled up anchor and slid graciously out of the harbor. We lined the decks looking back at the Arzew hills, happy to be leaving for a while at least. I wondered how many of us would be lucky enough to come back to Arzew.

Without escort we raced out to sea, soon losing the mountainous shoreline. That very night would find us anchored off the island, clambering into the assault boats ready to launch our much-trained-for attack.

Never was the battalion in higher spirits. From the loud raucous songs that reverberated throughout the ship, it appeared more like a rollicking Cook's tour of the international Elks Club. Nye and Murray moved about from one group to the other, kidding, joking amiably. Sarn't El Siego and Torbett started a tremendous crap game that saw the decks littered with franc notes. Phil Stern bounded up and down the decks taking pictures. Stern was ecstatic about the *Princess Emma.* "What a sweetheart! She can outrace any ship in the world. She's got enough firepower to blow up a whole navy."

Father Basil with green beret could be seen bobbing from one group to the other, exchanging witticisms, telling a bit of the history of the *Princess Emma,* chiding a few of the boys who had not completely cleansed their vocabularies. Father Basil's presence made everything all right.

I was standing on the portside of the bow listening to Carlo Contrera yak about his days as a ballroom Romeo in the Roseland dance hall, when I noticed the ship making a wide turn. "Hey, Carlo," I said, "am I seeing things? It looks like we're making a turn."

Carlo looked back at the curved wake. "We sure in hell are turning. Maybe it's a part of the strategy—to zigzag."

"Yeah, maybe," I answered, " 'cept now we've made a complete turn and are headed back in the other direction."

Suddenly the ship captain's voice blared over the amplifying system: "Now here this! Now hear this! Rangers, we are now returning to port. Colonel Darby, your commander, will now speak."

Colonel Darby's voice was thick with disappointment. "We have just received instructions from Supreme Headquarters that owing to changes in the over-all strategic situation in the Mediterranean, our island raid has been called off. Our orders are to return to Arzew. I'm sorry, damned sorry. . . . I know you would have put on a good show."

There was complete silence for a long moment as we digested the harsh impact of Darby's words. It was unbelievable. My shoulders sagged. The built-up nervous tension of expectancy evaporated into a blah feeling of nothingness. What a buildup we had had. What a beautifully co-ordinated set of battle plans, encompassing every aspect of Ranger warfare at its best. What intensive preparations, all climaxed to fever pitch with the boarding of our dream ship, the *Princess Emma*. All down the drain.

Night after night I had lived through the raid, experiencing every emotion that the actual battle would bring. The terrifying ascent up the cliffs, the torturous trek over the mountains, the bloody assault against the garrison, the destruction of the battery and radar station, the long wait the next day when enemy planes would plaster us, till nightfall allowed us to slip back to the *Princess Emma*. It was like a fighter training diligently for a main bout, only to find when he entered the ring that the fight had been called off. Or like a play when all the actors rehearse to perfection only to find on opening night that the show has been canceled.

Fuller was the first one to voice his feelings. "I knew it! I knew it was all going too good. This damned outfit is jinxed. Some joker in Headquarters suddenly decides the island ain't important

184

any more. Well, why didn't these geniuses figure it out in the beginning?"

For most of the Rangers there was little to be said. The mood was ugly and talking would have only made it worse. Once again the future was uncertain. Once again we would go back into training. Once again we wondered for what. All the way back to Arzew, Rangers listlessly stared over the ship's side, glumly contemplating the ignominious ending of our much-heralded raid. We had started out in high spirits, with keen-edged anticipation, with assured confidence. When we returned to the harbor of Arzew, the saddest, most dispirited outfit in the United States Army disembarked like wooden robots from the assault boats and wearily threaded its way up the coast road back to our quarters on the beach. Nothing we could ever experience could equal our disappointment that miserable day. We had made a raid all right . . . but only in our minds.

CHAPTER 33

A DEEP, foreboding gloom settled over the battalion when the *Princess Emma* departed, taking with her our futile hopes that she would be carrying us on another mission. We knew then for certain that the concept of Rangers being used for hit-and-run raids in the Mediterranean was definitely canceled. Gone were the bouncy zest, the cocky wisecracks, the enthusiastic efforts in our daily routines. The terrible letdown of the raid that wasn't, the impatience for action, the uncertainty of our status as a fighting force—all combined to pervade the outfit with a futile sense of melancholia, the most insidious enemy an army could have.

Darby was concerned. We knew it wasn't his fault that higher command had canceled the raid, when the Rangers needed action at a crucial period to justify their training and existence. Many of us sympathized with his problem and position, but neither understanding nor patience could overcome the corroding effects of the long period without action. In an effort to brighten our morale, Darby for a few days maintained only a token training schedule at the discretion of the company commanders and permitted frequent passes into town and Oran.

It helped a little but not much. We were plain bored with Arzew, and the pleasures of Oran no longer appealed to us, particularly since Oran was literally infested with GIs from all over Africa. Not that we minded competition, but the sheen of the city had worn off. The wine tasted lousier, the girls looked harder, the prices were higher and even Stern complained that the souvenirs

186

one could send home now reflected inferior workmanship. When Sarn't Sieg came back home one morning just in time for reveille with the earth-shattering statement that Oran, Mostagenum, Siddi Bell Abbis and every other damned crummy town in Algeria were "off limits" as far as he was concerned, we knew things were bad.

As the days wore on the boys started getting edgy. Barroom and street brawls with soldiers of other units—particularly the port battalion—increased alarmingly. Each company began reporting A.W.O.L.'s. It was time for Darby to take a firm hand. And he did. At battalion formation one morning Darby told us in no uncertain terms that our holiday was over. "I know you people feel letdown about the canceled raid. I know you are impatient for action, that you feel overstrained . . . well, you can stop feeling sorry for yourselves. You're Rangers! Now that we have had our little fling and it has accomplished nothing but a big zero, we'll get down to the business of soldiering again. We had one mission called off—that doesn't mean that the next one will be called off. We are still on a standby alert from Supreme Headquarters. We may be called today, tonight, tomorrow. Until we are called we are going to continue training. . . . Effective immediately the First Ranger Battalion will train exclusively in night-fighting tactics. We will sleep by day and work by night."

Darby's announcement was received with stony silence. We had expected it and were mentally adjusted to our fate. November, December and half of January we had trained and trained. Combined with our training in Ireland and Scotland we had the staggering total of seven and a half months' intensive training behind us. And still there was no prospect of a letup. Never, since the Rangers were organized, had the future appeared more dismal.

As Darby promised we trained by night and slept by day. Phase Three of Darby's highly dreaded program became known as the Ranger Swing Shift. Night marches, emphasizing compass and stars for guidance, night attacks, concentrating on contact, control and co-ordination, became for us the order of the night. It was during this period that Darby introduced new concepts in night-fighting tactics that later became standard procedure throughout the army.

We learned how to move swiftly over the most difficult terrain and yet keep in close contact with each other. We learned how to walk as noiselessly as panthers, through shrub-splotched fields and pebble-lined gulleys. Through the use of taped flashlights, allowing only a faint pinpoint of light to be seen, we learned how to employ the entire battalion on a massed skirmish line under a pitch-black sky. Darby and Dammer worked out an ingenious system combining radio communications with the pinpointed flashlights. By flashing their lights rearward, away from the enemy, each company commander could reveal the position of his company to the command post. With radio Darby could direct each company commander to the exact position required for the attack, by merely observing the pinpoints of red lights, not visible to the enemy.

During these night problems we traveled with light packs, carrying the barest essentials we would use on an actual raid. An extra pair of socks, a chocolate bar, a shelter half and a toothbrush. Helmets had been discarded. In their place we used woolen skullcaps. This enabled us to hear better and move more swiftly. All loose metal on our weapons and equipment was taped securely to avoid clanking, and our canteen cups were left behind so they wouldn't rattle against our canteens. Even our shoes were saddlesoaped to avoid creaking. And our hands and faces were blackened with mud so that we would blend into the night.

Over and over again our company officers pounded home the key themes of our training. "Contact and control, speed and surprise, endurance and stamina, resourcefulness and initiative"—all the requirements that Darby demanded of us as Rangers were stressed. "The outfit that can choose the most inaccessible route of approach under cover of darkness; the outfit that can arrive on the scene of battle after a grueling march still fresh for battle; the outfit that can slip up on the enemy and stun him with shock and surprise—that is the outfit that will win battles—and that is the outfit I want," Darby repeated to us again and again.

As the training wore on without letup, a dark mood seethed through the battalion. For one thing the long, grueling marches were affecting some of the older men. Legs strong enough to endure all the Commando training and feet callused enough to be immune to blisters were now buckling. Not being able to keep up the daily grind, these Rangers, through no fault of their own, were transferred out to replacement depots for reassignment. Other Rangers, disillusioned about the future prospects of the Rangers and angered at Darby for the incessant, grinding training, began asking for and receiving transfers back to their old units. Because it was a volunteer unit, no man could be held in the Rangers without his consent. The battalion strength was fast declining.

"If this keeps up there won't be anyone left but Darby," one Ranger commented.

"We may not have many battle honors—but when this war is over the Rangers will have the top training honors in the whole Army," another barbed.

Good, trusted, dependable troopers like Sarn't Sieg and Ed Thompson were outwardly fed up, although they weren't prepared to go to extremes. Fuller became more vitriolic, and even Pete Preston, who took everything in stride, admitted that he was "browned off" at Darby.

On the other hand, Deacon Dunn, Randall Harris and Howard Andre openly championed Darby's program. Many times Harris would tell us: "Darby knows what he's doing. There's real purpose in everything we're doing. Let's stick with it, fellows. It'll pay off in battle."

Dunn kept reminding us of history. His favorite example was General Stonewall Jackson's defeat of Union forces at Chancellorsville. "Stonewall marched his barefooted soldiers forty miles and surprised and whipped the Union Forces at Chancellorsville. They did it because they never stopped training. It's obvious that Darby is a keen student of history. He even gets some of his stuff out of the Bible."

Andre, although not quite as vocal, declared, "We're damned lucky to get so many chances to make mistakes in training. We won't get a second chance when the stuff is flying. I'll take all the training Darby can throw at us."

Darby kept pushing us hard. One day after a particularly exacting night problem that saw four men in our platoon drop out, three Rangers went up to Lieutenant Nye and requested immediate transfers. "We've had it, Lieutenant," the spokesman for the three said. "This Ranger business isn't what we were led to believe. We didn't join to keep on training all our lives."

189

Lieutenant Nye calmly asked them if they would wait till after he spoke to the entire platoon, then decide. We gathered around him anxious to hear his views of the developing crisis.

Nye's six-feet-four frame was relaxed as he yanked out a cigarette, lit up, then spoke: "Fellows, the going has been damned rough. I'll be the first to admit it. I'm not talking to you as an officer, but as a fellow Ranger. We all joined this outfit for strong reasons; we all had some pretty fancy notions about what this outfit would be.

"Personally I believe I have with me the best platoon going. We have a damned good combination. But now there are some of us who don't believe the outfit has lived up to expectations and want out. I can only say this: Let's give the outfit a chance in real battle before we decide whether or not it's lived up to what we expected. You've all invested a lot of effort, a lot of guts in the Rangers.

"Personally I believe strongly in Colonel Darby. I think he is driving us to our limits now so he can fully measure our capabilities. He is preparing us so well that when we do see battle, we'll not be hurting a damned bit in any department.

"And let me add this: We have learned to work as a team, how to take care of each other. You're a family. Let's not break it up!

"Think it over, fellows. That's all I have to say."

That's all that was necessary for him to say. Lieutenant Nye never before had made anything resembling a speech other than to brief us or explain a situation. To hear him talk like that moved us profoundly. The three Rangers who wanted to quit stayed on. Even George Fuller quieted down—for a while.

190

CHAPTER 34

ON FEBRUARY 1 a caravan of trucks thundered down the beach strip bringing a hundred and six hand-picked volunteer replacements to bolster the sagging battalion strength. We gave them a rousing Ranger reception. With Tommy guns, BARs and rifles, we splattered the sand under the trucks with live hot bullets. Hand grenades tossed over their heads landed into the sea beyond with terrifying blasts.

"Pour it on, Rangers. Give 'em the works," shouted Torbett, working his rifle furiously.

"They don't know what they're getting into." Another Ranger laughed as he emptied his BAR under the floorboards of a truck.

The trucks stopped as drivers frantically ducked down behind the windshields. Terrified recruits dived into the floor of the trucks, with arms and legs tangled together. One truck driver turned his truck right into the ocean in an effort to get out of the fire. It kept going until the waves washed over the motor and it groaned to a stop.

We were merely giving them a taste of what was in store for them.

When they finally dismounted and lined up amid the heckling and jibes from the entire battalion, they were still trembling.

The training program for these new replacements had barely commenced, when Phil Stern burst into our quarters with the news that he was leaving with Darby and other Headquarters personnel for Algiers. "The ol' man is going for a conference on our next mission. I think it's Tunisia."

"How come you're going with him? What's he need a camera-man for?" asked Lodge.

Stern laughed. "El Darbo doesn't need a camerman. He just likes my company."

"Don't give us the business, Stern," said Fuller. "You're just going along to take some pictures of Darby doing some sight-seeing in Algiers."

"If it's sight-seeing, it's gonna be a long tour. I'm taking all my gear with me, and so is Darby. . . . Be seeing you guys . . . in Tunisia."

For four days the battalion stood by on alert, then on February 7 the orders came. We were leaving the very next morning for Tunisia by air transport. Nothing was said about the nature of our mission. We were only told that Darby would meet us in Tebessa, the main American base in central Tunisia.

Miraculously the news of imminent action transformed our spirits from moody indifference to zestful anticipation. Emotionally, phys-ically and professionally we were ready. Carlo Contrera was par-ticularly elated because D Company had turned in their heavy mortars and was now an assault company. "Now you just watch D Company go to town. We'll show the rest of the battalion a few things about assault tactics!"

Deacon Dunn, who kept close tabs on the military situation in Tunisia—without encouragement—gave us the lowdown on the American forces. "We're bogged down in Tunisia. The British First Army is fighting in the north, our Two Corps is in central and south Tunisia, holding a line of about two hundred miles. But it's not a front as we think of a front. They call it a fluid front, with scattered strong points. Maybe we'll be used as a raiding force—like Stonewall Jackson's foot cavalry."

George Fuller didn't think so. "We're gonna fight just like the dogfaces. You can kiss the Commando business good-by."

I tried to pry some information from Lieutenant Nye. "It must be a pretty important and urgent mission to fly us in by planes. Do you think we'll be thrown into the lines or pull some raids?"

"Honestly, I don't know. The ol' man's been pretty close with whatever's developin'. But I have a hunch we'll be seeing our kind of action."

192

Phil Stern

Rangers overlook Arzew after the attack.

A "skull session" en route to Arzew. Rangers
doing a final review of their operation orders.

Briefing aboard ship en route to Africa. Capt. Roy Murray, Jr.,
explains details of the impending invasion to Rangers
of F Company.

Fox Company in Arzew.

Phil Stern

Phil Stern

Colonel Darby and Rangers on HMS *Princess Emma* at Arzew.

Rangers rehearse amphibious assaults after the attack on Arzew.

Phil Stern

The battle at Arzew.

Phil Stern

A Ranger guards a camp at El Guettar.

Phil Stern

Relaxation after capturing the harbor of Arzew.

Phil Stern

A mixed session of entertainment between
Rangers and British Commandos.

The rest of the day the Ranger camp bristled with feverish activity. We drew extra rounds of ammo, discarded faulty weapons, drew new ones, drew extra socks, stripped to the barest essentials to be carried in our bedrolls, stacked our barracks bags for storage. Each squad leader checked and rechecked his men, their weapons, their equipment, their battle dress. Nothing was overlooked even to the extent of emptying wallets of letters and printed matter that might reveal information to the enemy.

Once again our time had come.

CHAPTER 35

ANGRY winds ripped through the olive grove, stinging our eyes with fine-grained sand as our trucks ground to a halt in the outskirts of Gafsa. Silently we unwound our aching bodies and leaped to the ground, pulling our weapons and equipment after us. The long plane ride from Oran to Tebessa three days before, the short stay at Tebessa and the grueling all-night truck ride, winding through the tall djebels of central Tunisia were now behind us. Gafsa, a sprawling Arab town, held lightly by some French troops supported by American artillery and tank-destroyer units, was the southernmost anchor of the extended, loosely held American front. Less than seven miles away, perched on the towering heights of El Guettar, the enemy was firmly entrenched.

We moved away from the road into a tangle of bare trees. It was bitter cold, far colder than we expected Tunisia to be. Woolen scarfs and gloves helped but not enough. The chilling winds whipped through our light field jackets and penetrated our khaki shirts and heavy woolen underwear.

"I want every man to dig in. The enemy planes and artillery have been plastering everything around here," Nye said when the platoon halted. "Get a good night's rest. Tomorrow night we raid."

We dug in furiously, thankful for the opportunity to warm up. Wrapped in blankets and shelter halves, we sank into blissful sleep, oblivious of the cold, the bombers and the oncoming raid.

We slept late. At ten o'clock the next morning Torbett's whistle split the air. Each of us bounced up, shaved with the canteen of

194

water allotted, then rushed over to the chow line for steaming coffee and oatmeal.

Phil Stern, a cocky grin on his puss, elbowed his way to where I was sitting with Carlo Contrera. "Well, fellows, this is it."

"This is what?" asked Contrera.

"This is the turning point."

Carlo looked at me quizzically. "What's with this guy?"

"Darby knows it too. He kinda loosened up when we went to Algiers and Tebessa ahead of you guys."

"What did he loosen up with?" I asked.

"Darby said the high brass is giving him a free hand to pull some raids up and down the front. What we do here in Tunisia will decide whether or not the army will organize more Ranger Battalions."

"What does Darby think will happen?"

"He thinks the Rangers will even surprise themselves."

"Surprise themselves how good they are or how lousy they are?" asked Carlo.

"He didn't say. But he didn't seem to be worrying." Stern walked away.

"Big-deal Stern," grunted Carlo. "Always making like he's Darby's right-hand man."

"Stern's got a sense of destiny, Carlo. He sees the big picture."

"Yah, I guess the guy's okay. Me, I got a sense of destiny too— I know I'm gonna wind up at least a sergeant after these raids we pull. Now that we don't have those heavy mortar carts to pull around, I'll show my stuff—one, two, three."

"Then you'll have all the privates bitching at you like you been bitching at sergeants."

"Just let 'em try it. When I'm a sergeant nobody gives me any crap—nobody—unless he's bigger'n me."

It was late afternoon when Captain Roy Murray, flanked by Sergeant Torbett and the two lieutenants, called us together for a briefing. Up to this time we had known little of our over-all mission in Tunisia or the nature of this raid, aside from what Snapdragon had told us. Darby and Dammer we knew were out somewhere making a reconnaissance of the enemy terrain. Torbett held a large map to which Murray pointed as he talked.

"Our first mission is right down our alley. We're hitting three heavily fortified strong points guarding the approaches to Sened Pass. The troops are crack Bersaglieri—supposedly the best in the Italian Army. Behind them the German armored forces are building up for a power punch."

As Murray paused my mind flashed back to the day I had been interviewed by the Ranger officer in Ireland. "How would you feel about fighting the Italians?" he had asked. Now I was face to face with the chilling reality I had always hoped to avoid.

Murray continued: "Sened has been won and lost by our side twice. It's the key to Maknassy plain. The main purpose of this raid is to knock the enemy off balance; to bewilder and confuse and make him think there are more troops in this area than we actually have. Another purpose is the psychological effect it will have on the enemy's entire Tunisian army. We're gonna throw the Commando book at them—bayonets, knives, grenades—the works! Our orders are to terrorize and demoralize to our fullest capacities."

Murray was not smiling as he usually did when briefing us. Never had we seen him so intent nor his speech so crisp. "For this raid only three companies will be used—A, E and F. We'll be carted by trucks twenty-four miles to a French outpost on the edge of our lines. Between the French outpost and Sened are twenty miles of desert and mountains and the area is crawling with enemy patrols. We'll move out from the outpost tonight, then hide in the mountains during the day. We attack tomorrow night."

Using the map he continued to explain the high points of our raid. It was to be a slashing, hit-'em-and-run raid, employing all the techniques of Commando and Ranger night operations. Darby and Dammer would meet us at the French outpost tonight and lead us through the enemy-patrolled mountains to our hidden jump-off point. The final battle plan would be revealed the next day after close-up reconnaissance of the enemy positions. The trucks that transported us to the outpost would go back to Gafsa that night, then return to the outpost to pick us up the following night. They couldn't operate during the day because the entire road was under

196

enemy observation and artillery and exposed to enemy patrols. We were told that a British recon unit was patrolling the area around the outpost.

We listened intently. There was no need to ask questions. Everything was spelled out. Helmets were to be left behind. Only one ration and one canteen of water. No entrenching tools; no extra bandoliers of ammo. We were to be stripped for speed. Only a shelter half, to be used for daytime camouflage, would be carried in our packs.

"There's one thing I want to hammer home," Murray concluded grimly. "We've got to leave our mark on these people. They've got to know that they've been worked over by Rangers. Every man uses his bayonet as much as he can—those are our orders. And remember this: we're only bringing ten prisoners back—no more and no less."

After the briefing we drew our rations, sharpened our knives and bayonets and cleaned each round of ammo meticulously. With a few hours on our hands some of us wrote short V-mail letters, some of us joined Sergeant Torbett in a rip-roaring high-stakes crap game—and many Rangers just wrapped themselves up in their foxholes and tried to sleep. Deacon Dunn, Howard Andre and Sarn't Sieg were in a singing mood. With a half dozen other Rangers they gathered around a brush fire.

> "Oh, I'm a hayseed, a hairy sea weed,
> And my ears are made of leather,
> And they flop in windy weather.
> Gosh, all hemlock,
> I'm tougher'n a pine knot,
> For I'm a Ranger can't you see?"

Song followed song until voices became hoarse. The songfest ended dramatically when Deacon Dunn stood up and recited that famous Civil War poem, "That's Stonewall Jackson's Way":

> "He's in the saddle now, fall in,
> Steady the whole Brigade.

197

Hill's at the Ford, cut off. We'll win
Our way out of ball and blade.
What matter if our feet are torn,
What matter if our shoes are worn,
Quick step, we're with him before dawn,
That's Stonewall Jackson's way."

CHAPTER 36

It was nine-thirty when we lined up to board the trucks that would take us to the French outpost, our jump-off point, twenty-four miles away. The sky was black and starry and the winds whistled with eerie intensity. Our wool-knitted skullcaps were pulled down over our ears, blending with our blackened, tense faces. We looked like zombies.

Sergeant Mulvaney came down the line. "Al, Lieutenant Nye wants you." I followed Mulvaney to where Nye was standing a few yards away from our squad.

Nye pulled us over out of earshot of the others. "Al, Mulvaney has a high temperature. Doc Jarret doesn't think he should go on this raid. . . . I want you to take over the squad."

Stunned I looked at Mulvaney. My first reaction was a hopeless feeling of panic. Me lead the whole squad? Me who was struggling to muster up enough courage for myself, now saddled with the responsibility of twelve men, including two green Rangers! These were my first reactions. But swiftly I was flooded by another line of reactions, the exact opposite. I was yelling about initiative, here was the opportunity to show initiative. This was a challenge! Furthermore, even if I didn't want to take the squad, I couldn't back down now. To refuse to accept responsibility at such a critical time would be the same as cowardice.

All these thoughts crowded my mind for a long moment before I found my voice to answer. "Yes, Lieutenant, I'll do the best I can."

Mulvaney looked at me with a sickly stare. "Been feeling bad

199

for two days but thought I'd be able to make it. I just wouldn't do you fellows any good like this. . . ."

"That's okay, Mulvaney," I said not wanting to prolong the uneasiness.

Nye cut in: "Okay, Al, it's your baby—I'm sure we'll get along fine."

I turned around and moved back to the squad.

"What's up, Al?" Lodge inquired, as they gathered around me.

"Mulvaney's sick. You guys got yourself a new squad leader for this deal."

Lodge thrust out his hand. "Congratulations, Al. We'll all be right in there—you don't have to worry."

Pete Preston added, "Yeah, Al, the best squad in the company ain't gonna let you down." He patted his BAR. "This ol' baby will do a lot of talkin' for you, Al, a lot of talkin'."

"Thanks, fellows, thanks a lot," I answered with a tremendous feeling of gratitude and pride. Their confidence and support at this crucial period seemed to lift a good part of the load off my shoulders. I prayed I wouldn't fail them.

"All right, Rangers. . . . Load up!" Torbett's voice rang out.

Quickly we mounted the open six-by-six trucks and crouched down on the floorboards, guns at the ready, facing toward the outside. We were taking no chances of being caught with our backs toward the enemy in the event of an ambush.

The motors roared, then slowly the long line of trucks moved forward through the pitch-black darkness on the thin ribbon of sandy road that led across the plain of MacKnassy to our destination. Huddled together to keep warm, we were silent, thoughtful, each man wrapped deep in his own private hell, each man probing his inner soul for the strength and courage to prove equal to the battle ahead.

An hour later, after a cold, dusty ride across the flat barren plain, our trucks came to a halt. Barely visible, the outline of a small, stone-walled fort loomed ahead. This was the French outpost where Darby and Dammer were waiting. Swiftly we unwound our cramped legs and jumped to the ground.

"Platoon column of twos," Nye commanded tersely.

Quietly we fell into our places. It seemed strange to me to be at

200

the head of our squad instead of at the tail end. I looked at Ray Rodriguez behind me, his Tommy gun cradled under his arm. Even in the black night his eyes sparkled with bright intensity— eyes that I knew could see better and farther than anyone in the company. I felt good having Ray right next to me.

Nye took his place in front of the platoon behind Murray and Fronk. He turned to me: "We're marching fourteen miles through enemy mountains tonight. Nobody drops out. One straggler caught by the enemy will tip our hand."

I moved down the squad column repeating what Nye told me. Each man nodded his head.

The column moved forward. There was complete silence as we made our way over the pebbled plain. No weapons clanked, no leather creaked. Even our dogtags had been taped to prevent their clinking. The line of a hundred and eighty men led by Colonel Darby slithered ahead like a gigantic black snake. The pace started off mildly, then after three miles over open plain it picked up to a near run. A Company was in the lead, followed by Easy Company.

We all felt good about Easy Company being with us on this raid. Easy and Fox Companies worked well together. We knew each other individually better than we did men in the other companies.

Soon we were in the mountains. Swiftly, without breaking pace, we climbed up winding, steep draws clustered with rocks and boulders. As we climbed higher the air became thinner and our breath shorter, but the pace never slackened. Mountain after mountain we climbed through gorges, crevices and ravines. Occasionally we halted momentarily to boost one another up over small cliffs, then we sprinted to keep up with the Rangers ahead.

A bluish-gray dawn greeted us as we finally wound our way into a large bowl-shaped saddle between two towering peaks. The column slackened its pace and slowly the weaving line of Rangers moved along the inner rim of the saddle, away from the direction of Sened. The column halted.

Lieutenant Nye came down the line with Sergeant Rensink, a large, pleasant-faced Ranger of the second squad. Nye spoke slowly: "Have the men take cover among the rocks, and keep under the shelter halves all day. I don't want anyone moving around, unless absolutely necessary. We're behind their forward

201

lines now. Enemy planes will be scouting all over the area and there's always the chance a patrol might wander up. Put out flank guards down the ravine. Everybody conserve their water and food. When that's gone there isn't any more."

I went back to my squad and passed on Nye's instructions. Immediately they wedged themselves in between rock formations and crevices, covering their bodies completely with shelter halves. I gave Lodge and Ray the first tour of flank guard duty and told them to wake up Fuller and Dunn in two hours for their turn. Then with Pete Preston I eased down between two large boulders and covered myself and went to sleep, hoping I would wake up and find that it was all a dream.

I slept for what seemed an eternity when I felt a hand tugging at my shoulder. The glare of the bright sun blinded me as I rubbed my eyes and looked up to see Sergeant Rensink bending over me. "Nye wants the squad leaders up front. We're gonna take a look at the enemy positions, Al. Darby and Dammer just got back from a recon. . . . They got up real close and got all the dope we need."

"The ol' man went up himself? . . . How close did he get?"

"Close enough to read their mail."

I looked around me. The men in my squad were still huddled under the shelter halves, dead to the world. The entire saddle seemed empty of life. It was hard to realize that a hundred and eighty Rangers were hidden among the rock crevices right in the enemy's front yard. I picked up my rifle and followed Rensink along the outer rim of the saddle, ducking low to keep our silhouettes off the skyline. Finally we came across Lieutenant Nye, Captain Murray and the rest of our squad leaders, crouched low behind some jagged rocks overlooking the enemy plain. Their eyes were glued to field glasses.

Wedging myself between two rocks I pulled out my field glasses, covering the lenses with cupped hands to prevent the sun from flashing. Visibility was perfect. In the distance—six miles east—three gently sloping hills dominated the plain where two roads converged to a juncture. These were the positions we would take. Beyond the three hills I could see a wide split in the background mountains. This was Sened Pass. To the left of the hills some moving objects were stirring up clouds of dust. "The plain is lousy

202

with armored patrols," said Nye. "Darby spotted four of 'em in three hours. They're Jerry armored cars, part of Rommel's Afrika Korps."

As we studied the enemy positions, Murray unfolded the attack plans. I marveled at its simplicity and daring. As darkness approached we would move down from the saddle into the foothills. There we would wait until the moon went down, then we would march on a compass bearing directly on line with the center hill. At six hundred yards from the position our three companies would deploy on a battalion front. A Company would swing far to the left, E Company would be in the center, and our company would be on the right. Controlled by Darby, using the flashlight and radio technique, the three companies would advance silently until we were on top of the Italians. Only then would we open fire. After annihilating the garrison, destroying the cannon and then the supplies, we would withdraw back to the French outpost taking with us only ten prisoners and our wounded.

The enemy, we were told, had at least four machine guns and two cannon on each hill. Each of the three strong points was honeycombed with rifle positions. The troops were hardened veterans of Rommel's Afrika Korps. They were not pushovers. They were expected to fight hard.

"One point I want to stress," Murray concluded, "nobody fires until I give the order. I don't care how much stuff they throw at us. . . . We'll hold our fire till we're right on top of 'em, then every squad is on its own."

The men in my squad listened intently as I repeated what Murray had told us. After I finished Dunn spoke first. "It's a good plan—a typical Commando operation with the Darby touch."

Pete Preston grinned broadly. "Man, there's gonna be more dead Italians piled up in front of our squad than any squad in Fox Company."

George Fuller was skeptical. "I don't like that idea of holding fire till ordered. We may all be dead before we get a chance to open up."

"We'll all be dead if we don't hold our fire," I answered. "We'll be able to see where they are by their gun flashes. They won't know where we are unless we start firing."

203

"You hope!" Fuller added sarcastically.

Ray Rodriguez asked a logical question but one I wished had not been brought up. "How about land mines . . . ?" Land mines were a very likely possibility. I hated the mention of mines. They were my most pressing fear.

"I don't know," I truthfully answered. "Nobody mentioned land mines."

After our discussions ended I moved off from the squad with George Fuller to a rocky crevice where we wouldn't be overheard. Fuller's face was grimly tense and I could see he anticipated what was on my mind. "George," I started, "I want you to do me a favor—cut out your negative bitching in front of the new men. They're having a hard enough time. In fact I think it will help us all if you will just this once keep your bitchin' down."

Fuller glanced at me. "You been on my tail since you took over. Well, you can't buck for those sergeant's stripes on my hide."

My temper flared. I was stunned by his crude assumptions and hurt by his lack of consideration for the job I had on my hands. My first impulse now was to smash him to the ground. But that would accomplish nothing! It would be disastrous to the morale of the entire squad at a time when the highest spirits were needed. Considering these factors, I decided to appeal to his own pride as a squad member, rather than force the issue through mandatory force.

"I'm sorry you said that, George," I said. "There's nothing personal involved. For the good of the squad, let's cut out the guff."

"You sure changed damned fast soon as you took over."

"Look, Fuller, I got a job to do and I need everybody's co-operation. Now knock it off and start soldiering!"

I turned abruptly and walked away, leaving George looking as if I had just asked him to cut his jugular vein—that's how much bitching meant to him.

CHAPTER 37

THE saddle was shrouded with dark shadows when we lined up for the march into the foothills. Once more I checked the squad, repeated instructions. Once more we scooped up handfuls of dirt, spit in it and rubbed it into our faces and hands. I marveled at the seemingly calm, businesslike zest and assuredness with which the members of my squad fell into formation. Some of the fellows seemed downright casual about the whole thing, as though night raids were part of the daily schedule.

Colonel Darby, followed by Major Herman Dammer and the communications sergeant, Dick Porter, a tall strapping blond who had helped conceive the flashlight and radio communications technique, moved past us. Behind them came the ex-cook Sergeant Major Peer S. Buck. Seeing the strident, confident command group zip by was the best morale booster we could have at this time. Darby and Dammer had painstakingly engineered this raid—and now they were personally leading it. Somewhere behind a voice cracked.

"El Darbo hits the trail tonight."

"El Darbo hits the trail again," another voice corrected. "Don't forget he was out there last night and the night before."

The line moved. Like flitting ghouls our black-faced column glided noiselessly down the mountainside. It was dark when we reached our jump-off point on the fringe of the enemy plain. A half moon bathed the area in eerie brightness. Hidden behind a low hill we sank to the ground and waited for the moon to go down.

205

Randall Harris slithered up to my side. "How we doin', Al?" he whispered solicitiously.

"Fine, Harris. How's the mortar squad holdin' up?"

Both greetings were, of course, trite but I appreciated Harris' gesture. I needed some buckin' up myself. "Looks like a good night for a murder, doesn't it, Harris," I tried to kid.

"A mass murder," Harris corrected. "This is just like one of our problems back in Arzew—just think of it that way."

The moon went down, plunging the night into stygian blackness . . . and we were on our feet. Now tense, I followed closely behind the long loping strides of Lieutenant Nye. Ray Rodriguez and the rest of my squad closed up to less than three paces from one another. I knew it was going to be a fast clip over the open plain. Silently we stalked over the pebbled terrain with its occasional splotches of clump grass.

We had marched about a half hour when suddenly the line halted. We hit the ground, rifles at the ready. Nye whispered back to me, "Enemy patrol!" We strained our eyes in trying to probe the black wall around us. A muffled scream pierced the night, followed by complete silence. The Rangers ahead of me got to their feet and started moving as Nye again whispered back: "A Company's scouts got 'em." I knew what that meant. Ranger knives had had their first taste of enemy blood.

The pace picked up. As we drew closer, the frightening sound of enemy tanks could be heard in the distance from beyond Sened. A million thoughts entered my mind. What if the tanks got behind us and cut us off; what if they were lined up in front of the positions waiting for us? It would be a massacre. Swiftly I tried to dismiss these negative reactions from my mind. Darby, I convinced myself, wasn't going to lead his men into an ambush. Darby had made careful reconnaissance and had developed an audacious and foolproof plan. The odds were all in our favor. We had the surprise, we had the initiative and we had the most powerful ally of all working for us—the black night.

It was 0200 hours, just one hour since we jumped off from the foothills when the wraithlike column slackened pace slightly. Nye turned to me: "Pass it back: company in line formation!" I imme-

206

diately turned to Rodriguez, who whispered to Lodge behind him. Company in line formation meant that A Company had swung over to the left toward its objective, while Easy Company had remained in the center. It was now up to Fox Company to wheel around toward the right. Swiftly the Second Section, led by Sergeant Rensink, came up to our left while the Second Platoon, led by Lieutenant Young, moved over to our right, with Murray and Fronk between platoons. The maneuver was completed deftly, without any confusion. It had been one of Darby's favorite experiments back in Arzew, and every Ranger could go through it in his sleep. I could see Murray's pinpointed red light flashing our position back to Darby. The three companies now were marching side by side through total darkness on a half mile front. There was nothing but the enemy six hundred yards ahead.

There was no one in front of me now. Nye had moved over to the left so that he could be directly between my squad and Rensink's squad. We kept our direction between squads by observing Nye's green flashlight pinpoints. The platoon kept its direction by following Murray's red pinpoints. Murray kept the company's direction by following Darby's commands over the radio. From his position in the center and rear, Darby controlled the direction of all three companies, marching steadily toward battle with an enemy we couldn't see.

As we marched closer and closer, it seemed incredible to me that the enemy was completely still. Were they asleep? Any moment I expected to see the sky bathed in a bright flare, exposing us as surely as broad daylight. Any second I expected the chattering of machine guns, the pop of rifles and the boom of cannon. To catch three companies of Rangers on the open plain in front of well-buttressed positions was a defender's dream. But there was nothing but mysterious silence ahead. . . .

Then it happened! The stillness of the night was shattered with a long raking burst of machine-gun fire to our left toward A Company. Like a chain reaction a dozen more machine guns joined in a deadly chorus, spewing out green and red tracers into the plain. Ahead of us, less than fifty yards away, we could hear excited Italians as they scurried around to their positions, but still no fire opened up on us. Relentlessly we moved forward still undetected, though by now the entire front to our left was crisscrossed with searing fire from the enemy.

"*Que va la? . . . Que va la?*" Several voices yelled out to us in Italian. They were confused, but not for long. Almost at once the entire hillside erupted with a terrific roar as thousands of hot searing tracers banshied over our heads and ricocheted into the rocks on the plain beyond us. With the first flash I hit the ground, pulling Ray down with me. The rest of the squad, I could see through the eerie glare of the tracers, were already down. I looked toward Nye, his head buried in his arms, now on the walkie-talkie. After a short moment Nye yelled, "Let's move . . . but hold your fire!"

I took a deep breath and stared ahead into the inferno of molten steel, now stabbing the night with high-pitched frenzy. This was not the Commandos firing. This was not the French. This was for real. This was the enemy!

As I turned my head to shout back, a horrendous blast plowed into the dirt less than two yards to my right. Sharp rocks tore into my legs and a shower of pebbled dirt covered my head. *Whoom!* . . . *Whoom!* . . . Two more shells landed directly ahead of me, then miraculously ricocheted over my head into the black void beyond. The enemy was now raking our lines with direct fire from his 47-millimeter cannon.

I felt naked. There were no rocks to hide behind. There were no helmets to give us the illusion of protection. There was nothing between the enemy's field of fire and our crablike forms. Our only chance was to move forward. I shouted back at the top of my lungs: "Let's go! On your bellies!" As Ray repeated the command to the rest of the squad, I cradled my rifle in my arms and slithered forward into the hell of fire crackling over our heads like a hot blowtorch. I could hear the rest of the squad behind me, grunting, gasping. I could hear the babble of Italian voices ahead, bewildered, shouting commands. And I could hear an occasional cry of pain as some of our men were hit.

For forty yards we crawled under the enemy's searching, scorching fire. Rifles and machine guns spewed out their whining, screaming fingers of death in a crazy chromatic pattern of blues,

208

greens and oranges. Cannon shells *swooshed* by our faces like massive express trains furrowing up rocks and dirt in their spiraling wake. And still we moved forward, shutting out the terrible hell around us as though it didn't exist.

It seemed like a million years before I felt the damp ground rise on the enemy's forward slope. Miraculously we had reached the bottom of his positions, and chattering guns were now stitching their fire harmlessly over our heads. I couldn't see to my right or left, but I could hear the slight sounds of bodies moving up all around. Ray was right behind me, and so was Vernon Lodge. "Get into skirmish lines," I shouted over the crackle of fire. Swiftly the men in my squad slithered up to the protective ground rise and formed in their assault positions.

A long moment passed before I heard Nye's voice over to the left: "You all set, Al?"

"All set," I shouted back.

Another long moment . . . then, "Give 'em hell!" Nye's voice rang out.

"Grenade first," I yelled, as I pulled a pin on my grenade and hurled it up toward the stabbing flames of a machine gun. The explosion threw dirt down on us, and the earth ahead shook convulsively as a dozen other grenades hit home. Swiftly we were on our feet, screaming at the top of our lungs, charging up the slopes, firing our rifles and Tommy guns from our hip.

Tracers stabbed out from the black void in front of us. Rifles barked and automatic weapons rattled caustically. The crash and roar of battle swelled to a thunderous din as we wove up the slope like crafty Indians toward the flickering orange flashes.

Fear had no meaning. I was now a black-faced, conscienceless killer, and my only thought was to destroy the tormentors who had given me my first vivid impressions of hell. Gone too were my silly compunctions about fighting Italians. If my own brothers had shot at me like this, I would be just as anxious to kill them as these faceless people.

Ray Rodriguez was alongside me when I came on the first machine-gun position. The gunner was firing aimlessly over our heads, unaware that we had crawled right under his position. Ray, less than a foot from the muzzle blast, just stood up and sprayed the gunner with a sharp Tommy-gun burst as I fired three shots into the gunner's assistant. They never knew what hit them.

We moved swiftly up the slope toward other gun flashes. I could hear the shouts of other Rangers to my right and left and the blood-curdling screams of Italians as Ranger bayonets found their marks. Lodge was now on my right. I could see him firing his rifle with methodical efficiency. The sharp staccato of Preston's BAR sounded next to Lodge. I could hear Dunn's voice yelling far to the right, *"Yarrr, yarrrr,"* his own war cry. I couldn't see him, but I had the intuitive feeling that he was not neglecting his bayonet drill.

There was no time to check my squad to see who was where. The battle was on. Each Ranger knew what his role was. It was attack and kill everything in front of you. I wondered, however, how Fuller was making out with Hermes.

Now the enemy was screaming. Shrill cries of *"Non Fiermati! Non Fiermati!"* bleated all around us. I could tell by the flashes of our own gunfire and the roaring, cursing shouts of Rangers that our entire company was sweeping up the slopes in an unbroken, unremitting line. The first terrace of the slope was cleared but above us several machine guns and both 47-millimeter cannon were still blasting away. Somehow in moving up the hill I had veered toward the left, near Sergeant Rensink's squad. I could hear him yelling to his men as they surged ahead abreast of my squad. Suddenly a blast from a 47-millimeter cannon directly overhead illuminated a patch of hill just long enough for me to recognize Garrison, firing on his knees toward the cannon. I was two feet to his right when another horrifying blast *swooshed* by me, followed by a brilliant, bluish flash that revealed Garrison still on his knees— but without his head.

A booming explosion from one of our grenades silenced the gun as I continued upward, stepping on squashy bodies, slithering on squirming entrails. A blast from a concussion grenade picked me up, lifted me through the air and hurled me down with a crash flat on my back. Millions of shimmering silver dots whirlpooled around in my head as I staggered to my knees in time to see a dark form hurtling toward me. Instinctively I pumped three shots into the blurry form, then sidestepped as it crashed to the ground. A bluish flame flickered from a hill rise directly above me. Still hazy, I moved up, yelling like a demented savage, and then I felt myself falling.

I tried to check myself but coudn't. Before I knew it I found myself in a deep slit trench, wedged in face to face with an Italian soldier. He was as surprised as I was. He just stood there for a long moment transfixed. My rifle was still in my hand but the trench was too narrow for me to bring it to my hip and fire. In that flashinglong second of indecision I nearly panicked. Then I remembered my Commando knife snugly sheafed around my right leg. Almost mechanically I released my grip on my rifle, reached down, gripped the handle of my knife, then with a lightning thrust brought it up with all my strength into his stomach. *"Mamma mia,"* he cried. *"Mamma mia."* I felt the hot blood spurt all over my right arm as I pulled the knife out, then rammed it home again and again. As the body sagged and slid to the ground, I reeled and vomited.

I climbed swiftly out of that gruesome hole in time to crash shoulders with Vernon Lodge, who was firing his M-1 like a slow-paced machine gun. "You okay, Al?" Vernon shouted as we moved forward toward another flash of gunfire. . . .

"I'm all right," I answered as a tremendous blast detonated on our right.

A piercing howl erupted, followed by George Fuller's voice: "They got Pete Preston. . . . Let's give it to the bastards."

Without breaking pace we swarmed over the remaining centers of resistance, grenading, bayoneting, shooting, screaming, cursing and grunting. The remaining Italians never had a chance. We worked them over furiously, giving no quarter. We had taken all they could throw at us. Now it was our turn to dish it out. . . . It was sickening, it was brutal, it was inhuman, but that was our job—and we were stuck with it.

Now the enemy's guns were no longer crackling. Now the air was filled with the screams of their wounded and the cries of Rangers calling for medics. Now the sound of Torbett's lusty voice could be heard: "Don't kill 'em all—we need some prisoners."

Lodge and I reached the last of the enemy's dugouts in our path. Two Italian soldiers were standing with their hands over their heads, begging for mercy in Italian. Only then did we stop killing.

As suddenly as it had started the crackle of fire ebbed and died. Only the moans of the wounded and voices of Rangers checking their men could be heard as Lodge and I prodded our prisoners down the slopes. We bumped into Harris coming out of a bunker with pistol in hand. Harris was a mortar sergeant whose position was supposed to be down on the plain with his squad. Lieutenant Nye came up at the same time. "What are you doin' up here?" Nye asked Harris.

"We shot up all our mortars, Lieutenant, so I just joined the shoot."

When we reached the bottom of the slope George Fuller and a medic were working on Pete Preston, who was lying flat on his stomach with his shirt ripped off. The medic was taping bandages on his back. "How's it going, Pete?" I asked.

Pete looked up, winced, then grinned: "I sure made that BAR talk, Al . . . it was just startin' to sit up and growl when that lousy grenade landed on top my back. My pack caught the blast—they can't kill this ol' coal miner."

George on his knees spoke up. "Ol' Pete dug into those Eyeties like he was digging West Ginny coal."

Torbett's voice cracked through the still night. "All squads fall back to the medic post with wounded and prisoners." Twice he repeated the order as Rangers in groups of two and three scurried down the slopes, carrying their wounded and prodding their prisoners.

Ray Rodriguez and Vernon Lodge came up with two Italians between them who kept saying *"Non uccidere, Non uccidere!"* (Don't kill.) I quickly assured them in my broken Italian that they were not going to be killed unless they didn't keep their mouths shut.

Howard Andre with some other men of Rensink's squad came up with more prisoners.

"Boy, you're a loud mouth, Al. You must have alerted the whole German army with those weird yells."

212

"They said terrorize. That's what I tried to do!"

"Yes, them, not us!"

Dunn and two other men in our squad came down the slope as two loud explosions rent the air. The enemy's 47-mm. cannon were being destroyed.

Now our only concern was to get the hell out of there before the German forces behind Sened counterattacked. All my men were accounted for and I breathed a sigh of relief. Only one man wounded. I felt good about my whole squad. They had moved up that slope with deadly precision. I was amazed how easy my job as squad leader had been. Every one of them had been self-sufficient, requiring no further commands once the attack was launched. I felt particularly good about George. His attitude had changed surprisingly. I could only reason that it was mainly because of the opportunity to unlease his bottled-up fury and frustrations on the enemy.

By some strange miracle every Ranger reunited with his own squad in the pitch-black darkness. By the time we reached the medic post where Doc Jarret and his aides were working frantically on the wounded, my whole squad was assembled. Eighteen Rangers had been wounded. Some could walk with assistance. Some were badly mangled from grenades, machine guns and cannon fire and would have to be carried the entire twenty miles to the French outpost. Fox Company had seven wounded and I had seen Garrison killed. One man, Garland Ladd, of the Second Platoon, had his left foot shot off at the ankle. Swiftly, under the calm supervision of Doc Jarret, the men were patched up as best as humanly possible in the black night. We improvised stretchers for the badly wounded, using shelter halves and rifles.

More wounded were still limping in when Colonel Darby came up to the medic post with Major Dammer. His voice sounded sharp and exultant as he spoke to Murray and Schneider. "A helluva shoot . . . every company came through . . . a beautiful job. Now we got to get our tails out of here."

Darby looked at his watch. "Two and a half hours till dawn. . . . We've got to move these wounded men back to that outpost or we'll be cold bait out there. We'll split up into two columns. One

213

column will speed back before dawn . . . the trucks'll be waitin'—
they can hightail it to Gafsa. The second column will carry and
protect the wounded. I want volunteers for the second column.
Dammer, you take the first column. I'll take the second. . . ."

CHAPTER 38

THE nightmare of the raid was nothing compared to the agonizing, harrowing forced march across the spines of the rugged mountain range. Each one of us took turns carrying stretchers, supporting walking wounded and pulling rear-guard duty. Step by step, slowly, painfully we inched our way up steep mountainsides, slid down precarious draws and trotted across occasional level expanses of terrain in a desperate effort to make time. Our throats were parched, for what little water we had was given to our wounded. Our hands were blistered raw from holding rifle stretchers and our backs ached from the sheer weight of our burdens.

Back behind us toward Sened, the loud roars of enemy tanks could be heard throughout the march back. The enemy had been stunned by the lightning attack. Finding his three strong points littered with its dead defenders he would quickly evaluate that a strong raiding force had uncoiled like a whip from the mountains and was now speeding back. He would come barreling down the road—the long route skirting the mountains—with his tanks, his trucks and his mobile artillery. His planes would search the mountains while his armor probed the plains. He might even press forward as far as the outpost . . . and if he did we Rangers would have had it.

With these thoughts in our minds we pushed on, calling upon every inner resource, every ounce of courage and strength and faith to get ourselves and our wounded safely over those fiendish mountains that yesterday had been our closest ally and tonight were our

215

bitterest enemy. Again and again, as I struggled along, Lieutenant Cowerson's words kept echoing in my mind. "It's all in the mind and the heart. You can do the impossible if the mind and heart will it." Now I knew why our Commando instructors had hammered home the importance of tenacity, stamina and endurance. Now I fully understood Darby's unrelenting insistence on physical conditioning and night training. And now I was thankful that the man who had organized and trained our outfit was with us, exhorting everyone to push on to our fullest capacities.

Darby was magnificent. His very presence gave us amazing strength, both morally and physically. He took turns carrying stretchers. He did his best to cheer the wounded. Up and down the strung-out column he ranged, giving an encouraging word here, a reassuring pat there, a spirited challenge wherever and whenever needed. To Sergeant Butt Torbett he shouted, "Sergeant, you're walking like you still have that Commando lead in your rear!" To another Ranger, near collapse: "Our Commando friends should see us now! They'd learn a thing or two about mountain marching." Once he came alongside me and Fuller struggling with Pete Preston: "Take it easy with that Ranger: you're treating him worse than the enemy."

The wounded were magnificent too. Without a whimper they clenched their teeth as we jostled them up and down the mountains. Pete Preston, delirious with fever, never once complained, although he kept urging us to leave him behind and get away while we could. Several other Rangers on our makeshift stretchers kept moaning to their carriers to leave them. Garland Ladd, the fellow who had had his foot blown away, kept saying, "You guys are nuts foolin' around with me. I knew what the score was when I joined."

We knew what he meant. When he had first joined the Rangers, we were told that we shouldn't expect to be evacuated on hit and run raids. Wounded Rangers would only encumber the getaway of able-bodied troops and risk the capture of all. We all knew well enough that this was the unwritten code of our trade. But no Ranger from Darby on down would have considered following that code—not while there was the slimmest chance of pulling them through with us. Anyone left behind in those hills, we knew, would be killed by the enemy, after what we had done to his forces.

216

The sun was just coming up over the gray peaks in the east when the first limping Rangers cleared the last of the mountains and reached the pebbled desert plains. Slowly, painfully, the long, strung-out column snaked its way out of the last winding ravine. The worst was over but we still had six miles between us and the French outpost, six miles over open terrain under the hot glare of the morning sun.

Darby, his blackened face now glistening with sweat, his uniform ripped and tattered, stood at the foot of the mountains, waiting for the last of the stragglers to come down. As Fuller and I approached with Pete I could hear him shout to the men ahead. "Now we can march, fellows, now we can make time. Keep pushin'." Soon we were abreast of Darby. "How many more behind you, Altieri?" he called.

"Captain Murray and Lieutenant Nye are bringing up the rear with Torbett. The wounded are all through by now."

"Good . . . now stretch those legs, Rangers . . . eat up that ground!"

Spurred by Darby we stretched our legs and we ate up that desert plain as if the very devil was at our heels. Sleepless and aching from hunger and thirst, we marched the remaining six miles, carrying the wounded, prodding the prisoners, in a little less than two hours. When the French outpost finally came into view at the bottom of another mountain range, we saw several armored cars of the British Recon unit moving out to meet us. The worst was over. Now all we had to worry about was a counterattack against the outpost. We knew that the trucks that had sped the first column back toward Gafsa before dawn could not return until night to pick us up. We were still twenty-four miles away from our main lines.

The French soldiers gave us some hot broth and bread, which we devoured like animals. There were blankets and medical supplies for the wounded. Doc Jarret and his aides now went to work in earnest to try to save those critically wounded. The ten prisoners, several of whom were wounded, huddled in a corner of the courtyard under heavy guard.

The courtyard of the French outpost teemed with tired, tattered but still excited Rangers. The sheer joy of being alive, the exuberance of complete victory, completely overshadowed the seriousness

217

of our predicament. The hot broth had pulsed new vigor into our depleted systems and lifted our morale tremendously. There wasn't much we could do but wait, rest and try to collect a comprehensive picture of our smashing raid.

Rangers talked freely. From Fronk we learned that Captain Murray had stumbled into a machine-gun nest and wiped it out singlehandedly. Moving on up the slope Murray had captured two prisoners and turned them over to Torbett for safekeeping. "But, Captain," Torbett answered, "I want to do a little fightin' too."

Fronk, who carried the walkie-talkie for Murray, also filled us in on Darby's impatience about the 47-millimeter gun still firing blasts into his command post. "When are you people going to knock out that cannon?" Darby had demanded.

Just then Pop Ferrier and Sergeant Ed Thompson parked two grenades into the gun position with shattering blasts. "Cannon reached and destroyed, sir," Murray promptly answered.

Fronk didn't tell us about himself, but we learned from Sergeant Torbett that Fronk had not confined his duties to being Murray's runner. Junior Fronk, the baby of the Rangers, had kept close behind Murray and twice had sprayed Italians that Murray had bypassed.

From the men of Able and Easy Companies the stories were the same but with different variations. These companies, encountering stiff opposition, had swept up the slopes with relentless fury, silencing everything in front of them. The results of the raid were far beyond expectation. Counted dead were over a hundred Italians, and innumerable wounded had been left behind on the slopes. Destroyed were six cannon and twelve machine guns. The heavy barrages from our mortars destroyed completely their motor park behind the hills.

Only one Ranger was killed—Elmer Garrison. His premonition of death had been ironically fulfilled.

All day we remained at the French outpost, sweating out the enemy tanks that never came. Word was reported back by the British Recon unit that enemy tanks were spotted moving toward us, but for some mysterious reason had stopped and turned back toward Sened. Darby wisely assumed that the enemy was still confused, was wary of being hit by larger forces if he ventured out

218

further. Possibly the enemy was now on the defensive, assuming that the Americans were preparing for a major attack. If so, we had fulfilled our mission to the letter—to confuse, terrorize and demoralize.

It was two hours after dusk when the roar of our trucks sounded. Our purgatory of suspenseful waiting was at an end.

CHAPTER 39

THE thunder of falling bombs mingled with the tormenting drone of enemy planes as our trucks came to a halt in the olive grove. Clustered flares dropped by the bombers bathed the Ranger bivouac area in an eerie, yellowish half light, revealing dark forms scurrying for cover. The harsh metallic clack of our .50-caliber machine guns rose to crescendo volume as tracers stabbed skyward groping for the invisible invaders. Our tense, chilly ride from the French outpost to Gafsa had ended ironically with a bitter reception.

"Hit the dirt!" roared Torbett as he bounded out of the cab of our truck. He could have saved his breath. We bolted out of those trucks in a mad scramble and clawed into the ground, covering our helmetless heads with ours arms.

"This is a helluva way to die after what we been through," roared Sarn't Siego, half in jest and half in earnest. . . .

Crrruuumphhh . . . crummmmmmpphh—two whistling bombs crashed less than a hundred yards away, shaking the ground convulsively. Rocks and bits of trees showered down on us and acrid smoke left us coughing in spasms. Fortunately our wounded had arrived ahead of us and were now en route to the field hospital on the other side of Gafsa.

Two more bombs fell close by. "Winged retribution for our evil deed." Dunn laughed sardonically.

For ten long minutes the bombing continued as we remained frozen on the cold ground. Each terrifying explosion filled me with the most frightening fear I had ever known. My already frazzled

220

nerves were near the breaking point. Nobody wants to die under any circumstances. But to die by enemy bombs so soon after our harrowing raid was bitter irony. It wasn't fair. What right did the Luftwaffe have to punctuate our mission with a severe plastering? If I had to die, I would have much preferred getting it on the field of battle against an enemy soldier than getting killed impersonally by bombs dropped from the heavens. And even if the fates of war were so unkind that we must die by bombs, then at least they should allow us a good night's sleep and a good breakfast before doing us in. These were some of the far-fetched thoughts that crowded my mind as the blasts came closer and closer.

Thankfully the earth ceased its convulsive shudderings and the drone of planes faded away in the night. Relieved we stood up, brushed ourselves off and began checking our casualties. "Anybody hit in the Second Platoon?" Lieutenant Young's voice sounded off first.

"Who got it in the First Platoon?" Nye asked anxiously.

One by one squad leaders sounded off that all were unharmed. Suddenly Fronk's voice yelled. "Hey, fellows—Ol' Butt Torbett is our only casualty . . . he dived into a latrine instead of a slit trench."

Our roars of laughter took the edge off our tension. "Poor Torbett . . . he always gets the crappy end of the deal!"

Nye's voice again sounded off. "There's coffee and chow at the field kitchen for those who want it."

Most of us, although hungry, were too tired even to think about food. All we wanted was to curl up and sleep a million years, and try to forget the gory experience we had miraculously survived.

Stumbling through the bivouac area I found my foxhole and sagged into it, covering myself with a dew-frosted blanket. I was too tired to wipe the black mud off my face. I closed my eyes and tried to sleep—but I couldn't. The built-up terror and suspense of the raid, the close call of the enemy bombing, converged on me with shuddering impact. Garrison's headless body kept flashing in my mind, and his words back at Arzew kept echoing: "I know I'm gonna be next." Then the agonized face of the Italian I killed with my knife loomed into focus. *Mamma mia! Mamma mia!* I kept hearing. His sticky blood was still on my sleeve. Over and over I relived every horror of the preceding nights.

I couldn't believe that I—who couldn't stand the sight of a chicken being killed when I was a kid—had actually killed another human being with a knife. I felt stained, sodden, guilty. I had seen war in its most intimate brutal form—close fighting face to face—and I was full of revulsion at its ugliness.

All night long I tried to take my mind off the raid but I couldn't. I tried to think of peaceful days before the war; I tried to muster up all the pleasant experiences I had enjoyed during my twenty-two years of life, but I couldn't erase the gruesomeness of the raid. I knew it would be indelibly seared in my being for a long time to come.

Strangely my real crisis as a soldier and a Ranger—my real battle—did not occur during the raid. It was determined this night as I shivered under a thin blanket in the cold Tunisian dirt. Again and again I reasoned with myself that when I first joined the Rangers I knew what the score was. Hadn't the officer asked me if I would be able to kill a man with a knife? Hadn't I blithely told him I could do it? "What's the difference in killing with a knife or a bullet? They die all the same," I had reasoned. But I had found there was a difference, a big difference. A bullet was clean and less personal. Blood didn't bespatter you when you fired a bullet. You didn't hear your victim scream when a bullet thudded into his body.

It was one thing to conjure up pictures of Rangers as hard-hitting, bayonet-wielding Commandos marauding in the black night, putting terror in the enemy's hearts—but it was another thing physically to experience plunging a knife in another human's stomach.

But as much as I hated killing by the knife, as much as I knew I would be tormented with gruesome memories, I knew that I must and would continue the war with the Rangers. I had seen and experienced enough on that raid to know that I was in one of the best-trained, best-led and best-spirited outfits in the Army. I knew that Darby, although an exacting, firm and resolute leader, was a brilliant planner who made careful reconnaissance before he committed his men to battle. Our leaders had proved that they were men of personal daring. And Darby's concern over the wounded men, staying with them till the last had reached the safety of the outpost, proved he was a man with heart and compassion, genuinely concerned for the well-being of his men.

222

For these reasons I knew, that night as I lay shivering in the foxhole, that the die was cast as far as I was concerned. I had too much at stake in the Rangers. My natural abhorrence for killing was a price I had to pay to keep that stake. And I was comforted that I wasn't the only Ranger that hated to kill with the knife. Vernon Lodge, the mild-mannered, sensitive musician who went up those slopes so relentlessly, I was sure hated it as much as I. Lieutenant Nye, the quiet, even-voiced Nebraskan, who emptied his pistol in a foxhole full of Italians, wasn't the cold-blooded killer type either. And who could imagine little Junior Fronk or the loud Torbett as ruthless toughies? But they did kill and killed well because that was their job, and that's the way I must look at it. We were specialists in a certain kind of combat that we alone had mastered.

We were now bloodied in the goriest type of fighting in the world. From now on there would be no illusions about what the future held for the Rangers and what would be expected of each man who wished to remain with them. The personal price was high, but so were the compensations—the self-satisfaction that one could keep up with the best in the Army, the knowledge that Ranger tactics were one of the most effective ways to defeat the enemy, shorten the war and save lives; the exhilarating comaraderie that comes only to soldiers who believe in their leaders and believe in the men they are fighting with. These factors, I reasoned, more than compensated for my revulsion of knife killing. With these thoughts on my mind I finally dozed off into a merciful sleep.

CHAPTER 40

IT WAS noon the next day when I finally woke up. Rangers were scurrying toward the chow line, their faces clean and freshly shaven. As I threw the blanket aside and stood up, I saw Howard Andre's tall angular figure moving toward me, a messkit jangling in his hand. "Hey, Sleephappy, snap out of it. Ol' Smiley's serving up steak today."

"Steak! Right here on the front?" I asked incredulously.

"Yep, and that's not all. General Fredendall, the big chief in Tunisia, is coming down to pass out some medals. He wanted to do it this morning, but El Darbo said nothing doing, not until the boys have had some rest. How do you like that? Ol' Darby tells generals when they may come to unload their hardware."

I liked that. It was characteristic of Darby's concern for his men. Andre's mustache-topped lips were smiling broadly and his eyes crinkled as he continued: "Looks like the big brass is really shook up over our night party. They usually take months to hand out medals."

"You're right up with the scuttlebutt," I answered. "I thought Snapdragon Stern was the only guy who knew what was cooking."

"Well, like Stern always says, 'I get around!'" replied Andre as he walked away.

Swiftly I picked up my helmet, poured water from a nearby can, washed the mud off my face and sponged the caked sweat off the upper part of my body. Without using a mirror—because I had forgotten to pack one—I shaved rapidly, nicking my face badly. I

224

didn't put the bloody shirt back on. Instead I put on my field jacket over my brown undershirt. I didn't want to see that shirt again, nor did I want any other GI to wear it again after it was cleaned. So I sprinkled some lighter fluid over it and watched it burn into black, evil-smelling smoke. Feeling refreshed and cleansed, I hurried over to the chow line.

The chow line was buzzing with excitement as I took my place at the end. Rangers who had been on the raid were being pumped for information by those who had not. Buddies were shaking hands and many of the Raiders were telling of their close calls. For the first time men were openly expressive of their admiration for Darby.

I caught the tail end of the conversation of the Ranger in front of me with his two buddies. "I always thought that kind of leader was only in the history books, but believe me, brother, after the ol' man's performance last night, I'm sold on him! He could lead me right into hell—and I'd be right there behind him."

Another Ranger eating chow on the sidelines was telling about his commander, Max Schneider: "So Darby says on the walkie-talkie, he says, 'Max, how many prisoners you got?' Well Cap'n Max says right back to him: 'Sir, I got two.' But just then these two Eyeties make a fast break for it and Cap'n Max just nailed 'em with two shots, then he yells back in the radio: 'That is, I had two, sir!' "

I heard Sarn't Sieg up ahead put in a good word for his mortar crew: "I'm up there on the top of the hill radioing fire instructions back to Ryan and Gallup. Two rounds and they're zeroed right in on that motor park. So I tell my crew to lay it on. Throw in the kitchen sink too, I says. . . . They do—the next thing I know the motor pool is now a junkyard."

"Man, those tracers made so much light you could have read a paper . . . that is, if you had had the paper and felt like readin'."

Smiley the cook was all smiles as he forked two huge steaks into my plate. "There's more where that came from. Eat up, buddy," he exhorted each Ranger as though nothing were too good for the famished warriors.

With my messkit loaded, I sank to the ground, crossed my legs like an Indian and tore into the steak. But before I had eaten two chunks, Carlo Contrera came running up. "Hey, Altieri, I heard

225

you guys really knocked the piss out of those Berr—Berr shag-mieri. . . ."

"You mean Bersaglieri," I said.

"Yeah, that's them, those Bersaglieri. My ol' man used to tell me about 'em—them guys wear the feathers in their hats when they go marching. They're really big shots in Italy."

I dug into another mouthful of steak as Carlo continued: "Say, how do you like them apples? Nobody tells us a thing about the big deal. Suddenly we hear that A, E and F Companies go tearing off on a raid. They just sneak away from the rest of the outfit and leave us behind. A helluva note . . ."

"Don't worry, Carlo, your turn will be next."

"Yah, but it ain't like being the first to draw blood—you guys get all the glory."

"If it's glory you can have it."

"Ahhh, I'm just kiddin'. What I mean is, you know—you guys kinda set the pace. Now the rest of us got to prove ourselves too. You got your first deal over with, but we're still sweatin' ours out."

Phil Stern and Howard Andre, with a strange sergeant, spotted us and came over. I noticed the sergeant had a combat correspondent's patch on his right shoulder. "Hey, fellows," Stern bellowed. "Meet Sergeant Ralph Martin. He's with *Stars and Stripes*. Gonna write up a story about the raid with my pictures."

"Whadda ya mean your pictures?" growled Contrera. "You wasn't on the raid."

"Wait a minute, fellows. I didn't mean pictures of the raid. I mean he's gonna use some of the shots I already took, some close-ups, some training shots, to go along with the article."

Poor Snapdragon was squirming uncomfortably. He wasn't used to being on the defensive, especially when he had no reason to be. Stern hadn't been included simply because he wasn't considered essential to the nature of the mission, which demanded that every Ranger contribute the maximum of firepower and mobility. Furthermore, he couldn't have taken any pictures at night.

But Contrera wouldn't let up. "How come, Stern? You're supposed to be Darby's righthand man. How come you miss out on the big deal?"

Stern laughed uneasily. "Well, Carlo, it's like this—Darby's sav-

226

ing me for the real big show. This was only a warmup. He didn't wanna waste his first team on the first little deal."

Carlo winked slyly, then poured it on without mercy. "Big-deal Stern. Darby oughta send you right out there to Sened all by yourself to take pictures of what's left of the joint. Anybody can take trainin' shots."

Stern ignored him and asked if we would give Sergeant Martin some information for his article, personal impressions. Few of us had much to say . . . not right then. Finally, after some hard digging, Sergeant Martin jotted down some notes and ended by saying he would try to capture the spirit and daring of the raid. "Just pin to story on Darby," said Andre with finality. "You'll have all the spirit and daring you'll need."

"Yeah," growled Contrera, juggling his Commando knife. "And if you don't come up with a good story, you'll be next on our list."

Stern and Sergeant Martin moved on to another cluster of Rangers as Deacon Dunn ran up excitedly. "Hey, you should have heard what Axis Sally just said about us over the radio. She called the Rangers 'Black Death.' She said we're all a bunch of gangsters and convicts. Darby was listening too. He just laughed and said: 'Well, I guess we made a bit of an impression on them.' "

"What else did she say?" Andre prodded.

"She said that no Ranger will ever be taken prisoner—they'll be killed like they killed the Italians."

"Ha! As if they'll ever get us," Andre laughed.

"You guys sure stirred up a hornet's nest," added Contrera. "Too bad I wasn't on that raid, then they would be right in calling us gangsters."

CHAPTER 41

THE rumble of heavy guns thundered in the distance as Torbett called the company to formation and marched us down to a clearing between two rows of olive trees. The rest of the battalion was already there, formed in a huge semicircle, facing a cluster of officers standing with Colonel Darby. The battalion adjutant, Captain Karbel, and Major Dammer stood alongside Darby. Behind them at a distance of three or four paces stood General Fredendall, with members of his staff. Torbett led us to the left flank of the semicircle, and our two lieutenants took their places in front of the company.

"Men to be decorated, front and center," Major Karbel's voice boomed.

Immediately Sergeant Rensink, Pop Ferrier and Captain Roy Murray moved forward and took their places in front of Darby. The group was joined by Captain Max Schneider and Rangers from Easy and Able Companies.

As the men to be decorated stood at attention, Major Karbel sounded off, reading from special orders he held in his hand. It was surprising that in less than twenty-four hours since we returned from the raid, citations were already written. Someone in Headquarters must have stayed up all night.

"The following enlisted men and officers were awarded the Silver Star for gallantry in action . . ."

"Gerrit J. Rensink, Sergeant, Company F. Under heavy fire from two places, single-handed, Sergeant Rensink charged one en-

228

emy position and reduced their resistance. . . . With fixed bayonet he continued the assault on the second position and then destroyed the enemy. Sergeant Rensink's devotion to duty and display of courage was an inspiration to all members of his section which was directly responsible for the successful raid conducted by his group. . . ."

"Austin W. Low, Technician 5th Grade, Company F. Corporal Low came to the aid of his Browning automatic rifle operator when he was wounded in action, carried him to cover, then manned the gun and continued the assault. His action was directly responsible for clearing out a machine-gun position and allowing the advance of our troops without loss."

"Leslie M. Ferrier, Pfc., Company F. Pfc. Ferrier charging a 47-millimeter gun position with a hand grenade was individually responsible for destroying the gun that was holding up the advance."

"Roy A. Murray, Captain, Company F. Captain Murray led his company in the assault of the high ground which was protected by machine gun and cannon replacements. He was personally responsible for the mission of knocking out a .50-caliber machine gun. . . . The courage and leadership of Captain Murray inspired great effort on the part the men in his company played, which is highly commendable."

"Max F. Schneider, Captain, Company E. Captain Schneider displayed courage and devotion to duty while leading members of his company on a frontal attack which held up the advance of our forces. Captain Schneider's leadership and direction inspired confidence among the men of his unit to carry off their successful assignments which is deserving of the highest praise. . . ."

Captain Karbel continued reading citations as General Fredendall moved down the ranks, pinning on medals, shaking hands vigorously with each Ranger. "Donald G. McCollam, Sergeant, A Company . . . Owen E. Sweasey, T/S, E Company . . . Edwin L. Dean, Pfc., E Company . . . Joseph Dye, Pfc., E Company . . . Jacques M. Nixon, Pfc., E Company . . . Leonard F. Dirks, First Lieutenant, A Company . . . Mervin T. Heacock, Sergeant, A Company.

"Herman W. Dammer, Major. Major Dammer executed the details of the plan and personally led part of the battalion in the attack set down by the commanding officer. . . ."

After General Fredendall pinned the last of the Silver Stars on Major Dammer, the men saluted and withdrew back to their respective companies. With Darby and staff following, the general walked closer to the huge semicircle of Rangers and spoke.

The general congratulated each Ranger for his part in the raid and emphasized how its success had exceeded all expectations. He stressed the great confusion and terror which would follow as reports of the carnage left by the Rangers circulated through the enemy's ranks. He also mentioned how essential the capture of the prisoners were, which enabled our G-2 to gain much valuable information on the German and Italian units massing on the Tunisian front. He ended his talk by saying that the entire American Army in Tunisia was stirred by the Ranger exploits, and thus our action greatly contributed to the over-all morale.

Then the general turned toward Darby, smiled slyly and beckoned him front and center. Darby moved forward with alacrity, and stood at attention, his arms straight by his side, his shoulders back, a picture of strength, purpose and assuredness.

General Fredendall reached into his pocket and pulled out another Silver Star.

"I'm sure that you men will agree with me that Colonel Darby, your brave commander, is deserving of the Silver Star."

The general's words were drowned out with a thunderous and rousing roar, as, to a man, every Ranger, whether he had been on the raid or not, shouted his approval. Smiling broadly, General Fredendall pinned the medal on Darby, shook his hand, waited for the shouts to die down, then said:

"Now that I've had my pleasure pinning these medals on you people, now you can get back to the most pressing business on hand—the killing of more Germans and Italians. Now you can show them how appropriate that name is they call you—Black Death."

Darby saluted. General Fredendall returned the salute, then, followed by his staff, he made his way through the olive trees to his waiting jeep.

Darby, his face now showing deep emotion, spoke out for the first time. "I want to say this, Rangers. I'm damned proud to command this battalion. I told you back in Arzew, among other things,

230

that the outfit that could slip up on the enemy and stun him with shock and surprise—that is the outfit that will win battles, and that was the outfit I wanted. Well . . . I can tell you fellows right now: after Sened . . . that is the outfit I know I now have!"

Once again the battalion roared en masse. Never before had Darby so well exhibited his personality, his strident poise. And we loved it.

"You men have proved to me that commanding the Rangers is like driving a team of spirited horses. No effort is needed to get them to go forward . . . the problem is to hold them in check."

With his last sentence left hanging in air, Darby abruptly did a sharp half turn and strode out of the clearing, leaving behind five hundred cheering Rangers who from that day on would never doubt, never falter, never complain and always follow wherever and whenever Darby led.

PART II

"And the Rangers Will Lead the Way...."

CHAPTER 42

WE DIDN'T get much time to rest up after the Sened raid. Two days later—on Saint Valentine's Day—Rommel's Afrika Korps hurled several Panzer divisions against the American positions at Seibtla, Faid Pass and Kasserine. All American forces in the south were ordered northward to bolster our strength in those critical areas and to shorten our extended lines. The First Ranger Battalion—for the first and only time in its history—found itself rearguarding the entire II Corps withdrawal.

We moved out of Gafsa four hours after all other troops had left, and the next morning we found ourselves entrenched in a mountain pass outside of Feriana some forty miles north. We stayed there all day under air and artillery bombardment until the last of the American units had left. During the late afternoon Rangers scouts reported two Panzer columns approaching Feriana in an encirclement. As we prepared to dig in and fight, Headquarters radioed orders to pull back to Dernia Pass. Without any transport, without any armor to shield us, the battalion was faced with a twenty-four-mile march across an open plain.

We knew the situation was desperate when Darby gathered us around him and gave us the facts of war: "Rangers, we are the last unit to pull out of this mess. Behind us and on our flanks are enemy armored columns looking for straggling units to cut up. We have no tanks, we have no trucks. We have only a few rocket guns and sticky grenades to fight against armor. . . . But I know you won't

235

let them get us cheap. Onward we stagger . . . and if the tanks come, may God help the tanks!"

The tanks came, but a low overhanging mist and strong Ranger legs saved us from total decimation. It was then—with two enemy armored columns paralleling our route of march—that the Rangers made the most important speed march in their history. Though we had been without water, without sleep in forty-eight hours, Darby's inspiring words sparked us to dig in and make time—precious time. Three and a half hours later we hit the foothills of our forward mountain positions at Dernia Pass just in time to escape an advanced armored patrol that fired machine guns and cannon at the tail end of our column.

We all owed our lives that day to the Commandos and Darby. Once again our rugged training had paid off.

For several weeks the battalion was strung out on a six-mile front on the flanks of the strategic Dernia Pass astride the Feriana-Tebessa road. Four miles away, near Telepte airfield, the enemy forces threatened. Each night Ranger patrols moved out, harassing enemy positions, keeping tabs on his movements, radioing back artillery instructions. Each day the patrols moved back, took up defensive positions, waited for the enemy attack. Several feeler attacks developed during which thirty Italian and German prisoners were captured. But accurate reconnaissance on the enemy's movements prevented him from marshaling enough strength to launch a full-hearted attack. Artillery and air concentrations kept him at bay.

Here at Dernia Pass Father Basil held Mass in an open field, unperturbed by the heavy volume of enemy artillery that came crashing in. We less brave Rangers spent some anxious moments during services, but Father Basil seemed as unconcerned as if he were back in a parish church. Robert Ryan and Bob Chesher, the battlefield altar boys, and Sergeant Crandall, the battalion operations sergeant who served as field organist, manfully carried on their religious functions throughout these bombardments which seemed miraculously to just miss the saintly circle.

Meanwhile the full fury of the German offensive spent itself

236

against the American forces at Kasserine, eight miles away, where Terry Allen's First Division, parts of the Thirty-fourth and the First Armored Division were holding. General George S. Patton then assumed command of the II Corps and once again the American forces prepared to assume the offensive.

For a few days we rested, replenished our equipment and weapons and caught up with our mail. Some changes were made in our assignments. Sergeant Wojic, of the Second Platoon, won a battlefield promotion to second lieutenant. Andre then moved up to squad leader with a sergeant's rating. Captain Murray promoted me to leader of our squad with the rating of sergeant. This promotion really impressed Carlo Contrera. Instead of calling me Al, he started calling me Sarge, with heavy emphasis on the *aaaa*rge. "I don't understand it," he moaned. "Nobody gets promotions and medals like you guys in Fox Company. Every day in your company they make somebody a lieutenant or a sergeant. In our company we get nothing. . . . I guess I'll end up the war nothin' but a Pfc."

"Why not come over to Fox Company?" I kidded. "I'll ask to get you in my squad. Then if you do a good job, maybe I'll give you a break myself."

"I already tried—" he shook his head sadly—"but they say I'm too essential."

Deacon Dunn finally knocked out the poem he was always threatening to write when the occasion was worthy enough. It was an eighteen-stanza job about the Sened raid, and as he read it to us we relived it all over again—it was that vivid. In fact it was so good that Vernon Lodge suggested he should turn it in to the psychological warfare troops so they could drop leaflets of it in German and Italian behind the enemy lines. "The poem would scare them more than the raid," was Lodge's reasoning. But Dunn was particular about where his poetry ended up. In fact, he wasn't even going to submit it to *Stars and Stripes,* as many soldiers do, because its quality was so superior to the usual doggerel that appeared in that esteemed sheet.

We didn't have much time out of action—but it was enough for some of the fellows to get in hot water with General Patton. General Patton insisted, in his first general order to the troops, that everyone must wear helmets and ties at all times—front or rear areas. We Rangers somehow didn't hear of this new order. Captain Roy Murray was marching with the Second Platoon one day, when two jeeploads of MPs roared up and zealously took each Ranger's name and fined each one forty dollars. Murray protested to Darby. We didn't wear helmets miles behind the enemy's lines, but we must wear them behind our own areas. It was stupid. Darby agreed. He went personally to see Patton. The fine was lifted. El Darbo didn't take any stuff from generals, not even Patton, and we loved him for it.

Sensing something was in the wind, a new burst of spirit surged through the battalion. We were now veterans. We had proved ourselves. We knew we could march and fight in any kind of battle we were called to. Darby had more than proved that he was the man to lead the Rangers. His philosophy of training and leadership had paid off on every occasion. There was no doubt we were in the best damned outfit in the Army, and we were proud as hell.

The battle orders weren't long in coming. General Patton attached the Rangers once again to the First Infantry Division and sent them wheeling back to Gafsa with the terse orders: "Find 'em . . . attack 'em . . . destroy 'em." Arriving at Gafsa the First Division and the Rangers found the enemy had withdrawn to the high mountains east of El Guettar. In and behind the towering natural defense line, the Axis forces waited with two Panzer divisions and four Infantry divisions. Against these forces General Patton designated the First Infantry Division, supported by the First Armored, to launch the first major American offensive in the Tunisian war. And spearheading this attack were the Rangers. The entire Tunisian war hinged on the outcome.

The key to the whole operation was a funnel-like pass that commanded two important roads that led to the east. From positions blasted out of solid rock, the enemy covered all approaches with heavy machine guns and antitank guns. At the mouth of the pass barbed wire, road blocks and mines were laid out. To attempt a frontal attack was out of the question, as it would be smashed by

238

converging artillery and automatic weapons. The entire American force would be severely mauled and a great many lives lost. There was only one way to clear the pass—to stun and paralyze the enemy with shock and surprise, to swoop down on him from his own rear. This was a mission made-to-order for the First Ranger Battalion.

On a daylight reconnaissance Colonel Darby carefully studied the left side of the pass. He found the Italians were firmly entrenched with excellent observation. To their rear and flanks, seemingly impassable, cliff-faced mountains formed a natural protective barrier. The pass looked impregnable from every approach. The odds were all in the enemy's favor. Darby knew a way must be found to get his Rangers up those mountains to the enemy's rear. It was a situation that demanded Indianlike craftiness, guile and great daring. And there Darby relied again on the proven capabilities of his Rangers, forged through months of hard training and night problems.

For two nights Ranger scouts, led by Lieutenant Walter Wojic, carefully reconnoitered the mountains behind the enemy. Undetected they found a series of cuts, fissures, small cliffs and saddles, which—when linked together—formed a precarious route leading to a rocky plateau directly behind the enemy's strongest positions. The enemy was clearly unaware this route existed—for it was unprotected.

On the night of March 21, with an Engineer Mortar Company trailing behind, Darby led the battalion nearly twelve miles up the winding, steep-slanted mountain walls. In total darkness the Rangers struggled through the difficult gorges, fissures and draws, helping one another over the rough spots. Shortly before dawn the Rangers found themselves in position on the rocky plateau overlooking the enemy. So difficult was the going that the mortar company had not yet arrived.

With the first streaks of dawn a terrifying bugle call split the air. Shouting shrill Indian calls, skirmish lines of black-faced Rangers surged down on the sleepy Italians, whose guns were facing toward the plain. Leaping from rock to rock, the attacking groups closed on the enemy with stunning surprise. The first twenty minutes of battle were swift and stunning. The Italians never had a chance. Grenades, small-arms fire and bayonet charges completely overwhelmed them. "Give them some steel," Darby exhorted his Rangers again and again during the battle.

By 0830 Djebel El Ank, the left side of the strategic pass, was in Ranger hands and more than two hundred enemy prisoners were captured. Scores of dead Italians of the Centaura Division littered the mountainside, most of them grotesquely sprawled beside their unused weapons.

By noon the Rangers had moved across the pass, attacking the right side, knocking out a dozen machine guns and a battery of 88's. Prisoners by the hundreds were rounded up. Only one Ranger had been wounded. An exultant Darby radioed back to General Terry Allen: "You can send in your troops. . . . The Pass is cleared."

It was here that Father Basil helped save many lives—both among the Rangers and Italians—by talking an Italian officer into surrendering his unit peacefully. Father Basil's expert knowledge of the Italian language and people was invaluable to the Rangers on many occasions.

Thus ended the opening phase of the battle of El Guettar. Net result: an impregnable pass captured, along with fourteen hundred prisoners. The speed, surprise and ferocity of the attack had caught the enemy completely off guard. By continuing his attack relentlessly Darby had kept the enemy from recovering. Once again Commando and Ranger tactics were proved successful. No one could ever accurately estimate the number of American lives that were saved by this one operation.

But the opening of the pass was only the prelude to the fiercest battle fought in Tunisia. The Germans, reeling from the initial shock, swiftly counterattacked against the high ground now held by the First Division and Rangers. Sixty heavy tanks supported by Panzer Grenadiers waded into the battle. American tank destroyers and Artillery fought valiantly, stopping the main brunt of the attack. Several times the First Ranger Battalion was cut off completely in exposed positions as they protected Infantry and Artillery positions. At one time D Company, with Father Basil, was completely surrounded by a battalion of Panzer Grenadiers, but held on until relieved by other Ranger companies. Again and again a platoon of C Company, led by Lieutenant Chuck Shundstrom, sped from ridge to ridge, routing the German defenders.

Shundstrom's tough platoon made a surprise attack against a strong German and Italian defensive position on Djebal Berda, a towering mountain. They grenaded and bayoneted their way into the positions, and wiped out the defenders. In the course of battle one American Infantry battalion was completely overrun by German Grenadiers, and the positions were retaken by Rangers.

For six days the battalion fought it out alongside the First Division, supported by the First Armored Division and the Ninth Infantry Division. Then, on March 27, the battalion was withdrawn and sent back to Gafsa, placed in division reserve. The main part of the battle was now over. The enemy's counterattack had been decisively smashed. The enemy withdrew, leaving the major part of two Panzer divisions, two German infantry divisions and two Italian divisions destroyed.

The way was now open for a juncture of Patton's army with General Montgomery's Eighth Army advancing from the east.

Back in the battle-scarred olive grove Darby called his Rangers together and told us our fighting in Tunisia was now history. We were going back to Algeria to organize and train two more Ranger battalions. General Eisenhower was sold on the Rangers. A handful of Rangers would go back to the States to help train the Second and Fifth Rangers. The original First Battalion would be split up into three groups. A and B company would form the nucleus for the new Third; C and D would cadre the new First; and E and F Companies would cadre the new Fourth.

Snapdragon Stern wasn't there to hear the good news. Snapdragon was in a field hospital suffering from artillery shell wounds. Stern had been on the forward slope of a hill with Captain Martin, who was radioing back fire instructions to the artillery against a squadron of tanks. A heavy 88 barrage plastered them. Martin got wounded, so Stern took over the radio, accurately calling the shots that stopped the tanks. But a last salvo caught him. Ironically it was his heavy camera hanging in front of him that saved his life. A thick shell fragment spun into the camera, spending itself before piercing his skin slightly above his heart. This was one time

241

Snapdragon was too busy helping win the war to take any pictures.

It was here in the olive grove that Father Basil said good-by to the Rangers. "The grand and glorious alliance of our armies is in jeopardy unless I return," he told us. "I have stayed away far beyond my legitimate A.W.O.L. period. I can't tell you how sad I am to be leaving you. I will never forget you. I hope you will remember me . . . and I hope you will remember me best by never taking the Lord's name in vain."

There wasn't a dry-eyed Ranger when he finally turned and walked toward the British lorry that was waiting to take him back to his own Army. Father Basil's green beret was the only piece of his British clothing left. The rest of his uniform was now all GI.

For his part in leading the Rangers in the crucial El Guettar Battle, Darby received the Distinguished Service Cross from General Patton. . . .

For extraordinary heroism in action March 21 to 25, 1943. Leading his command over twelve miles of almost impassable mountain ranges . . . Lieutenant Colonel Darby struck with force and complete surprise at dawn in the rear of strongly prepared enemy positions. Always conspicuously at the head of his troops, Lieutenant Colonel Darby personally led the assaults against the enemy line in the face of heavy machine-gun and artillery fire, establishing the fury of the attack of the Ranger Battalion by skillful employment of hand grenades and bayonets in close-quarter fighting.

The success of this attack was largely due to the outstanding heroism of Lieutenant Colonel Darby, who, with complete disregard for his own safety, led and paced the entire assault. . . .

On 22nd March, again leading his Ranger battalion, Lieutenant Colonel Darby bravely directed his battalion in the advance on Bou Hamron, capturing prisoners and destroying a battery of self-propelled German artillery. . . .

The selflessness and courage displayed by Darby inspired his command to exceedingly greater efforts and proved an important factor to the ultimate success of our arms in that sector. . . .

General Patton also offered Darby a full colonelcy if he would leave the Rangers to take over an Infantry regiment. But Darby

242

said, "Nothing doing. You can keep your promotion . . . and I'll keep my Rangers!" General Terry Allen, who called the Rangers "my boys," wrote up a glowing commendation for the El Guettar battle which later became the Battalion's first Presidential Citation. It made good reading and convinced us we were a pretty hot outfit.

But the greatest significance of our Tunisian battles was not the battle honors but our low casualty lists. In the entire campaign we lost only four men—and two of these were from Stukas and artillery bombardment. We had actually come through with fewer casualties than during our Commando training and Arzew operation.

CHAPTER 43

AT NEMOURS, ALGERIA, a small port a few miles east of French Morocco, the birth of two more Ranger battalions began. Major Roy Murray now assumed command of the new Fourth Battalion and Major Max Schneider, became his executive officer. Captain Walt Nye became commander of the Fourth's Fox Company, and I became a platoon staff sergeant in the same company. Dependable Dunn, the poet-deacon, the peerless Ranger, at long last advanced to the position he was admirably qualified to hold—as a buck sergeant, leader of an assault section. Our first sergeant was an excellent choice, Ed Baccus, a quiet-spoken but rugged man around twenty-four years old, from Des Moines, Iowa. Ed Baccus had been platoon sergeant in the old F Company and was considered an able, level-headed noncom, well liked by all.

In a way it was sad to see old F Company splintered off to feed the new companies. I would have just as soon fought the whole war with the combination that had been tried and proved all through Tunisia. In fact, some of us felt so lugubrious that we got together one night and with deep-throated sentiment, somewhat lubricated by Algerian wine, sang "That Old Gang of Mine" till the early hours of morning. You would think that we were being split up and shipped to distant war theaters instead of to different companies in the same battalion. But despite our remorse that the new outfits were "breaking up that old gang of ours" we had good reason to be glad that some good soldiers were getting deserved promotions. Lieutenant Walter Wojic, who distinguished himself at Sened and

244

El Guettar, now became the commander of D Company, and Randall Harris, the quiet, unassuming mortar sergeant, became Wojic's first sergeant. Howard Andre, my ever-whistling, ramrod, mustachioed buddy from Philly, now became a platoon sergeant in D Company and Sarn't Sieg, the rollicking ex-Merchant Mariner who was competing with Andre in the mustache department, now became top kick of Easy Company.

Nearly all the old veterans moved up a rank or two to cadre the new outfits. Junior Fronk and Lodge and Rodriguez became squad leaders and moved over to Easy Company. Even Carlo Contrera got a promotion: he became a corporal and was assigned as Colonel Darby's personal driver, interpreter and—according to him—"the old man's chief tactical adviser."

For a while promotions were the order of the day. Old stripes were ripped off and new stripes sewn on. Gold bars became silver, and silver bars were doubled into tracks. Major Herman Dammer was picked by Darby to command the newly activated Third Battalion, and he truly doubled in brass as the executive officer of all the Rangers. Lieutenant Colonel Darby kept command of the First Battalion and supervised the organization and training of all three units.

We were officially attached to the Fifth Army for supplies and administration, and to Supreme Headquarters for operations. We were not a regiment, not a brigade, not even a combat team. We were three separate battalions, each with its own commander, and yet we were all directly under the command of Colonel Darby, who commanded the First Battalion. To us in the ranks it appeared that the sudden growth of the new Ranger Battalions had caught the Pentagon planners off guard, with the result that no tables of organization had been drawn up. Meanwhile we would continue fighting the war until a suitable T/O caught up with us, one that we hoped would also provide for an appropriate rank and staff for our esteemed commander. Until then we were satisfied to be called "The Ranger Force."

We had new outfits on paper, but we had to get volunteers to fill the ranks. And six weeks were all we had to whip the three new battalions into fighting shape for another invasion we knew we would again lead.

Spurred by Darby, Ranger officers and noncoms developed a new type of Ranger raid—raiding other outfits for Ranger volunteers. Tough, combat-hardened Rangers, like Captain Charles Shundstrom and Major Roy Murray, Lieutenant Warren (Bing) Evans and the irrepressible First Sergeant Scotty Monroe, wheeled into replacement depots and units scattered in Algeria and French Morocco, set up their tables, gave out their challenging recruiting talks and signed up somewhat awed but anxious volunteers.

We used reverse psychology in our sales talks. We spared no details in telling how rugged and grueling our training was, how dangerous. We told them the truth about our battles: that they could expect to be the first to spearhead the way in beach landings, mountain attacks and street fighting, and they could also expect to spend some time now and then paying visits behind the enemy lines. We told them the only thing we could offer them was furious fighting with top leadership in the best outfit in the army. No bonus, no special privileges, no special uniform, nothing special—except the very special privilege of wearing the Ranger patch. That and swift action.

Sometimes we would taunt them that there wasn't a man among them that looked as if he could take the tough life of a Ranger. Captain Shundstrom was a true master of this technique. He would stand on top of a jeep, with his legs spread out, chin outthrust and hands on hips, and roar a thunderous challenge to the sea of faces around him, then turn disdainfully away as though in disgust at the dearth of material available. Stung by the challenge men would swarm about him, determined to prove him wrong. Shundstrom's efforts resulted in truckload after truckload of eager recruits.

We learned that American soldiers love a challenge. From all over North Africa—to the dismay of their commanding officers who hated to lose good men—they flocked to volunteer. We recruited them from reppo depots, from Q.M. corps, from port battalions, from Infantry units, Armored units, ordnance; we even got a few paratroopers, and one Ranger recruiter blandly announced that he had actually brought in six recruits from a messkit repair outfit. Some of our more enterprising Rangers, like the colorful Sergeant Scotty Monroe (the new sergeant major of the Third Battalion), Sieg and his sidewick Sergeant Bob Chesher, went into bars and

246

bistros looking for able-bodied candidates. Their standard operating procedure was to swagger in, size up the crowd, then roar out a challenge to fight the whole bunch. The ones who waded in to accept the challenge were the ones that our erstwhile recruiters signed up.

Now we had a record and a tradition that the whole army knew about. That was the only thing we could offer the new recruits—that and action. It was enough. We got so many volunteers we soon began turning them away.

Under a blistering hot African sun we gave these new Rangers the works. For six weeks we poured it on—all that the Commandos had taught us in Scotland, all that Darby had taught us at Arzew, all we had learned the hard way in Tunisia. They learned fast, and they picked up the Ranger spirit. They knew how to sing, too. We taught them the Ranger marching chant, and a few other chants that will never get printed. And every day as we raced over the twisting Algerian hills, their loud, lusty voices could be heard for miles:

"We're the toughest and we're the best,
    You'll find us leading all the rest,
    Darby's Rangers . . . Leadin' Rangers.

We'll fight an army on a dare,
    We'll follow Darby anywhere,
    Darby's Rangers . . . Fightin' Rangers."

We old-timers poured it on relentlessly; we were even tougher than the Commandos had been with us because now the stake was much more personal. After the Commandos had trained us, they were through with us. But we would go into battle with these men. Our own lives, as well as theirs, depended on how thoroughly we trained them, and we were determined to eliminate as many of the weak ones as we could.

As the days wore on we old-timers got to know and respect the new men around us. What before were only faces with names now became distinct personalities—some more articulate, decisive and impressionable than others, most of them excellent soldiers, putting every ounce of drive and energy into their training.

At the end of six weeks Darby called a parade formation of the three new Ranger Battalions. Colonel Darby inspected each Ranger individually and stood by as the three battalions proudly marched in review. They looked so good you couldn't tell the difference between the new Rangers and the handful of old-timers sprinkled through each company. Darby looked pleased, and he told us how he felt: "I want to commend the old Rangers for the great job you've done in training the new Rangers. Not even the Commandos could have done better. And I want to congratulate you new people for the spirited way you pitched in in the training.

"But remember this: Rangers are made on the training field, but they prove themselves on the battlefield. Behind us we have Dieppe, Arzew, Sened, Dernia Pass and El Guettar. . . . Ahead of us are many more battles with the enemy, an enemy we have learned not to underestimate. The Rangers will lead the way in fighting them and defeating them. And as Rangers we will be proud that our actions will not only destroy the enemy—but will also save lives, the lives of our fellow soldiers who will come in after us. We are going into action soon. I know you will measure up to what the Army expects of you!"

Our training at Nemours was over.

The next day the three battalions packed gear, loaded into transports and sailed slowly along the Algerian Coast. The First and Fourth Battalions landed at Algiers, then with full pack we did a twenty-mile speed march to a place called Zeralda on the coast, alongside General Terry Allen's First Division. Here three weeks of dress rehearsals for a large invasion were scheduled. Meanwhile the Third Ranger Battalion continued on to Bizerte, to join elements of the Third Infantry Division, which were staging rehearsals in that area for the great assault against Fortress Europa.

248

CHAPTER 44

THE *Prince Charles* was a trim, sturdy British transport. For four days she had steamed lazily in a meandering pattern from Algiers to Malta through tranquil African waters. But today the *Prince Charles* was wallowing in deep troughs, her beams creaking and a raging wind roaring across her wave-lashed decks. Somewhere behind us was the *Prince Leopold,* carrying the other half of the Fourth Battalion, A, B, and C Companies; in front of us was the large U.S. troop transport, the *Dickmann,* bearing the entire First Ranger Battalion. Our destination was Sicily, and in four hours we would be spearheading the center task force of the Seventh Army commanded by General George S. Patton. Our mission: to storm and capture the heavily fortified coast citadel, Gela.

In the crowded, ill-ventilated holds, the Rangers of D, E and F Companies, part of the first-wave assault team, puked up their suppers, rolled in their hammocks and cursed the fates that suddenly blew in the turbulent norther that was now threatening to scatter the ships from hell to high water. For hours we had pitched and rolled and groaned as the *Prince Charles* valiantly clung to her course. Not only the veteran Rangers, but even the seasoned seamen, were groggy and green at the gills, and rumors spread throughout the ship that the invasion itself might be delayed. It was a wobbly and depressed group of noncoms and officers who gathered around Captain Nye for the final briefings.

Grim-faced and listless we clustered around him, our spirits badly bent by the merciless battering. But Nye seemed impervious to the storm and its effect on us, least of all on himself. Without any visible emotion and in his usual matter-of-fact manner, he repeated what we as a company had practiced over and over again during the dress rehearsals at Zeralda.

"Just to make sure there is no foul-up, we'll go over it once more. The First Platoon will land on Beach Green right next to the steel pier, clear the pillboxes overlooking the beach, then set up a defensive perimeter. The Second Platoon will go through our positions, fight their way up to main street to the cathedral square. There they will clean out all opposition and hold the square for Headquarters to be established. The First Platoon will then move through them, down to the edge of town facing the plain, cleaning out houses and pillboxes on the way. Easy Company will follow us. On our right will be D Company; on our immediate left, C Company. The First Battalion will land on the other side of the pier to the left on Beach Red. They have the tough job of knocking out the four gun batteries and capturing the west side of Gela. On our right, to the right of the Gela River, the First Infantry Division will land. Behind us will come the Combat Engineers to clear the beaches for traffic, and the Eighty-third 4.2 Chemical Warfare Mortar Battalion will follow. Any questions?"

No questions. We knew it all by heart, and we also knew the entire operation had the potential of another Dieppe. We were under no illusions that this would be an unopposed landing. The sandtables and photos we had studied had revealed that Gela—a three-mile cluster of sandstone buildings—was sprawled on a plateau one hundred fifty feet above the sea and was defended by a line of concrete pillboxes that overlooked a wide beach, littered with mines, tank traps and barbed wire. On both flanks of the town heavy-millimeter coastal batteries were emplaced. Intelligence estimated at least two thousand troops in the immediate area. And somewhere out on the plains toward Neciema lurked a mobile striking force of heavy armor and infantry, ready to counterattack. So we knew we were playing for keeps on this deal.

"All right, fellows," Nye concluded, "check your men once more, question them, make sure each man knows what his job is, and make sure they carry every piece of equipment they'll need with them. And get this straight—regardless of the storm, we're

250

going in and we're going to take our objectives. So those who are sick better get well in a hurry."

We all nodded assent, then quietly filed back into the holds to talk to the men.

Lieutenant Branson briefly repeated Nye's words to the First Platoon. As he spoke I studied each man's face, and I couldn't help feeling sorry that the new men should get their first baptism of fire under such depressing circumstances. But sympathy doesn't win battles, and when the lieutenant had finished I felt compelled to add a few of my own thoughts in an effort to buck them up, and in so doing to buck myself up.

"This storm is a Godsend," I said. "If those enemy shore guns open up, they'll have a hard time hitting us bouncing up and down these deep waves. They won't be able to see us half the time. Some of us feel sick now, but once we hit land, we'll be in fine shape. So the sooner we get in the better."

Although there certainly was some logic in what I said, most of the men cracked wide grins and accepted my effort for what it was—a gloom breaker. Pfc. Hoffmeister, however, didn't let me get away with it completely. "Yeah, Al, it's all part of Ranger planning—storm and all. Now all we got to do is tell their gunners about it!"

A ripple of laughter caught on, and I milked it for all it was worth. I took out a bag of chewing tobacco, and woozy as I was, I crammed a big ball into my mouth. Chewing tobacco was my favorite nerve relaxer, particularly before battle. "Hell," I said. "This storm's not so rough. I can still chew this moldy tobacco." The effort nearly killed me, but it brought a big laugh from the fellows, and this was one time a few laughs—even at my own expense—were at a high premium aboard the ever-rocking *Prince Charles*.

When the platoon dispersed I shoved my way back into the sergeant's quarters, where Sarn't Sieg, the top kick of Easy Company, Randall Harris, top kick of D, and Howard Andre, his platoon sergeant, were sitting, oiling their weapons once more. Andre looked at the tobacco drolling out of the corners of my mouth and roared, "Hey, Al, get rid of that chaw, please. It makes me sick just to see you with that crap in your mouth." By this time I had actually overcome the first nauseating effects and was beginning to enjoy my noble chew.

251

Before I could answer, Sarn't Sieg thrust a mimeographed sheet into my hands, saying, "Greetings from General Patton. He has a special message for you, Al." As I read he twisted the ends of his walrus-type mustache, very professional-like.

The Patton Manifesto Number One, as I later called it, was boldly etched in typical flamboyant Pattonese. It was a rousing clarion call to each soldier to do his utmost in the noblest traditions of the American soldier, etc. The meaning was good, because troops always like to have an encouraging message from top brass—but its contents was not particularly strong on logic. In particular, I was amused at the part that applied to Italian-American soldiers about to land on Sicily's shore. It went something like this: "There are thousands of soldiers of Italian descent who will be storming ashore with the Seventh Army. However, bear in mind that the real courageous Italians who loved liberty and who had the true pioneering spirit left Italy to come to the country of freedom where they have become good citizens. Those who were left behind were the cowards and weaklings who allowed Mussolini to come to power. Against them I know you as an American soldier will not fail in your duty, etc., etc."

I threw the sheet back to El Siego. "Ho hum," I said sarcastically. "Patton may be a great general, but he needs a good speech writer. Reminds me of the special morale booster he sent out when he took over the troops in Tunisia—you know, the one that said 'Get in there and kill the enemy, so you can go back home to your waiting girl or wife, a hero in her eyes!' "

"Patton writes his own stuff," chided Andre.

"Yeah, him and MacArthur like to give it a certain flair!" insisted Sieg. "They're Boswells of the Battles!"

"Now hear this! Now hear this!" the familiar British voice cut in over the loudspeakers. "All troops to their stations for departure to destination! All troops to their stations for departure to destination!"

Swiftly we jumped up and straightened our battle gear. All four of us hesitated for one moment before heading toward our respective companies.

"Good luck, fellow," said Randall.

"Now don't forget, the wine factory and that other place are part of my company's objectives," said El Siego.

"Hey, Al, don't you get shot, we need you," said Andre. "You're the only one who can speak the lingo!"

"See you all in church," I returned, meaning, of course, the huge cathedral which was my company's objective. Swiftly we threaded our respective ways through the milling troops, scurrying this way and that toward their battle stations.

Once again our time had come!

CHAPTER 45

THIRTY-FOUR tight-lipped, tense-muscled Rangers crouched low, hugging their weapons, as our assault landing craft, manned by a British crew, sank into a deep trough, then shot skyward into the piercing gleam of a probing searchlight. For a long split second we were bathed in a powerful glare that made us feel self-consciously naked and shy. Then, before we fully developed stage fright, our craft was thankfully swallowed into the blackness of another welcoming trough, only to hurtle skyward again for a repeat performance.

Each time we rode the crest of a swell we caught glimpses of a frightful hell awaiting us on the beaches of Gela. Blue and green cannon tracers—the Italians' favorite colors—were stitching through the black night and ricocheting off the turbulent waters along the entire beach front. Three or four giant searchlights were crisscrossing their blinding beams seaward, and the brilliant blue flashes of exploding mortar shells speckled the roaring swells. Far inland, behind Gela, we could see an eerie red glow caused by fires and flares from our bombers.

Directly ahead of us we could see the comforting taillight of the pilot launch that was leading our flotilla toward beaches Red and Green. Somewhere out there on our right flanks were the cruisers *Boise* and *Jeffers,* and on our left the cruiser *Savannah* and the destroyers *Shubrick* and *Maddox.*

It was a very unpleasant experience and retching seasickness

254

only made things uglier. Added to the weirdness of the sights and sounds of battle were the moments when our craft hung suspended on the crest of a swell while the propellers loudly churned the air much like those of a plane.

The time was 0245, D day, July 10. We had already advanced about five nautical miles from the *Prince Charles,* had reached our line of departure and were headed for our beach targets. Suddenly a snub-nosed armed support craft churned its way toward us from the left and slightly ahead. Through a megaphone a voice shouted, "Heave to! What outfit?"

Captain Nye cupped his hands and yelled back as our launch's motors slackened speed. "First Platoon, F Company."

The boat now idled directly alongside and we could well recognize the voice. It was Colonel Darby. "You're 'way ahead of the flotilla," he roared. "Stand by till the rest catch up!"

"Right, sir," yelled Nye.

"Good luck," roared Darby. "Have a good shoot!"

With that the command launch roared away as our boat tossed and pitched idly. By this time the swells had lost some of their fury and the winds were becoming less vicious. Again the foul-fingered shaft of light caught us, held us, then moved mercifully on to larger quarry. Pfc. Hoffmeister yelled back to me. "Hey, Al, how about dousing that light with a good spit of chaw terbaccer!"

From the stern of the boat a voice yelled: "Don't do it, Al. Save the juice for pillbox guys 'case we run out of ammo."

I laughed inwardly, thankful to both of them for helping relieve the awful tension.

The roar of flanking assault boats soon drowned out everything else as they came abreast, and once more our own launch bucked forward into the inferno awaiting us on the beaches of Gela.

It was now 0300. H hour was fifteen minutes away, each minute an eternity of fear—fear of the morbid reality that we could see and hear crashing around us, and fear of the unknown that we would meet on the beaches. As we surged forward a tremendous explosion erupted to our immediate left, lifting our assault craft high and slamming it down with an earsplitting crash that buckled the armor plate on the sides and hurled us into one another with

255

frightening impact. Helmets and rifles rattled and clattered and I felt as if my stomach had been squashed by the pressure. The enemy mortars were zeroing in and the biggest searchlight on shore once more held us in its relentless grasp.

At that moment a British support craft swished across our bow from out of nowhere, its pompoms blasting furiously toward the searchlight. Like a mad water-borne hornet, it bore in, straight as a torpedo toward the tormenting target, blasting it into darkness. We couldn't restrain ourselves; a cheer of relief erupted from our hoarse throats, a deserved tribute to the Navy. But that didn't stop the enemy mortars. A swift series of explosions bracketed the entire assault wave; and up ahead to our right I could see by the brilliant flash of an explosion that one of our assault craft had suffered a direct hit.

As we continued forward through the mortar barrage, once again my mind was bedeviled with a barrage of tormenting thoughts . . . "Will the next mortar get us? . . . Why didn't I increase my allotment and take out more insurance? . . . Shoulda gone to confession back in Zeralda . . . Well, I can confess to God now . . . But there isn't time to tell all your sins . . . Besides, you ought to be ashamed to confess only when you are in danger . . . God will understand . . . He's all-forgiving . . . Yes, but He must be getting tired of this last minute business. Wish Father Basil was here with us . . . Shoulda wrote a letter to Father Carr. What would he think—me his former altar boy, going into battle without confessing? And what about the cathedral we're going to attack? That's holy ground —it's a sacrilege to kill on holy ground. What would God think? But this is war. He'll understand. It's the enemy's fault if he uses the cathedral for defense. Besides, our side is in the right—that makes everything okay. Sure, they believe in God too, they pray too. But God won't listen to them, He'll listen to our side. . . . Well, that's what we're supposed to believe. Wonder if those Italians will really fight like the ones at Sened. I hope they wise up and give up without a fight once we land and show them we mean business. . . . Could be killing my own relatives, or one of my own relatives could kill me. . . . Will I hit a mine on the beach? Will I get emasculated? God, I'd rather die. . . . Stop thinking about you,

you, *you!* Think of them, them, *them*; your men, your platoon. What are you going to do to keep them alive? Did you train them right? Yes, you think you did . . . but did you really? You're a platoon sergeant, a leader. Are you really? Then prove it! Thought you'd make a few raids here and there and then live it up in between raids. Battle insurance, too, you said. Well, here it is, brother. How do you like it? The first wave. . . . You asked for it and you got it! There it is all in front of you—mortars, mines, pillboxes, street fighting—all waiting for you, and you'll get more of the same medicine in other landings. Oh, yes . . . there will be others if you are lucky enough to get through this. . . . Even tougher, until you die or get wise and quit this foolish nonsense of being a Ranger. Why didn't you stay with the First Armored Division? Or get in some nice outfit like your brother Gene back in the States? Cut out this whining! Two battalions of Rangers are with you on this deal. They can't be wrong. And Darby is right out there in front of you. Think of the enemy! They're twice as scared as you are. . . . You know where you're going and what you're after and how you'll do it. . . . How would you like to be in their shoes with a thousand tough Rangers opening up with all their firepower? And the paratroopers landing out there behind you, and the British and American navies backing them. Who's got the better end of this deal—you or the enemy? You have, so shut up! Admit it . . . sure, you're scared as hell now, because you just got to sweat it out till you hit the beach. Once you hit the beach, you'll have things to do . . . you'll forget yourself . . . you'll only think of your job and your men. You hate to kill, you hate destruction—true. Why don't they take death and destruction out of war? It would be a beautiful adventure, and everyone could enjoy it. Those screams out there ahead of us— those explosions on the beaches—some of our guys are drowning out there in the water, dying on the beaches. What were they thinking about when they got it? Wonder what the new guys are thinking? That Captain Nye—I'll bet he's not wasting his thoughts like this. His mind is right on that beach and what we're going to do. Wish I had his calm, cool nerve. Nothing bothers him, dammit! These new guys—they look up to us old-timers. Can't let 'em

257

know what's going on inside. Gotta play the part right down the line. It's against Ranger regulations to fraternize with fear, even when you're smothered by it. . . ."

A chorus of frenzied shouts up ahead shook me out of my apprehensive reverie. From the glares of fires along the shore we could see several figures struggling to keep afloat up ahead. Our beach target was still three hundred yards ahead and machine-gun fire was spitting out from its pillboxes. Captain Nye was faced with a grim choice—go straight ahead to the beaches and engage the pillboxes or lose a couple of minutes by picking up the struggling Rangers, who—weighted down with entangled web belts of ammo and other equipage—were sure to drown. I was grateful when he roared over the sounds of the motors to the Navy coxswain, "Let's pick 'em up!"

Swiftly the coxswain eased down the speed and we drifted over to the desperate Rangers whose anxious shouts of "Help . . . Help! We're going down!" wrung our hearts with pity. This act of mercy, it turned out later, saved the lives of our entire platoon.

While we were slowing down to pick up the drowning Rangers, assault craft 712, bearing the First Platoon of D Company, was coming in for a landing to our right on Beach Green. Up front, standing next to the British sailor manning the machine gun, was Second Lieutenant Walter Wojic, the curly-haired, blond physiology instructor from Minneapolis, Minnesota. Behind him was the second lieutenant who commanded the platoon; he was one of the new officers who had recently joined up at Nemours. In the rear of the boat were Howard Andre and Randall Harris.

The men sitting tensely, waiting for the boat to scrape bottom, had every reason to be confident of themselves. No company had been trained more thoroughly. Spurred by Wojic, Andre, Randall Harris and others of old F Company cadre, the new D Company's performance and spirit during training had been outstanding, and for this reason they had been given the privilege of landing on one of the toughest areas of Beach Green.

Lieutenant Walter Wojic—if he had been disposed to contemplate

258

his future—could look ahead to a brilliant career for the duration of the war. For his extraordinary qualities of courage and leadership at Sened and El Guettar, he had been singled out by Colonel Darby and Major Murray to be a company commander at the early age of twenty-three. Thus within eight months he had advanced from a buck sergeant leading an assault section to a lieutenant commanding the destiny of a Ranger company, the normal rank of which is captain.

But Walter Wojic was not the type to be disposed to contemplate his future or his past at a crucial moment. Built like a Roman gladiator and with a strong forceful face creased with lines of humor, Wojic had that rare quality of character that imbued his men with intense loyalty and *esprit de corps*. Although Wojic insisted upon and got from his men the best they had in them, he was no martinet, in the military sense of the word. Throughout the battalion he was known for his quiet modesty, his exceptionally high intellect, and his poise and dignity as a human being. Wojic as a sergeant was never known to raise his voice or use profanity, and he very definitely needed no act of Congress to make him a gentleman. The well-being of his men came first, in camp and in battle. To many of us Rangers, Wojic perhaps epitomized the ideal of a military leader in a democratic nation—one who leads by example, competence and innate qualities of human dignity and compassion, rather than one who leads mainly by mandatory military authority, cold and impersonal.

As the assault craft neared shore, Lieutenant Wojic was probably greatly relieved that the area of beach just head was a patch of black silence in contrast to the intense flashes of gunfire on both flanks. On his left, where F Company would soon land, six machine guns interspersed with two cannon, spurted their deadly flashes seaward.

But the quietness ahead of D Company might mean that the enemy was patiently waiting until the Rangers actually gained the beaches before opening up. So, like a good commander, Wojic decided that he would lead his men across the beach in a lightning-like dash and get them across as swiftly as possible to save as many lives as possible.

259

The British coxswain expertly piloted the assault craft into the surf and at exactly 0310 the bottom scraped against the steep gradient. Before the ramp had hit the waterline, Lieutenant Wojic had leaped over it into two feet of water, shouting, "Follow me!" Splashing through the rough surf, he turned around to note that the Rangers were right behind him and the launch was emptying swiftly. He could hear Andre's sharp, commanding voice shouting, "Move fast and don't bunch up!"

Wojic stretched his long muscular legs and hit the Ranger stride of forty inches as he raced across the beach toward the cliff. Now his thoughts must have been centered on his mission of smashing into the town and securing the entire right flank of Gela, connecting with the First Division which was making its landing at the same time. Panting hard, loaded down with heavy bandoleers and mortar shells, the Rangers of the First Platoon scrambled after him, urged on all the while by Randall and Andre.

So swift was the Ranger advance across the soft, sanded beach and so strong was the momentum of their surging bodies that when the first explosion blew Lieutenant Wojic into shredded bits, a good half of the platoon had also entered the mine field, and were tripping over mine wires before they could halt their forward charge. Around and under them, the dreaded Bouncing bettys and triggered hand grenades exploded, sending whirring metal ripsawing through their clothes, helmets and flesh. The officer leading the First Platoon was blinded and dazed and dropped to the ground holding his eyes. Four riflemen just behind Lieutenant Wojic, to his right and left, were killed immediately, and the awful screams of the wounded rang through the night. Randall Harris, who had found himself up alongside Lieutenant Wojic, felt his legs buckle under him and was lifted by a powerful blast backward into the oncoming Rangers. A moment later he picked himself up and yelled to the Rangers to hold still where they were, and then he heard the voice of Howard Andre, the platoon sergeant, yelling from the cliffside. Andre and several others had managed to get through the mine field.

Swiftly Harris moved among the Rangers still in the mine field, found a path back to the beach and guided the others with the wounded back to safety. Now Randall for the first time felt a sharp pain in his left lower abdomen. To his dismay his probing fingers found a gaping seven-inch wound and several smaller ones, and he had the terrible sensation of feeling part of his lower intestines slithering into his hand.

"Medic! Medic!" All around him were badly hurt men, some more, some less than he, shouting for succor. Some were too mangled to shout and just waited in silence for the mercy of death. But Randall had other things on his mind than shouting for medical aid. Half the platoon was killed or wounded. The other half was busy caring for the wounded, and several Rangers with Andre had gone safely through the mine field. The Second Platoon was now making its landing, and would have to be guided through the mine field. The blinded officer was out of action, so Randall quietly squeezed his intestines back into his stomach, lowered his web belt over the wound, tightened his belt and immediately took command of the situation.

By this time the Second Platoon had come up, already warned by a runner, and the new young lieutenant, on hearing of the disaster, went to pieces. At that crucial moment the most terrible thing that could happen to a human being—to fail as a leader, in competence and in courage in the eyes of one's own men—happened to that unfortunate officer. He just stood there and went to pieces.

Randall Harris, after a brief consultation with Andre, very quietly told the officer to fall in at the end of the company. He, Randall Harris, was taking over, and D Company would accomplish its mission as planned by Lieutenant Wojic.

And take over he did. With Howard Andre shouting directions from the cliffs, Randall found a path through the mine fields and moved the remnants of the company—minus a detail to take care of the wounded—up the steep embankments and onto a dirt road that paralleled a lower level of the cliffs. This road had been cut into the sides of the cliffs to service the concrete pillboxes and sandbagged machine-gun positions that were spitting out fire toward the First Platoon of Fox Company, now coming in for their landing.

Those pillboxes were not D Company's objectives. D Company on gaining the cliffs was to plunge into Gela and clean out the right

261

flanks. But D Company was in a fantastic situation; it was through the mine field and had access to the road that ran directly behind the pillboxes.

"F Company will be slaughtered by those pillboxes. We can't leave them firing. Our own mission will have to wait," said Randall to Andre.

"Let's go!" said Andre, pulling out his grenades.

Leaving D Company in a defensive position Randall, still holding his stomach and not revealing his condition, raced down the road toward the series of pillboxes, followed by Andre. Hardly breaking stride, Randall reached a pillbox that was firing a small cannon, came up to the concrete aperture from behind, flung in a grenade and raced on down the road, past Howard Andre, who had now reached the second pillbox. Within a few minutes Andre and Harris, playing leapfrog among the pillboxes, had used up all their grenades to silence seven pillboxes and kill some twenty Italians. The entire pillbox operation had taken less than five minutes. Now, weak from loss of blood and wincing with pain, Randall leaned against a sandbagged position. In the darkness he found his first-aid kit and sprinkled sulfa into his wound, once again pushed his oozing intestines back and tightened his canteen belt.

"You all right?" asked Andre as he came up to him.

"Just catching my breath," Randall lied. "Let's get back to our company. We got our work cut out for us!"

Back to their company they raced. The waiting Rangers of D Company, joined by their gritty leaders, were sparked into high spirits. D Company had tasted blood, their own and the enemy's. D Company was fighting mad. Following Harris and Andre, they plunged into Gela to make the enemy pay for Wojic and the others, and to show their noncom leaders they were worthy of inspired leadership.

While all this was happening, our assault craft, after picking up the drowning Rangers, had again been badly shaken by a tremendous explosion. The Italians had dynamited the pier on our left to prevent our ships from unloading troops and supplies. We drew

262

closer to shore, and, to our surprise and relief, the machine guns and cannon that had been blasting at us with angry fury were strangely silent. We had no idea of the drama that had been taking place as we came in. Since the Navy was not bombarding this sector of the beach, most of us assumed the Italian gunners had just lost their nerve and called it quits . . . or had decided to catch us on the beaches.

It was a wet landing. Into two feet of water jumped the long-legged Captain Nye and right behind him the giant Branson. We uncoiled our aching legs and streamed out of that boat like a pack of hungry wolves. The cold water oozed up to my crotch as I sloshed through the surf with other shadowy forms. In double file we streaked across the beach, praying the guns would remain silent and the land mines would be widely scattered, scattered enough to make a safe path for us.

A brackish burnt-gunpowder smell permeated the night air as we followed Captain Nye across the beach swiftly and silently. I couldn't believe it! Nobody was shooting at us; no mines were exploding. It was not supposed to be this easy. Surely there's a catch somewhere; they're playing 'possum, sucking us in and then— *wham!* But these fears proved groundless. Before I knew it we were safely across the beach climbing a wide path leading up to the cliff. A path, unguarded, unmined! Right past two pillboxes, still acrid with grenade smoke, we climbed. One of our scouts, who had already examined the insides of several pillboxes, passed the word along. Some outfit had beat us to the punch. Great!

Once across that beach and up the cliff we swiftly took up positions along a stone warehouse, by the water front on the main street leading toward the cathedral. This was Phase One according to our rehearsed plan—and the buildings and street plans were just like our own home town. The weeks of close study of aerial photos and practice on similar towns along the Algerian coast had paid off. I could sense that the new Rangers were already beginning to feel like veterans. We didn't talk because we didn't have to; every man knew his exact position in the darkness and each man gripped his weapon and waited tensely for the Second Platoon to come through us.

263

We waited for five suspenseful minutes, then Captain Nye held a whispered conference with Branson and me. "We can't wait for them! E Company is already here to follow, so it looks like we'll have to do the Second Platoon's job at the cathedral square. We'll move out in one minute."

I swiftly passed the word to Sergeant Green and Sergeant Wincompleck of the First and Second assault squads and to Sergeant Wilbur Gallup—our squad leader. We didn't take long to get organized, because we had rehearsed the Second Platoon's mission too and they had rehearsed ours, to ensure flexibility.

Captain Nye, followed by his runner, took the center front, close to Lieutenant Branson. I fell in a few paces behind them and, as the crash and rumble and crackle of battle flared up and down the beach fronts, the First Platoon of Fox Company, Fourth Ranger Battalion, at 0345, July 10, slipped silently and warily through the night to church—the cathedral square.

Meanwhile the Second Platoon of Fox Company was somewhere out yonder going round and round in circles. To avoid being hit by an Allied destroyer that was surging toward the enemy searchlights, the British coxswain had veered out of its path in the nick of time. But by the time the assault launch had turned about, it had lost the main flotilla. Now prodded by a platoon of furious Rangers, the coxswain was trying vainly to find the right beach.

On the left flank, the assault waves of the First Ranger Battalion had landed exactly on schedule against stiff opposition. Two assault craft had been hit by mortars and many Rangers had been killed and some drowned. Thanks to the U.S. Navy destroyer *Shubrick,* two of the large searchlights had been shattered just as the first wave closed in for the landing, otherwise casualties would have been much higher. Moving swiftly through the mine fields, elements of the First Battalion smashed their way through pillbox fire and by 0310 were well on their way toward their initial town objectives.

Far to the left flank a company of Rangers commanded by Captain James Lyle, while assaulting a large gun battery, found themselves in the unenviable position of being on the receiving end of a

264

six-inch shell bombardment from the over-eager Navy warships. Captain Lyle in the nick of time got word to Colonel Darby, who in turn got the Navy to raise their fire and "allow my Rangers to do their work." Lieutenant Donald Anderson, whose platoon had been interrupted momentarily by the naval intrusions, then continued to lead his men against eight machine guns, wiping them out and capturing many prisoners.

While Captain Lyle's company kept the Italians occupied from the front, another First Battalion company had sliced through enemy back fortifications and had enveloped the large coastal battery from the rear. In a surprise attack eight 170-millimeter coast guns were captured and a battery of mortars for good measure.

Meanwhile, Colonel William Orlando Darby, having touched Sicilian soil with the very first boat to land, with his lean, lanky Tommy gunner, Corporal Charles Riley, had come upon a Ranger unit furiously exchanging shots with Italians barricaded in a hotel. Always impatient for results and always anxious for some close combat, Darby, followed by Riley, led the way into the hotel, followed by the Ranger squad. A furious room-to-room battle erupted, punctuated by exploding grenades and Tommy-gun fire. When it was over Darby and his Rangers came out with what was left of some thirty Fascist officers.

To us Rangers advancing steadily and cautiously toward the cathedral, it seemed that we were moving through the only vacuum of nonresistance on the entire beachhead. We had covered three blocks without incident and were closing in on the cathedral square itself. Not a shot had been fired by us or at us, while on our flanks all hell was roaring wild. But if there were any Rangers who had been hoping for "some hot action" they were not to be disappointed.

Pfc. Richard Bennet had just reached the corner of the south side of the square when a machine gun erupted with a raking burst that cut him down immediately. He died before he hit the ground. Almost simultaneously a volley of rifle shots splattered the stone walls as Rangers dived for cover. Sergeant Leonard Green had seen the flashes from the machine gun, estimated the distance and

265

in the darkness—a difficult feat—had lobbed a grenade straight and true. The machine gun erupted again with its second and last burst when the grenade exploded. Nye and Branson moved swiftly into the center of the square, both firing their carbines from the hip. The first squad, led by Green, now turned the corner at right angles, and the second squad with myself and Sergeant Wincompleck laid down a barrage of cover fire, aiming at the dabs of orange and green flashes.

Every building bordering the square seemed to be crawling with persistent Italian gunners. It was still pitch-black night and we could hardly see the Rangers alongside us, let alone the Italians. But we knew the difference between a Ranger walking or running and an Italian; we knew the distinctive contrast between our automatic fire and theirs, our grenade bursts and theirs; even the sounds of our men reloading their clips, flinging themselves on the cobblestones, were different. Instinct, intuition, luck, ingenuity, all played an important part; but the most vital element in our favor was our systematic plan, learned from the Commandos. When the first squad peeled off to the right, the second assault squad peeled off to the left, while Sergeant Gallup and his squad, having parked their mortars, now came up to the intersection to lend us a hand with covering fire from the center. This left the two assault squads free to fan out and start working toward the cathedral in a pincer envelopment. But before we could actually close on the cathedral— from which strong fire was coming—we had to clean out the buildings, one by one, that were bordering the cathedral square. We had been warned by the Commandos in Scotland that such a situation at night was "right sticky."

Each assault squad on its own initiative found itself breaking down into small combat teams. In twos and threes Rangers darted into grenade-blasted doorways, sprayed the insides with rifle and Tommy-gun fire and moved up to the next building to repeat the process. Two men from Wincompleck's squad climbed a rainspout and gained the roof of a three-story building across from the cathedral. Directly under them were two snipers who were giving Green's squad a bad time. The Rangers silently crawled to the edge of the roof, lay down directly over the open window and gently lobbed in their fragmentation grenades, finishing off the offending Italians.

266

These two enterprising lads then swung themselves into the building through the open window, dynamited a hole through the adjoining wall, and knocked out two more Italians in the next building.

Pfc. Hoffmeister got separated from his assistant as he ran into a building, firing his BAR from the hip. Wounding an Italian who had been firing from an excellent vantage point, Hoffmeister moved him aside, then took advantage of the position to give cover fire to Captain Nye as he charged into another building. As Hoffmeister was firing, a figure ran in, kneeled beside him and started plugging away. Between bursts Hoffmeister gave the figure a gentle shove and said, "Go find your own window. This BAR draws enough fire!" The figure beside him suddenly yelled in Italian and threw down his gun in terror. The amazed Hoffmeister, not wishing to be encumbered by a prisoner, simply took off his helmet and gently tapped him on the head with his BAR to put him to sleep. Hoffmeister then resumed his firing.

Corporal James Hildebrant and I found ourselves converging toward a building where we had heard some Italians talking excitedly. A large alleyway emptying into Cathedral Square was between us and the Italians. We were ready to leap across the open alley when we heard the clop-clop of heavy leather shoes coming down toward the square. On an inspiration, I held Hildebrant's arm, and yelled out to the advancing Italians: *"Veni qua supita!"* (Come here quick!). Within seconds four stocky Italians carrying their rifles at the port double-timed up to us. Their leader, thinking I was an Italian officer, actually clicked his heels to attention. Hildebrant and I jammed our rifles at them and quickly disarmed them. Their leader, convinced it was all a dreadful mistake, kept saying in Italian: "But we're Italians, too." I hadn't realized my knowledge of the language was that good. We learned later that these men had been among a number that the Gela commander had ordered to the cathedral to hold it at all costs.

Later I bumped into a medic, bending over some wounded Italian. He was most solicitous about my state of health. "Are you all right, Sergeant? Did they hit you yet?" When I said no, he answered, "Doesn't anybody get wounded in F Company? I'm using up all my supplies on the Italians."

"Don't be so eager—have patience."

267

For nearly an hour the battle raged up and down Cathedral Square and in and out of the streets adjacent. Gradually and surely the First Platoon was closing the pincers until all resistance on the flanks was smothered and only a hard core of opposition remained within the embattled cathedral. Blistering rifle fire was pouring out of several stone apertures at various levels in the tower. And from the open doors of the cathedral, from deep within, an occasional shot would come pinging out.

CHAPTER 46

A PURPLISH dawn was breaking over the low, jagged Gela skyline when Sergeant Wincompleck and I, followed by Corporal McKiernan, Allen Merril and Big Pruitt, moved in and met Captain Nye and Lieutenant Branson just short of the cathedral doors. We were out of the fire line of the snipers on the other side of the tower above, and we knew that inside the large cathedral some Italians still held out.

Nye didn't lose any time. "Okay, Al—clean 'em out!"

Clean 'em out! Now I must spill blood on consecrated ground, in a holy cathedral. Of all the situations that a soldier can face, this was to me the most unpleasant. But Rangers can't waste time debating moral issues. A few more rifle pings from the tower apertures were convincing reminders that the enemy inside the holy ground was very much alive and very tenacious. Wincompleck and his men were crouched on the other side of the door, waiting for me to start the action.

"Okay, Winc, here goes!"

From my flattened position on the left side of the stone entrance-way, I kicked the door open wide, threw in a grenade, flung myself back as the grenade exploded and, before the debris had cleared, fired eight fast rounds into a corner of the cavernous cathedral. Wincompleck, followed by McKiernan, Allen and Big Pruitt, rushed by me, bounded over the altar rails, shot it out with two Italians holed up in a sacristy, then fought their way up the winding tower stairs. When it was all over we had flushed out three diehard Fascists of the Livorno Division; sprawled out grotesquely by the altar were two dead Italian soldiers.

As Sergeant Wincompleck herded the prisoners out the cathedral door, I crossed myself and knelt for a moment at the altar in silent prayer.

The sun was shining brightly when I came from the dark cathedral, exhausted from the terrific strain of the past few hours. The square was spotted with clusters of dead Italians, and in a corner of the square the medic was hard at work patching up a dozen or so wounded Italians. Forty prisoners were under guard in a sweet shop, and tired, red-eyed Rangers leaned wearily against walls and squatted cagily on steps, catching a breather while they could. Sergeant Leonard Green and his men came limping back from their rooftop-cleaning sortie with eleven prisoners, and Green reported laconically to Captain Nye, "Mission accomplished!"

At 0600 on July 10, the cathedral and the square around it were as quiet as Parkesburg, Pennsylvania, on a Sunday morning.

Captain Nye now contacted the battalion commander and received orders to move down to the edge of town facing the plain of Gela in support of Easy Company. Company C, under Lieutenant James O'Neil, had accomplished its mission on our left flank. All Fourth Battalion objectives had been taken with remarkably few casualties. Nearly four hundred and fifty prisoners had been taken by the Fourth, and more than five hundred by the First Battalion. Our engineer detachments had landed and were clearing the beaches of mine fields, and some companies of the Eighty-third Chemical Warfare Mortar Battalion were already setting up their mortars to support us.

The First Platoon of Fox Company was extremely lucky. We lost one man—Pfc. Bennet—and none wounded. We were in great shape—except for our missing Second Platoon. For all we knew, the erstwhile Second Platoon might have got so far off course that they had made their own invasion of Italy itself. We wouldn't have been surprised.

As we were organizing to leave the square a number of Sicilian citizens began venturing toward the cathedral. Two old ladies, sobbing loudly, approached two bodies lying on the cathedral steps.

270

They knelt, crossed themselves and began crying out their saddened hearts to God. I could just barely understand the Sicilian dialect: "Please, God, bring an end to this terrible slaughter of your children. *Dio Mio. . . . Beca . . . ? Beca . . . ?* (Why? Why?)" It was a sad moment and I could see most of our fellows were quite touched, even though they could not understand the words. Maybe those dead soldiers were the sons or relatives of these old women? I wish I could have told them why, why it was necessary for Americans to invade their lands and kill their sons. But I am sure they would not have understood. How can anyone understand or care which side is right or wrong, when one must witness the slaughter of human beings in and around a place of Christian worship, a citadel of faith and spirit and peace and goodwill to all men on earth?

I turned away only to witness an even sadder scene. A handsome young Italian sergeant lay in a puddle of blood just to the right of the cathedral entrance. Bending over him weeping was a swarthy, smooth-complexioned, young Sicilian woman, with straight long hair; she wore a plain black dress and long black stockings. Her head was buried in his chest and she was sobbing: *"Giovanni . . . Sienti . . . Sienti . . . Alsata . . . Veni . . . Giovanni, beca le non sienti?"* She was asking him to listen to her and get up, not to lie there like that. It was obvious that Giovanni was her *inamorato*. I couldn't take any more of this. It is bad enough for a soldier to be compelled to kill; but to witness the bereavement of the enemy's women is an anguish too torturous to endure.

As we queued up and marched out of the square, somewhere in the rear of the column some Ranger philosophized, "It's tough, dammit! Even if they are the enemy!"

"Yeah," said another. "But they died on their own land among their own kind. If we get it, they'll be no women to cry over our bodies!"

As we marched toward our new positions a loud cry was heard from our rearmost Rangers. "It's them . . . the Second Platoon is here!"

We all stopped and looked back. Sure enough, the warriors of the Second Platoon, led by Lieutenant Zazlaw, were actually double-timing to catch up with us, unadulterated disgust written on their faces. We gave them the works.

271

"The Lost Platoon—why didn't you guys stay lost?"

"Yeah—we don't need you now, after it's over!"

"We oughta send 'em back to guard prisoners!"

"Hey, Second Platoon! Did you stop for tea on the way?"

The Rangers in the Second Platoon were in no mood to parry jibes. They looked tired and mean. Bouncing around the sea in a small launch for hours was probably a much tougher ordeal than we had had. They just stared ahead and took our good-natured heckling stoically.

Artillery fire from the plain of Gela was beginning to crash into town as we took up positions in small stucco and plaster houses a few blocks from the square. Overhead three Focke Wulves screamed low in tight formation over the congested beaches, where Engineers and Naval personnel were laboring furiously to clear mines and land supplies. The earth shook as their bombs crashed home, and we prayed that our valiant Air Corps would soon be on hand to ward off these annoying bastards.

Not far from the beach, Captain Richard Hardenbrook, the dedicated young medical officer, and his able assistant, Staff Sergeant Karboski, had set up their first-aid station and were doing a rush business. Captain Hardenbrook looked up from bandaging a Ranger with a minor leg wound and spotted First Sergeant Randall Harris, holding his stomach in pain, at the tag end of the line. Doc Hardenbrook called to Randall to come on ahead of the others, who seemed in less painful condition than he. But Randall smiled and said he would just wait.

Doc went back to investigate Randall's wounds—all seven of them, carved out around and above, as Randall put it, "his family jewels." A few more minutes and it would have been all over for Randall Harris. Swiftly Doc fixed him up and ordered immediate evacuation to a hospital ship. But Randall was not through yet. While waiting for the launch to take him to the hospital ship, he picked up his rifle and started herding prisoners into a large compound.

The news about Harris' extraordinary valor spread throughout the small beachhead. Led by Harris, D Company had plunged into Gela, knocked out four more pillboxes on the right flank of the town, cleaned out several city blocks of snipers and machine

272

gunners, and, as Major Roy Murray put it, "were ready to be committed for additional objectives."

The two new Ranger Battalions, the First and Fourth, were now blooded and cocky and were prepared to defend Gela to the last man against anything the Italians and Germans could throw at them. We knew we were in good company and that helped bolster our confidence immeasurably. On our right were the spirited, tough veterans of the Fighting First, led by the colorful, dashing General Terry Allen. The First Division had taken all their objectives, and already the Sixteenth Regiment of that division was probing deep toward Ponte Olivo Airport. Somewhere out toward Prioli a valiant band of paratroopers who had been dropped during the night were raising hell with enemy tanks, hanging on till the First Division made contact. Behind us on the Gela roadstead was the most formidable concentration of naval power in the entire invasion, under the command of Admiral John Hall. All that was needed to make it a perfect team was the appearance of our air cover.

But as we tightened our belts and prepared for the worst with confidence, we Rangers were unaware that nature had conspired against us and was almost responsible for tipping the balance in the enemy's favor. To the despair of the Navy, the scuttling of the Gela pier kept our forces from using it as anticipated. Large sand bars prevented heavy tank landing craft from coming in, and the Navy was working furiously to assemble pontoon causeways across them. At several points the Engineers were trying to clear channels. Only the new Army ducks—sea-going trucks—could make it to shore, and these were not capable of carrying big guns. Here and there, smaller landing craft were able to get through the sand bars and unload some jeeps and ammo and a very few small 37-millimeter antitank guns. But what we needed desperately were tanks and heavy artillery, which could not be landed.

By 0830 another enemy air attack blasted the ships off shore, and when it was over the valiant destroyer *Maddox* was sunk. Among those lost was its commander, Eugene S. Sarsfield, with seven officers and two hundred three enlisted men.

CHAPTER 47

LIEUTENANT BRANSON and I were looking through our field glasses, studying the flat wheatfields of the Gela plain. From our rooftop position we could see scattered small, red-roofed farmhouses against a background of forbidding mountains, now shrouded in a bluish morning haze. It was a peaceful, pastoral scene, one that would make a good travel poster—except that there were some strange-looking black dots moving down the road from Neciema to Gela.

"What do you think, Altieri?"

"Too small to be German—could be those little Italian tanks."

Branson immediately picked up the field phone and clued Head-quarters in.

"Enemy tanks approaching Gela. Light Italian, Co-ordinates 35.9-26.8 Niscemi-Gela road. Request artillery and mortar fire. . . . What! No artillery? How about Naval fire? Good!"

As I watched through the glasses, the small black blobs became increasingly and incredibly larger, and I realized they were actually speeding at around thirty to thirty-five miles an hour, a fast clip for tanks. They were heading straight toward D, E and F Companies' positions.

Swiftly Branson and I spread the word to our squad leaders. Sergeant Gallup immediately zeroed in their puny 60-millimeter mortars, and within a minute were lobbing shells against the on-coming tanks. We set up our BAR-men at key points and instructed our Bazooka gunners. We were not worried so much about the tanks, but about the infantry that would be sure to follow.

274

As the tanks sped toward us a flurry of shell bursts speckled the plains around them and between them, some from the 4.2-millimeter mortars, some from the Navy guns, and some from our own small 60's. It was encouraging to see our fire landing out there—but it wasn't stopping the tanks. They just kept rolling blithely along as they were going to a Sunday church meeting—and that was precisely where some of them were destined—the cathedral.

At this stage there was nothing we could do but just watch in amazement. It was incredible! A whole Army supported by a mighty Navy had thundered ashore and here before our eyes were sixteen black Renault tanks coming to pay their respects and being received most cordially.

"Where's our mighty Air Corps?" a Ranger wailed.

"They'd be sitting ducks for an air sweep," another jibed.

"Where, oh where, are the Tankers?"

"Let 'em come—we'll beat off their bogie wheels with our rifle butts," Hoffmeister said with a grin.

Now the speeding tanks had reached town and were beginning to turn right, onto the very street that ran behind our positions. Once behind us, they would have free access to Cathedral Square, where Force Headquarters was set up, and would be in a position to blast their way down to the beaches. Lieutenant Branson quickly evaluated the situation and ordered the platoon to pull back to the buildings in front of Cathedral Square and fight them off with anything we had. Branson remained behind with a bazooka gunner to cover us. I led the platoon across the street and toward the buildings designated—and not a moment too soon. Just as we cleared the street, the leading tank let go with a thundering 47-millimeter burst that crashed into the corner building directly behind us, narrowly missing our rearmost Rangers.

Swiftly I put my men into position in the three-story stone buildings fronted with heavy ornate masonry. "Get as high as you can! The tanks can't elevate their guns too steep—and throw everything you have, grenades, dynamite, bazooka fire, mortar shells," I yelled.

"Even M-1 rounds?" the Rangers asked.

"Yes! Even M-1 rounds. Aim for the portholes, aim for the bogie wheels. But keep firing."

As I was giving these hurried instructions, Colonel William Or-

275

lando Darby and Captain Chuck Shundstrom came tearing down the street from the square. "What's going on here, Sergeant?" Colonel Darby inquired grimly. "What are you men doing back here?"

"Sir," I said, "the tanks broke through! They're coming right up behind us. Lieutenant told us to hole up here and try and stop 'em from overrunning your Headquarters!"

Darby looked at Shundstrom, then barked to me, "All right, we'll give them a fight! They won't get through, is that clear?"

"Yes, sir," I said. "They won't."

With that I ran into the building, up two flights of steps, and plunked myself down next to Sergeant Green and Hoffmeister. "You heard what the ol' man said," I shouted. "If we let those tanks get through, F Company is finished."

"You mean they'll wipe up the whole beachhead?" asked Hoffmeister.

"I'm not worried what the Germans or Italians will do," I answered. "It's what Darby will do to us!"

From our vantage points we could look down the street at the intersection where the tanks would turn. We had all inserted armor-piecing clips in our weapons—fat chance they had of penetrating!—but it made us feel better. Strangely, aside from the unique excitement and sensation of being under a tank attack, none of the Rangers around me seemed nervous or edgy—just tense—waiting for the drama to unfold.

We didn't wait long.

A tank had just started to make the turn—its machine guns and cannon spitting out death and splattering concrete and plaster off the buildings we were in—when it was hit by a shower of grenades and rifle shots. Though these heroic efforts proved ineffective, the tank paused for a long moment before resuming its turn.

I will never forget that moment as long as I live—or the moments that swiftly followed.

At the precise instant that the tank momentarily halted in its left turn, out of nowhere came a lone Engineer soldier, driving a jeep towing the most priceless object on the beachhead—a 37-millimeter, antitank gun. Colonel Darby bellowed out, "Hey there, soldier— swing that damned thing around here!"

Without blinking the soldier swung the jeep around, and Colonel

276

Darby, bareheaded, sleeves rolled up, and Captain Charles Shundstrom, helmeted, bounded over and began setting up the gun for action. But before they could get it fully set up for firing, the Italian tank—bearing a death's head device—clanked around the corner and came charging down on them.

Colonel Darby immediately leaped up to the jeep, swung the .30-caliber machine gun around, aimed it and splattered the ugly black turret of the tank with several withering bursts. The tank again halted momentarily. *Shhoommmmm! . . . Shhhhooom! . . .* two cannon bursts went whishing over the heads of Darby and Shundstrom and crashed into a building behind them. Now Darby sprang from the jeep to the 37 cannon and threw in a shell, as Shundstrom peered into the sights. Darby pulled the lanyard and the shot screeched into the turret of the Italian tank as the 37 bucked back from the recoil. Again Darby threw in a shell and again it thundered home with such accuracy and force that the Italian tank was actually flung back for several feet and then was enveloped by a sheet of searing flame.

We cheered wildly. Even as the drama unfolded before my eyes I couldn't believe it. Our Ranger chief and his tough right-hand man, Captain Shundstrom, had just performed one of the war's most outstanding and selfless acts of courage and daring.

That was all the Rangers needed. The rest of the tanks did not pass.

From alleyways and rooftops, Rangers inspired by our valiant leader, waded in and made short work of the remaining tanks that had the temerity and misfortune to enter town.

A tank following the one knocked out by Darby and Shundstrom was struck by a double salvo of bazooka blasts, followed by a thermide grenade that roasted the occupants beyond recognition. Another tank was blown up by Captain Jack Street and Sergeant Shirley Jacob as it bore into First Battalion's sector. They got up on top of a building, waited until the hapless tank was under them, then dropped a "pole charge" of dynamite on it.

Sergeant Mathew Polus of E Company, Fourth Battalion, slammed a bazooka charge at another tank. It struck square in midsection, but it was a dud. Before Polus could make another try, the tank swung its turret and fired its cannon killing his buddy,

Ranger Joe Marty. Polus then ducked back into the alleyway as the tank fired another salvo. The tank later ran into another knocked-out tank, and its crew meekly surrendered.

The rest of the Italian tanks got the message soon enough—Gela was too hot for them to handle. They turned tail and streaked across the open plain back where they came from. General Guzzoni's D day counterattack had failed miserably, but he had happily provided us Rangers with the means to stoke up our spirits for the bigger battles to come.

As the Rangers strengthened their front positions and prepared for the enemy's next move, enemy planes swooped low over the beaches, strafing and bombing with increasing fury. A thousand-pound bomb exploded right next to the command post and tore down a whole block of houses shortly after the noon hour. Later that day an Me 109 sneaked in on a low-level attack and dropped a bomb on LST 113, loaded down with much-needed artillery and ammo supplies. The bomb exploded below deck and the explosion ripped it apart and enveloped what was left in roaring flames. The enemy was drawing blood, and where it hurt most—our arteries of supply and support.

We prayed that our Navy would overcome the tremendous obstacles confronting them on the beaches and bring in the stuff we needed—on time.

CHAPTER 48

No RANGER slept on the tense beachhead that night. Every Ranger was on his toes, weapons at the ready; waiting for the counter-attack, for the tanks to come crashing at us again and for the infantry that would have to close with us before Gela could be taken Enemy artillery beat a steady tattoo in and around the Ranger perimeter, and out on the flat plains Ranger scouts set up listening posts to report any signs of enemy movements or infiltration.

July 11, D-plus-one, broke upon us tired Rangers. A hot glaring sun revealed the Sicilian wheatfields ahead of us crackling in flames. Black smoke clouded the plains and hid the tall mountains beyond. Again I probed plainward with my field glasses but could see nothing. But we could hear them—the unmistakable sound of diesel motors. Somewhere behind those burning fields German tanks were deploying into position for their attack on Gela.

Lieutenant Branson was crossing the street from Captain Nye's command post, when three 88 shells came swooshing in. Branson dived for the gutter just as the shells crashed into the houses beyond.

"Oh, no!" shouted a Ranger. "Why did they do it?"

"Why did they do what?" spoke up Hoffmeister. "The lieutenant is still alive!"

"It's not the lieutenant I'm crying about!"

"What's bugging you!"

"The sons of bitches just hit the whorehouse!"

Branson picked himself up and charged across the street into our command post. As he shook off the dust, he grinned widely.

"Kinda close, Lieutenant," I said. "Stick around a while—we wouldn't want you to miss what's coming."

"More tanks!" Branson groaned.

"Yes, sir . . . a double feature!"

We probed the plain again with our glasses. My eyes were squinted from the glare of the sun and for a moment what I was looking at was dancing spots in front of my eyes. Again I glued my eyes to the binoculars and stared hard. I had known tanks were out there somewhere, so it was no surprise to see them. But what sent a sharp tremor through my whole body—a tremor composed of fear, awe, wonder and utter astonishment—was to see a staggering three-mile-long line of Mark VI and Tiger tanks suddenly appear out of the smoke banks. In clusters of threes and fours, and followed by Panzer Grenadiers, they surged toward us; they were less than three miles away.

Branson whistled in amazement. "Must be a hundred big babies out there!"

"At least," I answered. "They want this place bad!"

Sergeant Green and Sergeant Wincompleck reported in. This was it! I gave final instruction. "Save your ammo for the infantry. These are tough Panzer Grenadiers of the Herman Goering Division. Keep the men concealed, and have them fire from in back of the windows, not sticking out of them. Make those Molotov cocktails count. The tanks may break into Gela, but they can't hold Gela unless they wipe out every Ranger. Before that happens our own tanks of the Second Armored will counterattack from Licata and Scoglitti. So it's not as bad as it looks!"

Sergeant Green roared: "How do you like that? A hundred tanks we see coming at us, and he says it's not as bad as it looks! Shall I tell my men it's all a mirage?"

"No! Just tell 'em to forget the tanks and keep score on the infantry they hit!"

Shells from the enemy tanks and artillery whistled and crashed around us as the awesome array of enemy armor thundered toward Gela and the First Division positions on our right. For a few moments I seemed completely oblivious of the ominous destructive force of the oncoming tanks. I was strangely mesmerized by the

280

fantastic scope and drama of the spectacle unfolding before my eyes. I seemed—only for a few moments—hypnotized into a ludicrous belief that I and those around me were privileged spectators, for whom two armies were about to clash with fury. The plain ahead seemed to be a gigantic Coliseum, and our shell-dented stone houses were the grandstands. The element of personal danger— the awareness that those tanks were out to destroy you—was completely missing those first few moments in the early morning of July 11.

A direct 88 hit on the house next to ours, which killed three civilians and wounded a Ranger, was all I needed to snap out of it and realize we were in for some big trouble.

As the tanks relentlessly bore down on us, a squadron of Italian bombers streaked across the skies and blasted the ships off shore. Hot steel fragments from the navy antiaircraft guns rained down on us, and all along the Ranger front men were saying:

"Where's our air support?"

"Hope our tanks get here!"

"Let's see some Navy firepower!"

None of us at that time could understand why our air support over Gela was not more active. The spectacular zigzagging line of tanks was a perfect target for a dive-bombing attack. Of course we realized our air fellows had other important things to do, like bombing enemy airfields and railroads and back-of-the-lines concentrations of supplies and stuff like that. But we sure would have liked to see them give us a bit of a hand with those tanks out there, and I think the Navy would have welcomed some protection, too. But they didn't come—not this morning. The Navy did come through, however—thank God. And so did our magnificent 4.2 chemical warfare battalion—and the few units of First Division artillery that managed to be ferried to shore by the new ducks in time to meet the tank attack.

Spellbound I watched the leading tanks of the Herman Goering Panzer Division advance to within two short miles. Suddenly they were enveloped by a crashing, blistering barrage of mortar, artillery and naval gunfire. The angry guns of the cruisers *Savannah* and *Boise,* the destroyers *Glennon* and *Butler,* had roared into action— and not a moment too soon. For half an hour the fires from these

281

naval vessels, joined by the 4.2 mortars and divisional artillery, crashed down on the vaunted Panzers, splintering them into slivers of junk. But other Panzer tanks, screened by their own smoke barrage and the smoke from our shell bursts, waddled into the battle, determined to smash our young beachhead back to the sea.

On came these tanks, past and through the Navy and mortar barrages . . . straight down the Niscemi-Gela road, and on its flanks . . . past the Ponte Olivo airport, smashing through an exposed unit of the Sixteenth Infantry regiment that valiantly stood up and fought the tanks with bazooka guns and sticky grenades . . . down the winding slopes of the Gela River and straight for the beaches between the First Division and the Rangers.

It was at this stage of the battle that General George S. Patton landed at Gela to find Colonel William Orlando Darby—the ex-Artillery officer—with a crew of Rangers firing several captured Italian 77's at seven German tanks that had advanced to within one thousand yards of the beach. And the Rangers were, according to General Patton, cut off from the First Division.

Meanwhile General Theodore Roosevelt, Jr., assistant division commander, at his advanced command post directly in the path of the oncoming tanks, phoned his division commander, General Allen: "Terry, look! The situation is uncomfortable out here . . . Third Battalion has been penetrated—no antitank protection out here. If we could get that company of medium tanks it sure would help."

As General Roosevelt concluded his urgent message, forty more Panzer tanks began a wide-arc swing across the First Division front that would send them crashing to within eight hundred yards of the Gela defenses.

And all the while we Rangers on the outer defense perimeter gripped our rifles till our knuckles whitened and awaited the fateful moment when the enemy's steel monsters would grind into Gela and pulverize our flimsy plaster and stone defenses with point blank 88 fire.

Back on the beaches, heavy tank fire crashed on the Engineers and Navy shore parties working furiously to bring in the "stuff we needed." Men groaned and sweated as they pushed and pulled artil-

282

lery pieces through the fine-grained loose sand, and trucks and jeeps shuttled back and forth between the frontline and beaches, towing antitank guns, artillery pieces and much needed ammo.

By 1025, in response to the urgent demands of General Patton, General Allen and Colonel Darby, the Navy had finally rammed a pontoon causeway across the treacherous sand bars and several tanks managed to come ashore. At the same time, an L.S.T. loaded with five tanks, bulled and chewed its way over a sand bar and crashed on the beach, allowing the tanks to speed directly into the path of the oncoming German Panzers.

These tanks, on Patton's direction, closed the gap between the Rangers and the First Division, and with First Division artillery knocked out the Panzers that had come so close to encircling us at our rear. By 1150 the first German attempt to annihilate the beachhead had been decisively smashed.

We cheered wildly, grateful for the reprieve, grateful for the Navy's helping hand. The plain of Gela ahead of us was now transformed into a graveyard of burning tank hulks and blackened bodies. We knew then that Gela was ours to hold and keep, and, instead of crumbling as the Germans had hoped, we would soon move forward.

But General Alfred Guzzoni, the commander of the Italian Sixth Army wasn't yet convinced. Mussolini still hoped to make good his boast to the world: "Our mobile reserves will sweep down from the mountains and push the invaders into the sea." General Guzzoni ordered the badly shattered remnants' of the Herman Goering Division to attack once more, and he sent a regiment of the Italian Livorno Division down the winding mountains from Butera to attack the Rangers from the left.

Again the Navy guns thundered. Again the valiant First Division antitank and artillery gunners worked over their smoking guns till their hands were burned raw and their ammo was expended. Again Darby and his picked cannoneers manned the captured guns . . . and again the Gela plain was transformed into Dante's Inferno. This time the enemy tank attack was hopelessly smashed, and those tanks that could turned tail and streaked for the mountains.

Now the infantry on the left flank, in scattered skirmish lines, was approaching within two miles of Gela. Through my glasses I could see the color of their uniforms—a brownish sand color in contrast to the blue of the Gela Italians. I thought of the poem, "The Charge of the Light Brigade," marching bravely and stupidly into the Valley of Death. I knew I was about to witness one of the most futile and needless lost-cause attacks in the history of warfare. equivalent of 155-millimeter artillery shells—and all the shells that the sweating seaman could ram into cruiser *Savannah's* six-inch guns, were sent crashing into the ranks of the exposed Italian troops. I saw bodies by the score disappear into mushrooming bursts, and pieces of equipment and flesh and bone were falling all over the flat terrain. For five agonizing minutes the barrages pummeled the Italians mercilessly. When it was over the Livorno regiment was no more, save for four hundred or so who had managed to find cover along a railroad embankment.

Colonel Darby, with a couple of halftracks and a Ranger company, sped out to the plain and took the remnants prisoner.

Now—thanks to the Navy's heroic efforts—tanks, artillery and halftrack cannon were flowing ashore, building up for the power punch that would uncoil from Gela across the plains to Butera, a mountain citadel, and Niscemi, headquarters of the late-lamented Herman Goering Division. Under special orders from General Patton, Colonel Darby quickly organized a small task force comprised of three First Battalion companies, a company of halftracks from the combat engineers, two companies of armored infantry of the Second Armored Division and the dependable and resourceful 4.2 Mortar Company.

As dusk approached, Darby led his Rangers across the plains for an attack on the enemy stronghold of Mount Della Lapa, a junior Maginot line complex guarding the approach to Butera. Meanwhile, another company of Rangers moved out with the First Division to take the Ponte Olivo airport, seven miles inland, which was needed for our air support.

Company F, Fourth Battalion, found itself ordered to the west side of Gela where we occupied a captured enemy artillery battery to guard against a flank attack. Thankful for a chance to catch some sleep, we tried to make ourselves comfortable in the enemy

284

dugouts, knowing that tomorrow would find us once again on the move.

But sleep was not for us.

The Luftwaffe again blasted the offshore ships. Twenty-four JU 88's came over in one of the heaviest attacks, and a Liberty ship, loaded with ammunition, suffered a direct hit. For hours exploding ammunition rocked the area, and by nightfall her fire illuminated the waters for miles, exposing our ships at anchor.

She was a perfect beacon for enemy bombers. Again and again between 2150 and 2300, D-plus-one, wave after wave of German Focke-Wulves and JU 88's attacked. The clatter of antiaircraft guns, the clump of exploding bombs, the dazzling aurora borealis of tracers, kept us in wakeful suspense. Twice large bombs dropped right by our positions, and Rangers cursed loudly up and down the line.

It was just about 2400 hours when we Rangers heard the mighty thundering drone of what we believed would be the enemy's greatest air attack yet. Already one wave of bombers had dropped their loads and gone. This wave sounded like the roar of a thousand planes. Up and down the lines noncoms yelled to their men, "Take cover! Deep cover! This is it!"

It was a clear night and a bright moon bathed the waters with a silvery gloss. The burning Liberty ship's red glare gave the scene a surrealistic contrast. It was the most beautiful face of war I had ever seen, but before the evening was over I was to find it the ugliest.

Looking up we could actually see the planes, almost wingtip to wingtip. They looked too graceful to be bombers, and they were flying unusually low. They were bearing directly over the Gela roadstead, where our transports, surrounded by our cruisers and flak ships, rode the swells.

"Everybody keep your helmets on and dig in!"

We didn't want any casualties from our own flak in case the bombs missed us. It was a chore to keep reminding the new men to keep their helmets on.

Now the formation was directly overhead and the itchy-fingered antiaircraft gunners on land and on the sea gripped their guns and aimed them toward the oncoming planes. This time, alert, red-eyed

285

gunners were on to the enemy's attack patterns and knew how they would peel off this way and that after dropping their deadly cargo. The *Maddox* L.S.T. 113, the Liberty ship *Robert Warren* and other casualties of the Luftwaffe—they would all be avenged.

The first gun to fire was a slow-paced .50-caliber machine gun that stitched its red tracers like an angry finger pointing out the transgressors. A split second later, one thousand, two hundred and forty-three guns blasted skyward, transforming the Gela night into a terrifying latticework of hot red tracers. Cruisers, destroyers, flak ships, support craft, transport ships, beach guns, rooftop guns, cannon, pompoms, machine guns, rifles—it seemed that every man on land and sea was throwing up his weight in lead, at the attacking planes.

And strangely the planes dropped no bombs, but dived this way and that way to elude the fire which would not and could not relent.

"That'll fix their wagon!"

"Yeah, Navy—pour it on—the bastards!"

"Give 'em the full treatment!"

"Get every. one of the sonsofbitches!"

We could see several planes burst into flames and come plummeting down at sea and over the Gela plain. Each time a plane exploded we cheered till our throats were hoarse.

"Great shootin', Navy!"

"Give the swabs a Marine sharpshooting medal!"

"Tickle their livers!"

As we were shouting, Captain Nye sent a runner to tell us enemy paratroops were landing down near the beach. I was to get a patrol down there and pick them up. All Rangers were alerted against paratroop attack.

"Okay, Sergeant Wincompleck, let's go!"

But Sergeant Green spoke up. ."How 'bout me and my squad? I got a special score to settle with those bastards."

"After you, Alphonse!" obliged Sergeant Wincompleck. "The privilege is all yours."

"One squad is as good as another. Let's go!"

Swiftly we bounded over to the bluffs overlooking the sea, slid down the cliffside and soon were fanning out in both directions up and down the beach. The first paratroops we saw were in the surf,

286

trying to untangle from their chutes. Green was up ahead of me and I saw him drop to the ground and prepare to fire. There was no reason for him not to fire, and there was no logical reason why I shouldn't let him fire. They were as far as we knew enemy paratroops—the toughest and most brutal of German troops. In the surf or out of the surf they were best handled when they were dead.

But something I can't fathom told me to fling myself down beside Green and put my hand over his trigger finger. "Let's take 'em alive if we can!"

Green in a whisper mumbled something. We got up and moved down the beach, rifles at the hips, and met the Germans just as they stamped their feet on solid ground, their weapons still slung across their backs. Two Rangers covered us from behind as we slammed our guns into the paratroopers' guts.

It was evident the paratroopers were still under shock from their terrific ordeal, and they muttered something incoherently as they put up their hands. I noticed their faces were blackened, and I was amazed to see they were wearing the American flag patch on their shoulders.

"They're paratroopers—our own!" I shouted.

"What outfit?" one of them asked, obviously relieved to know we were not German.

"Rangers," I answered.

"Thank God!" the tall one answered. "We're from the Eighty-second Airborne Division. We were supposed to jump over Farello Airdrome."

"They been shooting down our own planes!" Green exclaimed.

"All those planes that got hit—our own men!" I shook my head incredulously.

"We're all that could get out alive from our plane. The rest of the platoon was blown to hell! A helluva war!" the paratrooper bitterly spat out. "A helluva way to fight a war!"

We found that both were wounded. Gently we carried them up a winding path to our positions where we were met by a medic, who patched them up swiftly.

I had already sent a runner to Captain Nye so that he could pass the word to other companies not to fire on the so-called "enemy" paratroops. Reports soon came pouring in from all beachhead points. Paratroops—our own—were being picked up in the offshore waters, were scattered all over the Gela plain, were found dead inside crashed planes—C-47's.

Later we learned to our horror the devastating toll our own guns had taken of our own men. Out of one hundred forty-four troop carriers that had thundered over Gela that moonlit night, twenty-three never made it and a good part of those that did were badly damaged and many of the passengers killed and wounded.

This terrible fiasco saddened us. We Rangers felt a deep kinship with the courageous paratroopers—not only because we were both specialized volunteer troops, but because we knew they were faced continually with daring risks, and they, like us, knew the terrors of a first wave assault. By air or by sea—the risks were the same. We knew too that as the war progressed the paratroops and the Rangers would find themselves in situations where each needed the other.

To all of us the plight of the valiant paratroopers was felt deeply, and it took away the luster of our Gela victories. And it reminded many of us that war, however valiantly waged, brings tragedy and heartbreak to the victors too.

CHAPTER 49

THE NEXT day, D-plus-three, was a day of heavy fighting for the Darby force attacking Mount Della Lapa. Here the Italians were firmly entrenched on high ground and had two batteries of heavy artillery in support. These troops were no pushovers, and they had orders from General Guzzoni to stop the Americans at all costs. But with the aid of our 4.2 mortars and cruiser fire, the Darby force, after a day of repeated bayonet charges, finally broke through and, with tanks in support, reached and took Italian secondary positions at Mount De La Zai. Six hundred more prisoners were sent back to the Gela cages.

While this was taking place, another Ranger Company helped the First Division capture the Ponte Olivo airport, and Allied fighter planes from North Africa and Pantelleria were soon landing there.

Meanwhile barreling down the dusty Sicilian road toward Licata —through no-man's land—were two jeeps on a historic mission: Major Murray and driver in one, and Captain Nye and myself in the other. Our mission: to make contact either with the enemy or with the Third Infantry Division commanded by General Truscott that had landed at Licata, fifteen miles west of Gela. Five miles out we spotted a staggered line of troops about platoon strength, stopped our jeeps, hit the ground and prepared for battle. The troops saw us and they too prepared for battle by advancing toward us in skirmish lines. It was a tense moment with each side holding fire until targets could be identified. We could see by the way they deployed that they were good soldiers, and they outnumbered us ten to one. It looked like a rough deal for us. But as they advanced we heard a voice yell, "Hey, Murph! Over to the right, work your way behind 'em!"

"I'll be damned!" Captain Nye laughed. "Paratroops!"

It seemed all of us yelled out at once, "Hey! Hold your fire! We're American Rangers!"

"Rangers! Great!"

It seemed we all stood up at once—the paratroopers and our party. A heavy-set sergeant with ripped trousers and bloodstained shirt came over, gripped our hands warmly and told us they had been shot down and thought they were among enemy forces. We gave them what water and cigarettes we had, told them the road was clear right into Gela, and wished them better luck on their next jump.

Three miles later we ran into an armored recon car of the Third Infantry Division, and our handshakes sealed the historic merging of the American forces that had landed at Licata with the forces that came ashore at Gela. We were now no longer beachhead forces. We were an invading army.

By the evening of July 13 Darby's forces had become a self-contained army, with the addition of an armored field artillery battalion with eighteen self-propelled howitzers. Through the winding roads up the steep forbidding mountains the Darby force surged, up to the outskirts of Butera. Perched atop a towering almost vertical mountain and astride the road to Enna, a key Seventh Army objective, Butera resembled an impregnable medieval fortress, accessible only by a twisting mountain road. High-ranking officers thought that the capture of this citadel would require divisional strength.

Following the First Ranger Battalion the Fourth Battalion moved into position on the shell-scorched slopes in front of Butera, prepared for another major battle. The armored artillery drew up, laid in their guns and waited for the signal to blast the town into rubble.

But Colonel Darby, without revealing his intentions to the supporting units—in an effort to save lives—decided on a bold, audacious plan to catch the defenders off guard and capture the town by shock and surprise. To execute this plan, a company of Rangers commanded by the rugged, daring Captain Shundstrom was ordered to attack at night.

On the night of July 13, fifty black-faced Rangers followed Captain Shundstrom boldly up the winding road. Ahead of them was a detachment of Fascist rear-guard suicide troops, armed with flamethrowers and supported by pillboxes and tanks. Ranger scouts soon made contact with the Italian roadblocks and drew their attention with heavy Tommy-gun and BAR fire. As this skirmish raged, the rest of the Rangers following maneuvered off the road in a flanking assault against the antitank and machine-gun positions behind the forward outposts. Completely surprised and outfought by the gritty Rangers, the positions were reduced within fifteen minutes.

Now Shundstrom and his Rangers moved up the road to the very walls of the fortress city. A prisoner was sent to give an ultimatum to the German garrison commander, demanding the immediate surrender. The commander said, *"Nein!"* meaning he would defend to the last Italian.

Captain Shundstrom didn't waste any time calling for support. With his fifty eager Rangers he deployed into skirmish lines and opened up with all the firepower that fifty small arms could muster, raking the parapets over the road entrance. The Italians, thinking a whole army was upon them, wilted. After a token show of resistance the Italian troops defending the gate quickly surrendered and the German commanders fled. Shundstrom and company boldly marched into Butera, accepted the surrender of the entire garrison, and radioed Colonel Darby that the town had fallen.

The Citadel of Butera then became an inland base for the drive on the mid-island road center of Enna. Once again Darby's brilliant and bold leadership and Shundstrom's great courage and combat cunning, using proven Ranger tactics of night fighting, speed, and surprise, had gained an important military objective and, in doing so, had saved countless lives.

Thanks to Captain Shundstrom's Rangers, dawn found the rest of the Darby force and supporting troops surging through a peaceful Butera hot on the heels of the crumbling Axis forces withdrawing toward Enna.

That evening, camped on a terraced mountainside six miles north of Butera, I found time to bring my diary up to date. Since the North African landings I had kept careful notes of our important engagements. These notes were the subject of a great deal of kidding among both new and old Rangers—particularly Sergeant Dunn, the poet laureate of the Rangers. Rangers would ask me each day how my notes were doing and who received "honorable mention" for the day! I concluded the Gela phase thus far with the following entry.

Somewhere in Sicily—July 14th. We leave for Butera. On way we see miles of scorched fields, pockmarked with shell craters. We pass through fortified positions evacuated by enemy that would do justice to a Maginot line. As we approach Butera we see bloated and burnt bodies of fallen Italian soldiers and the smell of burnt flesh mingled with the smoke from burning fields is gagging us. And the dust is choking us and blinding our eyes. We also see abandoned enemy tanks and destroyed vehicles and some of our own. Butera looks like old medieval fortress. Shundstrom and his men took it last night after swift surpirse attack—now we walk in like tourists. So far the Sicilian people seem very happy to see us. They even clap their hands now and then, and some shout "Viva Americano!" After talking to quite a number of them I find that they truly hate the Nazis and they feared the Fascists. They say they have been waiting a long time for the Americans to come, that the Nazis had taken all their wheat and other products of their fields and they are nearly starving. They are extremely poor and badly dressed and sanitation is nil. They bring up the water to the towns by mules from outside wells. We treat them cordially but we don't go overboard. They are definitely tired of war. Small wonder that the Sicilian soldiers don't offer too much resistance in contrast to the Fascist soldiers from Italy. Often I heard stories from captured prisoners about the Germans forcing them to fight, then mining the roads behind them, leaving them to face the Americans.

Fox Company was preparing to move out toward Caltanissetta the next day when Carlo Contrera came barreling down the road in a cloud of dust in the command jeep. Carlo, his jaw jutted out, his shoulders hunched over the wheel, his helmet cocked rakishly, looked like a man of destiny, as befitted the driver-interpreter of El

292

Darbo. He braked the jeep to a screeching stop when he saw me.

"Hey, Carlo! Where you going in such a rush?"

"Hey, Altieri! How you doin'?"

"Just fine, Carlo, just fine. What's with you—what's the latest from H.Q.?"

"Man, ain't you heard?"

"No, what was we supposed to hear?"

"About General Patton and Darby?"

"No! What happened?"

"I was right there. I heard Patton say it!"

"Where? What did Patton say?"

"Well, before he said it he gave Colonel Darby the Distinguished Service Cross—said he was the hero of Gela—right in front of all those big generals. So many stars there I was blinded. Too bad Stern wasn't there to take some pictures. Roosevelt, Bradley—all the bigshots were there!"

"Hurry up, Carlo—we're movin' out!"

"Well, Patton shakes Darby's hand after he personally pins the DSC on him and he says: 'Colonel, you and your Rangers did a great job! Would you like to take over a Regiment in the Forty-fifth Division and be made a full colonel?' And Darby says, 'You mean I get a choice, General. I'm not used to choices in the Army.'

"And Patton says, 'Take the regiment and I'll make you a full colonel in the morning. But I won't force your hand! There are a thousand colonels in this man's army who would give their right arm for this chance!' "

"What did Darby say?" we asked breathlessly.

"What do you think he said? He said, 'General, thanks anyhow, but I think I'd better stick with my boys. . . .' And get this—he winked at me when he said it! Boy, was I proud! All those big generals standing there—'nuff brass to sink a battleship—and he winks at me!"

"Gee, Carlo, that's great. Sure glad he turned it down!"

"Well, so long, Sarrrgeent," kidded Carlo. "Me and Darby got big things to do. Gotta get going on another reconnaissance job."

"You sure get around, Carlo . . . good luck!"

Carlo waved his hand, slammed the jeep into gear, and roared away in a cloud of dust to join Darby somewhere up front. Before long the news about our chief's turning down another promotion to stay with his Rangers rippled through the entire battalion. It seemed that each Ranger quickened his step and thrust out his chest a couple more inches. We felt proud—proud of Colonel Darby putting his men before his own advancement, and proud of ourselves for meriting such selfless loyalty.

By July 16 the Sicilian campaign was in full swing. The British Eighth Army had taken the port of Augusta and was now attacking toward Catania and Mount Etna. The Forty-fifth Division, after light resistance at Scoglitti, was now battling valiantly across the center of the island in what General Omar Bradley was later to describe as "one of the most persistent nonstop battles of the Sicilian war." The Fighting First, known also as The Big Red One, after capturing Niscemi, was now pressing hard against the German stronghold at Enna. Already over twenty thousand prisoners had been taken, and Allied planes were operating from quickly repaired enemy airfields.

Meanwhile, fanning westward from the Licata sector on our left, was the Third Division, part of the Eighty-second Airborne Division, a task force of the Second Armored and our own Third Ranger Battalion. These units were opposed by formidable Axis forces, including a regiment of the Fifteenth Panzer Grenadiers, two regiments of Italy's toughest troops, the Bersaglieri, and armored and artillery units, seasoned by North African veterans.

The Third Ranger Battalion, commanded by Major Herman Dammer, had spearheaded the beach landings at Licata on D day with the Fifteenth Regiment of the Third Division. All objectives were taken on schedule, and, like Gela, Licata was in American hands by dawn. The next few days for the Third Ranger Battalion were a marathon of marching and fighting through a string of Italian strong points, roadblocks, artillery positions and fortified towns. Compobello, Naro, Favare, Monteparte—all capitulated to Dammer's Rangers, some with mild resistance, some after sharp skirmishes, others after all-out battles. By the time the Third Battalion had reached the outskirts of its major objective—Porto Empedocle, twenty-five miles west of Licata—some six hundred and fifty prisoners had been taken, ten armored cars and vehicles destroyed, and twelve artillery batteries overrun and reduced.

294

Porto Empedocle, named after the ancient Greek philosopher Empedocles, boasted a fine artificial harbor that was vitally needed by the Seventh Army to supply its cross-Sicily drive. General Patton wanted it badly but General Alexander ordered him not to attack either Agrigento or Porto Empedocle, because he feared the strong forces there would involve the Seventh Army in a heavy battle and thus weaken the left flank of the Allied invasion. Characteristically General Patton met with General Alexander and insisted that the Americans should not remain in defense but should attack westward toward Palermo. Alexander finally concurred, but only if the forces used were a "Reconnaissance in Force." Thus the Third Ranger Battalion now preparing to attack the vital port of Empedocle was in effect a forward finger of this so-called reconnaissance force. The success of this westward advance, which was directed by General Lucien K. Truscott, commander of the Third Division, was so important to General Patton that he said later: "Had I failed I would have been relieved."

The forces in and around Porto Empedocle were strong in numbers, high in quality and well supported by artillery and antiaircraft batteries. From staunchly constructed concrete fortifications, they could hold off an army. Among the garrison troops were several hundred German infantry and artillerymen newly arrived from the Russian front. Although the cruiser *Philadelphia* and a couple of destroyers had traded shells with the tough German battery and with an Italian railway battery, the garrison remained defiant. Further bombardment would only destroy the fine harbor and render it useless to the Seventh Army. A Ranger attack was the expedient answer.

After a short rest in an almond grove two thousand yards from the city walls, the weary Rangers—using every terrain feature for concealment—deployed into skirmish lines. The battalion was split in half—three companies under Major Dammer and three under Major Miller his executive officer. At exactly 1420 hours on the hot sunny afternoon of July 16, the attack got under way, supported only by the perky Ranger 60-millimeter mortars.

Major Dammer's force lost no time in blasting its way into the eastern fringe of town, meeting stiff resistance from rooftop snipers and machine gunners. After a sharp battle the Dammer force

295

methodically worked its way down to the port area, cleaning out strong point after strong point. Large numbers of prisoners were taken, handicapping the attackers considerably.

Meanwhile the Miller force was delayed by even tougher resistance. Entrenched in a walled cemetery and in coastal defenses and in antiaircraft positions on the west side of town was a stubborn group of German defenders, determined to fight it out. But the Miller force assaulted position after position with desperate flanking attacks covered by automatic weapons, until finally all resistance was smothered. With the capitulation of the Germans the entire port of Empedocle fell into Ranger hands. On that day alone over six hundred seventy-five Italians and one hundred Germans were captured and two hundred of the enemy killed.

The Seventh Army now had a major port. Its cost: twelve Rangers wounded, one Ranger killed. Ranger training, tactics and leadership had again taken a major objective with the minimum of American lives.

After the Rangers had taken Empedocle, the cruiser *Philadelphia* —unaware that the city was already captured—launched two spotter planes flying white flags. In one plane was a high-ranking officer with a message from the admiral demanding "unconditional surrender." The planes landed safely in the harbor and to their surprise were greeted by Major Dammer and his Rangers, who informed the Navy that the United States Army had the situation well in hand. However, the naval mission was by no means in vain. The Rangers were hungry and needed medical supplies. Would the Navy lend them some grub? The magnificent United States Navy that had supported the Rangers so heroically throughout the landings once again magnanimously came through. They gladly furnished Dammer's starving Rangers with two whaleboats full of "good Navy grub," which even the most loyal mess sergeant will admit is far superior to Army chow.

The remainder of the Sicilian campaign was for us Rangers a period of mixed and often novel assignments. All three battalions formed part of the spearhead for the American westward sweep toward Palermo. Over roads choked with burning enemy guns and tanks, across shell-pocked wheatfields, through towns and cities teeming with now-cheering Sicilians, the three Ranger Battalions

296

marched and, once in a rare while, rode. Caltanissetta . . . Sciacca
. . . Memfi . . . Castelvetrano . . . Marsala . . . Trapani . . . and
countless other fly-speck villages fell swiftly before Patton's hard-
hitting "Reconnaissance in Force." For the most part, however—
thanks to the forward elements of the Second Armored Division—
our main job was rounding up prisoners and herding them in barbed
wire enclosures. By mid-August the First and Fourth Battalions
were camped near a place called Corleone, about thirty miles south
of Palermo, relieved from battle to rest up and train for another
invasion.

But the Third Battalion was not so lucky. The Third Battalion
was off on another cross-country marathon through the tall North
Sicily mountains, with the Third Infantry Division, now known as
the "Truscott Trotters." From August 9 to 17, the Dammer Rangers fought and marched over a hundred miles of steep mountains
and jagged ridges, with little rest between. Operating most of the
time in advance of other units, the Third made several surprise
night attacks, delivered from routes the enemy least expected. Colonel Darby, however, didn't want Dammer's boys to have all the fun.
Colonel Darby and a company from the First Battalion commanded
by Captain Alex Worth, of Durham, North Carolina, organized a
mule train for supplies and pack artillery and remained with them
up to the fall of Messina. Again Darby's past experience in the
Artillery paid off.

We didn't get much time to rest at Corleone. There were new
Ranger replacements to train, and more advanced training for the
coming invasion, with more emphasis on night tactics. But we
didn't mind it a bit. By this time every man in the Rangers knew
that more training was the best "life insurance policy" we could
get. And the news about another invasion didn't seem to upset us
either. In fact at this time the spirit of our outfits was so high that
if we had learned that an invasion was to be made without us we
would have felt a bit slighted.

We old noncoms of the original Rangers were mighty pleased
with our new Fox Company. The Sicilian campaign had been a
tough test for them, far tougher than our first test during the North
African invasion. There was not a man in my platoon who had
not measured up and then some when the chips were down. They

297

were a good bunch, cocky as hell and eager. And they were mighty proud, too—proud to sew on the Ranger patch for the first time. They had certainly earned the right to wear it.

Fox Company had a lot to be grateful for. In the entire campaign we had lost only one man killed and two wounded slightly, and we didn't forget that Randall Harris and Howard Andre did more than their share to keep our casualties so low on the beach at Gela.

The greatest morale booster at Corleone was the news that Randall Harris, now recuperating from his serious wounds at a base hospital in North Africa, was awarded a Distinguished Service Cross and had won a battlefield appointment to second lieutenant. Every one of us was as proud of Randall as if we had won the honors ourselves. In our outfit, medals were at a high premium. Distinguished Service Crosses were considered the equivalent of a Medal of Honor. In seventeen major battles, six campaigns and four major invasions, only two DSC's were awarded among the three battalions —to Colonel Darby and Harris. Even Silver Stars and Bronze Stars were awarded most sparingly. Heroic action was considered a Ranger's duty.

We members of Fox Company felt mighty proud that one of our men had won the Silver Star for "gallantry in action." Captain Walter F. Nye, our long-legged, level-headed, never-perturbed, front-running company commander received official recognition for his daring and courage in the "Battle of Cathedral Square." He certainly deserved it for his boldness in leading the nightmarish door-to-door, roof-to-roof, hand-to-hand street fight that captured the center of Gela before schedule. It was characteristic of Captain Nye to line the company up and tell us: "While I am proud to accept this medal and what it represents, to me this is not a personal award, but an award to all the Rangers of Fox Company. This is your medal, as much as it is mine!"

For most Rangers the Sicilian campaign had a profound impact that seemed to add to our stature as fighting men and contribute immeasurably to our purpose in fighting the war. After the harrowing experiences at the Gela beachhead we knew that we could stand up to anything the enemy could throw at us in future campaigns. Our confidence increased, not only in ourselves as Rangers, but in all the American fighting forces we were privileged to share battles with. Seeing with our own eyes how Fascism had deprived the people of Sicily of their personal dignity and liberty, and how it had impoverished the island, made us more keenly aware of the evils we were fighting against.

The fall of Messina on August 17, 1942, officially ended the Sicilian campaign. We Rangers of the First and Fourth Battalions, training hard at Corleone, were proud to hear the news that the Third Battalion, Dammer's hard-fighting, foot-slugging, mountain-climbing, mule-driving Rangers, were among the first American troops to enter the city, along with General Truscott's Third Infantry Division. To commemorate one of the most successful campaigns in American military history, General George S. Patton issued General Order Number 18 to the soldiers of the Seventh Army, which I called the "Patton Manifesto Number Two." With this he not only redeemed his literary reputation but produced—according to our man of letters, Sergeant Robert Dunn—"an enduring military classic, perhaps rivaling the best of Caesar's reports during the Gaul campaign."

HEADQUARTERS U.S. SEVENTH ARMY
August 22, 1943

SOLDIERS OF THE SEVENTH ARMY:

Born at sea, baptized in blood, and crowned in victory, in the course of thirty-eight days of incessant battle and unceasing labor, you have added a glorious chapter in the history of war.

Pitted against the best the Germans and Italians could offer, you have been unfailingly successful. The rapidity of your dash, which culminated in the capture of Palermo, was equalled by the dogged tenacity with which you stormed Troina and captured Messina.

Every man in the Army deserves equal credit. The enduring valor of the Infantry and the impetuous ferocity of the tanks, were matched by the tireless clamor of our destroying guns.

The Engineers performed prodigies in the maintenance and construction of impossible roads over impassable country. The Services of Maintenance and Supply performed a miracle. The Signal Corps laid over ten thousand miles of wire, and the Medical Corps evacuated and cared for our sick and wounded.

299

On all occasions the Navy has given generous and gallant support. Throughout the operation, our Air has kept the sky clear and tirelessly supported the operation of the ground troops.

As a result of this combined effort, you have killed or captured 113,350 enemy troops. You have destroyed 265 of his tanks, 2,324 vehicles and 1,162 large guns, and, in addition, have collected a mass of military booty running into hundreds of tons.

But your victory has a significance above and beyond its military impact—you have destroyed the prestige of the enemy.

The President of the United States, the Secretary of War, the Chief of Staff, General Eisenhower, General Alexander, General Montgomery have all congratulated you.

Your fame shall never die.

> G. S. PATTON, JR.,
> *Lieut. General, U.S. Army*
> *Commanding*

This general order we thought was a particularly great tribute, because it pinpointed the outstanding work of many services and branches that seldom receive their due credit. The Engineers, the Medical Services, the Signal Corps and the Quartermaster troops, in every campaign, are somewhat overlooked in press notices and official reports. But without them an army would be powerless.

We were also happy to see the Navy and the Air Force get full credit too. We learned later that the reason our air cover didn't appear when the tanks attacked was low mists over the Pantelleria airfields that prevented early morning takeoffs. However by July 11 and 12 the air people intensified their activities over the beachhead areas and did great damage to withdrawing Axis forces; they also rendered excellent support the remainder of the campaign. Nevertheless, we were still entitled to our prejudices—and from the Sicilian campaign to the end of the war we Rangers, when saluting a Navy officer, gave him the best we could deliver—both with arm and heart.

As our time grew shorter at Corleone our training and preparation for the Italian invasion stepped up in tempo and spirit. The

Third (footsore) Battalion was now back—but before they could soak their blistered feet, they were plunged into the hectic training grind. To bolster our firepower Colonel Darby added a Ranger Cannon Company consisting of six self-propelled 105-millimeter guns, commanded by Captain Chuck Shundstrom. A call for former artillery men went out, and the rugged Shundstrom went on a personal recruiting binge, raiding our own units for "qualified Rangers." He got more than enough. Shundstrom's fame had spread (we lost count of his Silver Stars), and there were no small number of Rangers who actually were anxious to share Captain Shundstrom's exciting adventures because he was known to be where the "fighting was the hottest." Having left a Field Artillery unit, I personally wasn't interested, and as much as I admired the daring Captain Shundstrom, I had found enough opportunities in my own Fox Company for exciting action.

Things seemed to be going too well. Four Red Cross gals descended on us at Corleone—exceptionally pretty ones—who made doughnuts and served coffee all day long and kept us on our toes in the personal appearance department. Rangers trimmed their beards and mustaches, put creases in their battleworn trousers, patted down their hair and tried to smile their winningest when they passed the sweet-scented girls. Just to look at them, smell them and receive a smile was all we needed to remind us what we had left back home and give us even more determination to win the war and get back as quick as we could.

They kinda liked us too, because they stayed with us for a whole week. Four girls among fifteen hundred Rangers—and they were treated with deference and respect.

Bop Hope made an appearance and did a terrific job, and several nights we saw some fairly good movies. After duty hours there was plenty of stateside beer, and once the ever-resourceful supply officer, Captain Joe Fineberg of Philadelphia, Pennsylvania, and his able sidekick, Sergeant Paul Perry, came up with the morale clincher of the Sicilian campaign—a truckload of ice cream from Palermo. How Fineberg managed it, no one knows, but there were some rumors to the effect that this cagey ex-burlesque theater manager had managed to make a fair trade with the Sicilian ice cream company—a truckload of Spam for a truckload of ice cream with several boxes of tasty C Rations thrown in as a special bonus.

Then tough luck hit us. Lieutenant Branson got hit with a short mortar round during a mountainside assault and was badly cut up in the face and shoulders. At Corleone we used live ammo on all our night and daytime problems and soon after Branson got it, Captain Ralph A. Coleby and Pfc. William Eger of the First Battalion were killed.

The casualties dampened our spirits. The boys in our platoon were mighty sad about Lieutenant Branson. He had come through just fine during the action at Gela and in later skirmishes, and most of the "infantry school approach" had been happily rubbed away by the realities of war and field life.

Then malaria hit us, followed by an epidemic of jaundice and dysentery. Half the Rangers were laid low with the shivering fever and the other half were spending fulltime duty racing to the crowded latrine boxes. With others in Fox Company I got it real bad. The doc loaded me up with pills, forbade me to run the company through the scheduled assault course, and gave me hell for not taking atabrine pills regularly.

Captain Hardenbrook finally ordered me and many other unfortunate Rangers to the hospital. The hospital proved to be an abandoned schoolhouse near Palermo that was crowded with troops of every division, suffering from malaria and wounds. Stretchers were laid side by side on the concrete floors and we were so cramped together that nurses could hardly walk between us. For several days my temperature stayed as high as a hundred and four. I couldn't eat or drink, and my hands trembled with the chills and shivers. For the first time in my life I had the most awful feeling that not only was I going to die but I was looking forward to the mercy of death to relieve me of this awful pain.

By the third day my temperature was down to a hundred and one. The chills were still with me, but the fever had declined enough for me to swallow some nourishment and gain some strength. I began to notice that the nurses around me were quite attractive and perhaps my hospital stay would be a bit more pleasant as the days wore on.

At noon a truck from Ranger camp brought some new malarial

302

cases and from the sergeant in charge we learned that the Ranger force was leaving that night to board ship at Palermo for the Italian invasion. Our outfits were going into battle without us.

It was then that we discovered our Ranger fever was higher than our malaria fever. Some seventeen Rangers, on hearing this news, suddenly threw off their blankets, grabbed their belongings and hobbled out the doors over the protests of nurses and medical attendants. Into the truck we scrambled as a whistle blew somewhere summoning the MP's to stop the mass exodus. The truck slammed into gear and away we went down the road in a cloud of dust, hoping to make Corleone in time for the departure.

We made it. I had just enough time to draw some ammo and rations and limp into line at the head of my platoon. As First Sergeant Ed Baccus took the company report I had just enough strength to answer, "First Platoon, all present and accounted for."

Once again our time had come, and the other hospital A.W.O.L.s and I weren't about to miss out on what we knew would be the biggest deal of all—the invasion of Italy with General Mark Clark's Fifth Army.

CHAPTER 50

AGAIN in the invasion of Italy the Ranger force helped spearhead the way, making a daring silent landing on a narrow mountain-hemmed beach at Maroi, west of Salerno. By dawn the Rangers had surprised and wiped out a loosely organized German armored recon-naissance company and had marched six miles inland over precipi-tous mountains to seize the high ridges overlooking the plain of Naples. Astride these strategic heights the Rangers dominated the enemy's main line of communications leading from Naples to Salerno.

A confident Darby radioed back to General Mark Clark: "We have taken up positions in the enemy's rear and we'll stay here till hell freezes over."

Finding the Rangers in control of this favorable high ground, threatening them like a knife at their jugular vein, the Germans swiftly counterattacked. Wave after wave of black-uniformed para-troops and elite S.S. troops stormed up the mountains, preceded by blistering mortar and artillery barrages. The thinly held Ranger front bent but never broke. Each attack was thrown back with heavy losses. So decisive was the enemy setback that captured prisoners later revealed that the Germans estimated the heights were held by a full division.

From mountaintop observation posts Rangers directed cruiser, artillery and mortar fire on the enemy below. Thousands of shells daily crashed into enemy troop and supply concentrations and forced him to abandon daylight traffic on the network of valley roads. At night Ranger raiding forces swept down the mountains

304

with savage, pin-pricking, harassing raids against German artillery and troop positions. These attacks confused and demoralized the enemy and caused him to rush reinforcements to the Ranger area—troops that were badly needed to smash the main Fifth Army beachhead at Salerno.

For eighteen days the three Ranger battalions, supported by the 4.2 Mortar Battalion and several companies of the Eighty-second Division Paratroops, held on grimly. During this period the Germans launched six full-scale attacks, determined to clear the heights and outflank our main forces at Salerno. But, although outnumbered nine to one—according to official Fifth Army records—every attack was decisively smashed and followed up with a Ranger counterattack.

At times the positions held by the Darby force were virtually isolated from the main Fifth Army front. On our right, near Vietri, a tough Commando brigade fought valiantly to keep its toehold on Italian soil. The entire brigade was nearly wiped out, but it held on.

Finally, on September 22, 1943, after thirteen days of the bitterest fighting in Ranger history, the Rangers led the way down the winding, Sals-Chinnzi Pass road for the big push to Naples. Two more Presidential Citations were added to the Ranger battle honors, and for his outstanding leadership and personal bravery Darby again was awarded the D.S.C.

After a short rest the Rangers were again called into action, this time to dislodge the Germans from the commanding mountains overlooking the Venafro valley, some forty miles north of Naples. Here the Germans were strongly entrenched in their famed Winter Line. Mountain after mountain was stormed and seized until the American lines were advanced to San Pietro. Each Ranger attack was followed by a German counterattack. Sometimes mountains would exchange hands several times in one day. Heavy enemy mortar and artillery barrages blistered the mountaintops and caused a great many Ranger casualties. After nearly forty-five days of continuous combat the three battalions were withdrawn to reorganize, recruit and prepare for the Anzio Beachhead. Nearly forty per cent casualties were suffered in the bitter mountain fighting. Again the Fourth and Third Battalions received Fifth Army commendations for their work.

By this time, December 1943, after four campaigns and thirteen major battles, the old-timers who had started back in Ireland were getting fewer and fewer. Nearly all of us who remained had been wounded at least twice. Malaria and yellow jaundice took their toll. Gone were Lodge and Rodriguez, who were captured on a raid behind enemy lines near Venafro. New faces kept coming in after each battle.

Christmas week at Lucrino north of Naples brought some cheerful surprises. Father Basil, who was serving with the Eighth Army, popped up and was greeted enthusiastically by the old-timers. Father Basil said special Mass for the Rangers and spent two days visiting all three battalions. Vainly he tried again to go A.W.O.L. with us. But Darby—much as he wanted him—felt the good Padre had already done enough for us. Sadly we said our good-bys again, after the good Father commended us on the tremendous improvement of our vocabularies.

It was here at Lucrino that Broadway star Ella Logan adopted the Rangers as her favorite outfit, and we made her a "Rangerette" in appreciation of the many shows she put on for us.

Howard Andre and I were especially happy this Christmas. Earlier in the morning at Fifth Army Headquarters, General Mark Clark had pinned second lieutenant bars on our shoulders. Our battlefield appointments were the tenth and eleventh such awards to be given to enlisted men in our outfit. Darby and Murray believed firmly that Ranger commanders should come from the ranks.

Murray and Nye moved up too. Murray was now a lieutenant colonel and Nye was a major, his executive officer. Major Schneider had left us before the Venafro fighting to go to Britain to train the Fifth and Second Ranger Battalions for the Normandy Beachheads. Randall Harris was now company commander of Fox Company.

For weeks we trained hard at Lucrino, whipping the new replacements into fighting shape. Then on January 21, we boarded British ships and sailed out of the harbor of Pazzoli, Italy, bound for the Anzio Beachhead, to write the final chapter of our fighting history.

Storming ashore on the cold, black night of January 22, 1944, the three Ranger battalions made a perfect, silent, unoppposed landing directly in the harbor of Anzio. Surprisingly, the enemy was caught completely off guard. Within three hours the entire port of Anzio was secured as Rangers struck out to enlarge the beachhead. Three armored cars, two machine-gun nests and a battery of 100-millimeter coast guns were bagged and forty Germans killed. The landing was the most successful in Ranger history.

The next day, as the aroused enemy pounded the port with Stukas and 88 barrages, the three battalions advanced seven miles, then dug in. We could have gone all the way to Rome if they had given us the orders. But Rome wasn't included in our battle plan. Our mission was to establish the beachhead with the British Tenth Corps on our left and the Truscott-led Third Division on our right . . . and then hold. The high command hoped that the beachhead would necessitate the reshuffling of Kesselring's hard-pressed forces at Cassino to meet the new threat, while the Fifth Army launched a gigantic attack against Cassino. They estimated ten days for a link-up of the main Fifth Army Forces with the beachhead forces.

Within seven days, while we were digging in and strengthening our beachhead forward lines, the Germans had ringed our seven-by-eleven mile toehold with major elements of ten divisions. Some were flown in by air, from Yugoslavia, some moved in by train from northern Italy and others wheeled in from nearby reserve concentration points. Without drawing from their Cassino forces, the Germans contained the beachhead with a ring of steel.

From January 25 to 28 the Rangers held the furthermost point inland, near the Carrocetta-Aprilla factory area. Heavy fighting raged here day and night. Enemy probing attacks trying to push through Ranger positions were beaten back, and each night Ranger patrols penetrated the enemy lines, raiding and harassing.

It was here near Aprilla that Howard Andre, who less than a month before had won his field commission, was killed as he led an attack against a fortified farmhouse. It was here too that Lieutenant

307

Randall Harris, his company commander, was seriously wounded for the third time and evacuated to a hospital. And it was here that I found myself in command of Company F. The inexorable law of averages was catching up with the old Rangers.

Tired, sleepless, battered incessantly by enemy artillery and air strafings, the three battalions slugged it out, farmhouse to farmhouse, ditch to ditch, from January 25 to January 28. Then suddenly on the evening of the twenty-ninth we were replaced by British troops for what we thought was a much needed rest. But we learned instead that we had another mission. General Lucien Truscott, the same general who was responsible for organizing the Rangers back in Ireland, ordered the three Ranger battalions to spearhead the Third Division attack against Cisterna di Littoria—a key beachhead objective.

The next day, after an all-night march, Darby called his officers together and revealed the hastily drawn-up battle plans. It was to be an all-out offensive—to capture Cisterna and cut highways six and seven, the main roads from Rome to Cassino.

The First and Third Battalions were assigned the daring mission of infiltrating the enemy forward lines at night—march six miles and storm the town by dawn. Their orders were to bypass all enemy forces en route to their objective. Sentries and outpost guards were to be killed noiselessly by knife or bayonet. If it met resistance, the First Battalion was to creep off toward the objective, and the Third was to engage.

The mission of our battalion—the Fourth—was to follow an hour later and clear the main road leading to Cisterna so that reinforcements could be rushed into town to assist the First and Third. The Fifteenth Infantry Regiment of the Third Division was to follow us.

At dawn the famous hard-hitting 504th Parachute Regiment was to support our drive with a furious attack on the right. The Seventh Infantry Regiment was to attack on our left, and link up with the Ranger force in Cisterna. Meanwhile, far to the left on the Carrocetta-Anzio road, our old friends, the First Armored Division, was to push forward toward Albano. That's the way it was planned.

We were singing "Pistol Packing Mamma" as we moved out of

308

our bivouac area and trudged over the frozen ground toward our jump-off area past the Mussolini canal. It was a tough mission, but we felt confident that we would accomplish it as we had every other mission. We had met and defeated the Germans before. We could do it again.

The First and Third moved out at 0100 hours, in single file. Snaking through a series of irrigation ditches, they crossed the enemy's outpost lines, killing German sentries noiselessly with knives. Skirting enemy artillery positions, so close they could hear the Germans giving fire orders, they continued their march deep behind the enemy's lines.

The Fourth battalion moved out one hour later, a file on either side of the enemy-held road. But less than a half mile up the road a lone machine gun opened up. Then out of the black night, coming from the fields on both sides of the road, machine-gun tracers suddenly magnified into a wall of flaming steel. Swiftly the leading Ranger company attacked at close quarters with grenades and bayonets. Two machine guns were wiped out, but others in depth continued firing. After two ferocious assaults that failed to penetrate the solid line, the company, with its commander, Lieutenant George Nunnelly, killed and many wounded, was forced to hole up in a shallow ditch. Every inch of ground was covered by deadly grazing fire and enemy shells were now landing on the road.

Colonel Murray directed another assault, with A and B Companies on the right flank. This attack also was stopped. A perfect system of crossfire was in effect, covering all avenues of approach with selected lanes of fire. Through the night the battle on the road raged with growing intensity. Two more company commanders were killed and numerous men were wounded badly. Paradoxically the First and Third Battalions were by now several miles past the very wall our Fourth was trying to breach. They had met no resistance in slipping through the flanks. We had met solid, strong, determined opposition—and worse, we weren't getting ahead.

As dawn approached, the leading company of the First Ranger Battalion found itself in the middle of a German bivouac area. At once the Rangers flung themselves upon the Germans, Tommy-gunning and bayoneting nearly a hundred before moving on toward

Cisterna now less than eight hundred yards away. But by now the Germans were alerted. The First and Third Ranger Battalions found themselves squarely in the middle of a German paratroop division that had moved in the night before. Then began the goriest, costliest battle in Ranger history.

From stone houses, from freshly dug earthworks, and from tanks hidden near haystacks, the Germans poured mortar, machine-gun and cannon fire on the two battalions strung out along a series of irrigation ditches. Rangers swiftly dug in on the banks of the ditches and returned the fire. None of the Rangers had expected to take Cisterna without a fight, so they were not particularly worried. The flank attacks would be reaching them soon as well as the Fourth Battalion in the rear.

Meanwhile, Colonel Darby back with the Fourth Battalion continued to direct the attack to break through to the two beleagured battalions. Again and again our companies swept across the fields, capturing strong points and farmhouses. But each avenue cost dearly. Fanatical paratroops were entrenched in depth in well-camouflaged ground-level dugouts. Ground-grazing machine-gun fire covered every ditch, and their mortars crashed all around us. In one attack I lost one of my platoon lieutenants and four key non-coms, as well as ten men badly wounded. We were desperate; we knew we had to crack through to save the First and Third—but each attack in broad daylight over open ground brought frightening casualties.

Darby kept his command post right up with the forward Fourth Battalion attacks. In desperation he called on General Truscott to get the flanker attacks moving. But both the Five Hundred Fourth Paratroops and the Seventh Infantry Regiment were meeting equally strong opposition and getting nowhere. The Germans were much stronger than expected, the entire American attack had bogged down and the two Ranger Battalions—the only units that had reached their objective—were now battling for their lives.

To add to Darby's despair, a heavy mortar barrage bracketed his command post killing his trusted staff officer, Major Bill Martin. Moments later another barrage killed his loyal runner, Corporal Presly Stroud, who had been with the old man ever since Achna Carry. A shell fragment struck Carlo Contrera's helmet, but Carlo

310

got out of it unscratched. Three of our medics were killed as they leaned over the wounded, near the command post.

In response to Darby's demands a tank destroyer unit moved up and attempted to smash through the road. Two of them hit tellar mines and were destroyed. The others tried the fields but were soon bogged down in soggy mud. Our artillery couldn't fire toward the Ranger pocket for fear of hitting our own men. Our 4.2 Chemical Warfare Mortar Battalion couldn't help because the base plates of the heavy mortars sank into the mud and couldn't be fired with accuracy.

Behind the German wall the two beleagured battalions fought desperately. Enemy tanks and flak wagons joined the battle. They blocked off the ditches with machine-gun and cannon fire. But the Rangers had been in tight spots before, and they knew how to fight tanks. With sticky grenades and rocket guns they attacked the tanks and flak wagons. The first enemy armored assault ended with seventeen tanks and flak wagons destroyed. But another wave waded into the battle to take their place.

While it was still early morning another column of tanks approached the Ranger pocket from the rear. The enemy, coming out of a low-hanging mist from the direction of American lines, was at first mistaken for friendly forces. But loud cheers gave way to bitter disappointment as the tanks bore down on the rearmost Ranger groups, firing machine guns and point-blank cannon.

Rising from the ditches alongside the road, Rangers again attacked the tanks with rocket guns and sticky antitank grenades. Many were killed by withering machine-gun fire and point-blank 88's. Some of the Rangers clambered aboard while the tanks were in motion, lifting the turret hatches to spray the insides with Tommy-gun fire. Fighting furiously with every means at their disposal—which were few—the beleagured Rangers exacted a heavy toll from the Germans. No quarter was asked or given by either side. For the Rangers it was a battle to the finish.

Suffering terrific losses, the initial German attacks were decisively smashed. For a while Rangers again assumed the offensive, attacking enemy artillery positions, storming strong-pointed farmhouses, but the preponderance of German strength was too much. The Rangers were outnumbered ten to one.

311

Among those who were killed as the Rangers fought back was Major Alvah Miller, commander of the Third Battalion. Major Jack Dobson, commander of the First Battalion, was badly wounded by shell fragments. Medics set up in farmhouses and ditches were working tirelessly, tending the ever-growing number of wounded.

Toward noon the Germans made another heavy armored attack. From the Appian Way and the maze of interlacing roads, both behind and in front of the Ranger pocket, Mark VI tanks supported by Panzer Grenadiers waded into the battle. By this time the Rangers' strength was badly sapped. Ammunition was almost completely expended. Some were fighting with whatever German weapons they could lay their hands on; some were fighting with only knives and bayonets. On the bloody fields, along the canal and irrigation ditches and in the shell-torn houses on the outskirts of Cisterna, the battle raged on. Beset from all sides by ever-increasing German attacks, the Ranger pocket became smaller and smaller.

Shortly after the noon hour, Sergeant Major Ehalt of the First Battalion radioed back to Darby for the last time: "They're closing in on us, Colonel; we're out of ammo—but they won't get us cheap! Good luck . . . Colonel . . ."

Darby, his eyes red, his face haggard, his voice thick with anguish, knew now that his two battalions—some nine hundred and fifty of his boys—were irretrievably lost. "God bless you, Sergeant . . . God bless all of you. . . ." were his last words to his stricken men. The radio was destroyed as Sergeant Ehalt rose to meet the German paratroops closing in on his command post.

Sergeant Scotty Monroe, the sergeant major of the Third Battalion, had already destroyed his radio after telling Darby the situation was desperate. Sergeant Monroe and many other Third Battalion Rangers continued to fight till late in the evening.

Darby was desperate. His invincible Ranger force was shattered. Two battalions decimated and another battalion, the Fourth, had suffered nearly fifty per cent casualties, with three company commanders killed in the last twelve hours. Darby, the iron-willed, resolute commander, fought hard to hold back his tears. But he couldn't. He went inside the farmhouse, asked his staff to leave and then, alone for a few moments, he sobbed out his anguish as enemy shells beat a steady tattoo around the house.

Carlo Contrera saw the colonel as he came out of the farmhouse, and noticed that the colonel's shoulders were now straight and his chin thrust forward defiantly. He had lost most of his Rangers; his dream was gone, but the war had to go on. As long as a Ranger lived, the enemy must pay and pay heavily. He was a soldier, a West Pointer, and he still had a command, however small. He picked up the field phone, informed General Mike O'Daniel of the loss of two battalions, and received orders to prepare what was left of the Fourth battalion for another attack the next morning.

The next day, supported by the Fifteenth Infantry Regiment, the Fourth Battalion once again launched an attack. This time we pushed forward another mile and destroyed a battalion of crack paratroops who were dug in in well-camouflaged earthworks. We killed close to three hundred of them and reluctantly captured the rest. But it was too late to save our two sister battalions.

In two bitter days we had lost more Rangers than we had during our entire six campaigns—through North Africa, Sicily, Salerno and Venafro. Later reports indicated that sixty per cent of the First and Third were killed and wounded, and the rest captured. The Fourth Battalion lost sixty men killed, and a hundred and twenty wounded. Five company commanders in the Fourth Battalion were killed—most of them in hand-to-hand combat.

Eighteen Rangers managed to infiltrate back from the corpse-cluttered Ranger pocket. Lieutenant Ed Harger, one of my platoon leaders, led a patrol behind the lines that brought out seven more wounded. Sergeant Fergen of the First Battalion revealed the full story of how our men fought to the bitter end. It was heartbreaking. Two of the finest and most spirited outfits in the Army were ground to bits by an awesome mailed fist—and all the while hoped vainly for help that never came. They fought tenaciously, they went down fighting, although hopelessly outnumbered. Their stand was the Rangers' finest hour.

But the loss of our two battalions was not in vain. Later German prisoners revealed the Germans had been marshaling strong forces in the Cisterna sector for an all-out drive to smash the Americans back to the sea. Elements of the reorganized Herman Goering Division, the First Parachute Division, the Twenty-first Panzer and

the Seventy-first Infantry—all crack veterans of many campaigns—
were the forces that met the Ranger attack. Two regiments were
chewed up by the Rangers before they went down. The sudden
attack behind the enemy's lines had completely disorganized and
disrupted the German offensive before it began and helped save the
Anzio Beachhead at its most crucial period.

CHAPTER 51

FOR SIXTY days the Fourth Ranger Battalion continued to fight on alongside the Five Hundred Fourth Parachute Regiment at Hell's Corner, the southwest patch of bitterly contested beachhead real estate. Fighting from dugouts and trenches reminiscent of World War I days, we fought off five major counterattacks. By now the Germans had stopped our main Fifth Army drive at Cassino and were desperately striving to fulfill Hitler's order. We didn't like this kind of defensive fighting, we weren't trained or equipped for it, but we knew the situation was so desperate that every soldier—be he paratrooper, Ranger, or Infantryman—was needed to save the Beachhead.

Darby meanwhile was commanding the One Hundred Seventy-ninth Infantry Regiment of the Forty-fifth Division, holding key positions in the center of the beachhead. His regiment took the full brunt of the heaviest German attacks during the month of February . . . and held firmly. The rest is history. Anzio—the grave-cluttered patch of hell—was held, and from it the Fifth Army launched its attack on Rome.

But we were never to see Rome. General Marshall in mid-March ordered the old, war-weary, surviving Ranger veterans back home to train other troops. One hundred and ninety-nine of us of the original battalion went back. The others—some two hundred and fifty Rangers who joined us after Tunisia—were transferred to the crack Canadian-American Special Service Brigade that later distinguished itself in spearheading the beachhead breakout and the

315

subsequent landings in southern France. As a special courtesy these Rangers were allowed to wear their Ranger patches in battle.

Of our original Fox Company, about one third survived. Sergeant Dunn, Corporal Fuller, Tech Sergeant Junior Fronk and First Lieutenant Harris, along with Major Nye, Colonel Murray and I, came back together. Lodge and Rodriquez later returned from POW camps. Dunn, a Regular Army man, was later killed in Korea.

Carlo Contrera—my old buddy—who had been with Colonel Darby throughout the bitter Anzio battle, came back to marry his Brooklyn sweetheart. Sergeant Smith, my old First Armored battery mate, came through unscratched. And Phil Stern—Hollywood's best photographer—was on hand to greet us when we landed, as a full-fledged photographer for *Life* magazine which did a spread on us.

Back in the States we old Rangers took it easy for a while, then we were split up into small groups and sent to various training camps around the country. We did our best to pass on our experience to the rest of the Army. They say we did a pretty good job.

The loss of the First and Third Battalions and the dissolving of the Fourth Ranger Battalion brought to an end the fighting history of the original Darby Rangers. But the spirit and fighting techniques of the Rangers was passed on to the entire Army. Tough realistic combat training patterned after the Rangers was adopted by all training camps. The Ranger amphibious know-how and night-fighting tactics became standard Army doctrine. These were used to good advantage and saved many American lives in later campaigns.

The Normandy landings in France found the hard-trained Second and Fifth Ranger Battalions proudly carrying on the Ranger traditions. These outfits trained and led by our own Lieutenant Colonel Max Schneider and Lieutenant Colonel Rudder, spearheaded the invasion by scaling towering cliffs on D day and knocking out enemy shore batteries. In the Pacific the Sixth Ranger Battalion led by Lieutenant Colonel Henry Mucci, of Bridgeport, Connecticut, distinguished itself by a daring raid deep behind Japanese lines to rescue American prisoners at the dreaded Cabanatuan POW camp in the Philippines. Throughout the war these battalions

316

played an important part in the final victory we were never to see.

A group of Rangers who had been captured at Cisterna also played an important part in the Italian campaign. These ingenious and tenacious fellows, quickly made good their escape from POW camps and organized Italian partisan troops into hard-hitting guerrilla raiders. Captain Charles Shundstrom, Lieutenant William Newman, Sergeant Scotty Monroe and many others led these partisan fighters on slashing raids against enemy supply points, communications lines and arsenals. These raids helped confuse and demoralize the enemy and seriously disrupted and hampered his war effort in Italy. Nearly ten per cent of all Rangers captured made good their escape.

On the sixteenth of April, 1945, Colonel William O. Darby, assistant division commander of the Tenth Mountain Division, was killed leading a combat team in the Po Valley. A shell fragment had pierced his brave thirty-four-year-old heart. Two days later all German forces in Italy surrendered.

We old Rangers were hit hard by the news. The old man had seemed indestructible. It was hard to believe that his luck had run out. Three months before his death I had lunched with him at the Pentagon where he was assigned to the General Staff. "I hate this damned desk," he told me. "I'd like to get up another Ranger outfit and go to the Pacific . . . would you come along?" I told him I would—right then if he was leading it—and I told him that every other Ranger would do the same. He just laughed and said, "That's the old spirit."

The Army paid him high tribute. General Truscott, commander of the Fifth Army, said: "Never have I known a more gallant, heroic officer." General Patton said: "He was the bravest man I knew." The Army made him a brigadier general posthumously. Later the Army named a large troop transport the *William O. Darby,* and an Army camp in northern Italy bears his name.

But the greatest memorial to General Darby—the memorial he would be most pleased with—is the Ranger Training Command at

Fort Benning, Georgia, which is turning out 1500 tough, spirited, resourceful Rangers every year. I visited this camp in April 1957 with Colonel Roy Murray, and we both agreed the training is even tougher than we got with the Commandos. Each Ranger after receiving his training goes back to his own outfit and helps infuse it with his spirit and know-how. Thus the entire army benefits. Eventually every unit in the Army will have a hard core of daring, spirited combat leaders, imbued with the same qualities of initiative and valor that Darby inspired in his original troopers.

Thus the Ranger spirit will never die.